GLOBET...

KU-769-415

Travel Guide

ICELAND

ROWLAND MEAD

NEW
HOLLAND

NEW HOLLAND

★★★	Highly recommended
★★	Recommended
★	See if you can

Sixth edition published in 2011
by New Holland Publishers (UK) Ltd
London • Cape Town • Sydney • Auckland
10 9 8 7 6 5 4 3 2 1
website: www.newhollandpublishers.com

Garfield House, 86 Edgware Road
London W2 2EA
United Kingdom

80 McKenzie Street
Cape Town 8001
South Africa

Unit 1, 66 Gibbes Street,
Chatswood NSW 2067
Australia

218 Lake Road
Northcote, Auckland
New Zealand

Distributed in the USA by
the Globe Pequot Press, Connecticut

This guidebook has been written by independent
authors and updaters. The information therein represents their impartial opinion, and neither they nor the
publishers accept payment in return for including in
the book or writing more favourable reviews of any of
the establishments. Whilst every effort has been made
to ensure that this guidebook is as accurate and up to
date as possible, please be aware that the facts quoted
are subject to change, particularly the price of food,
transport and accommodation. The Publisher accepts
no responsibility or liability for any loss, injury or
inconvenience incurred by readers or travellers using
this guide.

Publishing Manager: Thea Grobbelaar
DTP Cartographic Manager: Genené Hart
Editors: Thea Grobbelaar, Lorissa Bouwer, Nicky
Steenkamp, Melany Porter, Donald Reid
Cartographers: Nicole Bannister, Inga Ndibongo, Tanja
Spinola, Marlon Christmas
Design and DTP: Nicole Bannister, Éloïse Moss
Consultant: Richard Sale
Picture Researcher: Shavonne Govender

Reproduction by Hirt & Carter (Pty) Ltd, Cape Town
Printed and bound by Times Offset (M) Sdn. Bhd.,
Malaysia.

Photographic Credits:
Heather Angel/Natural Visions: page 114;
Gavin Hellier/awl-images.com: cover;
Jenny Forrest: title page, pages 9, 15, 21, 39, 49, 50,
54, 57, 62, 66, 68 (bottom), 80, 81, 82, 83, 85, 86,
87, 92, 95, 96, 97, 102, 106, 107, 112;
Gallo/Tony Stone Images/Paul Chesley: page 22;
Gallo/Tony Stone Images/Jonny Johnson: page 12;
Gallo/Tony Stone Images/Hans Strand: page 7;
Gallo/Tony Stone Images/Kim Westerskov: page 74;
Fiona McLeod: pages 13 (left), 18, 20, 23, 24, 35, 37,
38, 42, 43, 55;
Rowland Mead: pages 14, 25, 48, 53, 64, 65, 72, 76,
77, 78, 79, 94, 98, 100, 105, 108, 109, 110;
Richard Sale: pages 4, 6, 10, 11, 13 (right), 16, 17, 19,
26, 27, 28, 29, 30, 32, 33, 34, 36, 41, 46, 51, 52, 56
(top and bottom), 58, 60, 67, 68 (top), 69, 70, 90, 104,
111, 116, 117, 118, 119, 120.

Keep us Current
Information in travel guides is apt to change, which is
why we regularly update our guides. We'd be grateful
to receive feedback if you've noted something we
should include in our updates. If you have new
information, please share it with us by writing to the
Publishing Manager, Globetrotter, at the office nearest
to you (addresses on this page). The most significant
contribution to each new edition will receive a free
copy of the updated guide.

Cover: *Icebergs floating in the lagoon beneath
Breiðamerkurjökull Glacier.*
Title page: *Turf houses at Skaftafell National Park.*

CONTENTS

1
Introducing Iceland

Over the last two decades, Iceland has become one of the world's fastest growing tourist destinations. The reasons are easy to appreciate. First, and above all, is the scenery. A volcanically active zone runs through the country from northeast to southwest following a tectonic plate boundary. Active **volcanoes** such as Hekla and Krafla have reared above lava plains and **geothermal areas**, which include geysers, fumeroles, hot springs and mud springs. There are numerous **icecaps**, including Vatnajökull, which is bigger than the rest of Europe's icecaps put together. **Glacier** tongues flow from the icecaps, with icebergs calving from their snouts, sometimes into glacial lagoons, such as that at Jökulsárlón. Steep-sided **fiords**, formed by glaciers, punctuate the northwest and southeast coast, giving shelter for fishing villages. Iceland even has **deserts** – in this case the cold variety. In fact, because of the icecaps, lava fields and deserts, over 70% of the country is uninhabitable.

Iceland has a population of just under 320,000 (2009), of which 37% live in the capital, **Reykjavík**, and its suburbs. As well as being one of the least crowded countries in the world, it is also one of the least polluted – all its power is from geothermal sources – and the clear light will delight photographers. The country is a **bird-watcher's joy**, with teeming 'sea-bird cities' on its cliffs and abundant wildfowl on lakes such as Mývatn. Others come to Iceland for **outdoor activities** – hiking, whitewater rafting or snowmobile rides across an ice-

TOP ATTRACTIONS

*** Lake Mývatn: great range of birds and some fascinating volcanic features.
*** Geysir Area: geysers and other geothermal surprises; Gullfoss waterfall and Skáholt Cathedral.
*** Jökulsárlón: boat trip on a glacial lagoon amongst melting icebergs.
*** Hallgrímskirkja: modern church with superb views over the rooftops of Reykjavík.
*** Þingvellir: lakeside site of ancient parliament.
*** Blue Lagoon: hot-water swimming pools alongside a geothermal power station.

Opposite: *A snowy scene at Þingvellir, the site of Iceland's parliament.*

Above: *A distant view of Vatnajökull, Iceland's largest icecap.*

cap. But do not come here for sun-drenched beaches, as they are composed of black volcanic sand and pounded by massive Atlantic waves.

THE LAND

Situated in the North Atlantic Ocean, just to the south of the Arctic Circle, Iceland covers just over 100,000km² (38,600 sq miles), making it the second largest island in Europe. The nearest land masses are Greenland – 287km (178 miles) to the northwest; Norway – 970km (603 miles) to the east; and Scotland – 798km (496 miles) to the southeast. Iceland is the largest of a series of islands positioned on the submarine mountain chain known as the Mid-Atlantic Ridge, which marks a **plate boundary** separating the American Plate from the Eurasian Plate, which are moving apart at an average rate of 1–2cm (½–1in) a year. Geologists delight in stating that the west of Iceland is in North America and the east of the country is in Europe! It is also true that, geologically speaking, Iceland is the youngest country in Europe.

The **volcanic belt** runs in a northeasterly direction, from the southwest of the country in the Reykanes Peninsula area towards Lake Mývatn in the northeast. It varies in width from 40km (25 miles) to 60km (37 miles) and is typified by volcanoes and other forms of volcanic activity such as geysers, hot springs, mud springs, fumeroles and solfataras. The majority of the lava is of the scoria type, which is coarse, loose and sharp and which often solidifies into fantastic shapes. Volcanic activity has continued throughout recorded history, with the most recent eruptions being at Surtsey in 1963, Heimaey in 1973, Krafla in the mid-70s and Hekla in 1991, while in 2010 Eyjafjallajökull produced an ash cloud which grounded most of Europe's planes for over a week and played havoc with many people's travel plans. In the east and west of Iceland, away from the active volcanic zone, are mountains of basalt and rhyolite, the result of lava flows up to 20 million years ago.

Being on a plate boundary, Iceland often experiences **earthquakes**, the latest in May 2008 which recorded 6.3 on the Richter scale. The quake's epicentre was near Selfoss and although there was damage to property, there were no fatalities.

Another important feature in the shaping of Iceland is **ice**. The country is still in the throes of the Ice Age and enormous icecaps can be seen where the land is about 1300m (4265ft) above sea level. The biggest icecap is **Vatnajökull**, the largest in Europe and also the world's third greatest after Antarctica and Greenland. Tongues of ice, called valley **glaciers**, spread out from the icecaps, eroding deep U-shaped valleys and creating a number of spectacular **fiords**. The material eroded by the glaciers is eventually deposited on outwash plains or **sandur** – lowland areas covered with sand, gravel and

PLATE TECTONICS

The modern science of Plate Tectonics has its origins in the work of **Alfred Wegener**, who in 1912 published his work on **Continental Drift**. It was rejected then as he did not suggest a mechanism by which this drift could occur. It is now known that convection currents can move plates in various ways, causing three types of margin: **Constructive Margins**, with plates moving apart and volcanic material forming new land (as in the case of the Mid-Atlantic Ridge in Iceland); **Destructive Margins**, with plates moving together to form fold mountains; and **Passive Margins**, where plates move sideways, causing earthquake activity.

Below: *Lingering snow in the Landmannalaugar area on one of the main routes through the interior.*

VOLCANOES

Volcanoes are mountains formed when hot molten lava is forced through weak points in the earth's crust. The material may be liquid, as in the case of **lava**, or solid, as with volcanic **bombs** or ash. Steam and gases are also commonly found around volcanoes. Volcanoes generally have a distinct **crater**, which may fill with rain water to form a **crater lake**. The shape of a volcano depends very much on the type of material erupted. The most common volcanic material seen in Iceland is **basalt**, which is a very fluid lava, forming extensive **lava fields**. Those volcanoes which are erupting at present are known as **active**, while those which are totally dead are called **extinct**. Volcanoes which are temporarily quiet are said to be **dormant**.

braided streams. The largest of the sandur is Skeiðarár-sandur, situated to the south of the Vatnajökull icecap. The juxtaposition of ice and volcanic activity can have calamitous effects, such as the **jökulhlaup**, where volcanic activity under an icecap melts the ice to cause huge amounts of glacial flood water.

Mountains and Rivers

Many of Iceland's **rivers** have their sources on the ice-caps, particularly on Vatnajökull. The Skjálfandafljót and the Jökulsá á Fjöllum flow northwards to reach the sea to the west and east of Húsavík, while the Lagarfljót runs northeast through Egilsstaðir on its route to the Atlantic. The main river of the southwest is the Þjórsá, which rises in the interior and arrives at the sea east of Selfoss. The volume of water in Iceland's rivers gives rise to some spectacular **waterfalls**, including Gullfoss, east of Reykjavík, or the magnificent Dettifoss in the northeast. Iceland's highest **mountains** are called **nunataks**, or mountains which rise above the level of the ice. They include Hvanna-dalshnjúkur, at 2119m (6952ft), and Barðarbunga, at 2009m (6592ft), both on Vatnajökull. Just as spectacular, although not necessarily as high, are Iceland's volcanoes – particularly Hekla, at 1491m (4892ft), which has a perfect cone shape, capped by snow and ice.

Seas and Shores

The hard, volcanic rocks of Iceland have produced some truly majestic **cliffs**, alive with nesting sea birds in the summer. Winds, particularly those from the prevailing southwest, whip up strong waves which erode the cliffs into **sea stacks** and **arches**, such as those at Dyrhólaey, near Vík. In other areas, deep **fiords**

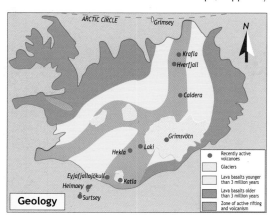

Geology

ARCTIC CIRCLE   Grimsey

N

Krafla
Hverfjall

Caldera

Grimsvötn

Hekla   Laki

Eyjafjallajökull
Heimaey   Katla
          Surtsey

• Recently active volcanoes
   Glaciers
   Lava basalts younger than 3 million years
   Lava basalts older than 3 million years
   Zone of active rifting and volcanism

provide safe harbours for fishing fleets. Less common are **spits** – these are long ridges of sand and shingle formed by longshore drift and marine deposition. They are best seen to the east and west of Höfn, where a narrow gap in the spit leads to a sheltered harbour.

Above: *The Atlantic waves attack the steep cliffs of basalt at Krýsuvíkurberg on the Reykjanes Peninsula.*

Climate

Iceland's maritime climate is noted in particular for its changeability. The people of Iceland are fond of saying, 'if you don't like the weather right now, just wait a few moments and it will change'. Weather conditions such as wind, rain, snow, hail and fog can all feature within a single day, so visitors to this destination need to be prepared for all eventualities.

Iceland's geographical position directly in the path of the **Gulf Stream** combined with the prevailing westerly winds means that winters here are milder than in cities of a more southerly latitude such as Toronto, New York and Moscow. The downside is that though they are less harsh, the winters can be extremely wet, particularly in the southwestern parts of the country around Reykjavík, where the wind makes the climate even more miserable. The situation barely improves in summer, when the capital receives on average only one fine day during the month of July.

COMPARATIVE CLIMATE CHART	REYKJAVÍK				AKUREYRI				EGILSSTAÐIR			
	WIN	SPR	SUM	AUT	WIN	SPR	SUM	AUT	WIN	SPR	SUM	AUT
	JAN	APR	JULY	OCT	JAN	APR	JULY	OCT	JAN	APR	JULY	OCT
AVERAGE TEMP. °C	-0.8	2	11	5	-1.8	3.5	11	3.9	-1.3	1.4	9.9	4.5
AVERAGE TEMP. °F	30.5	35.6	51.8	41	28.7	38.3	51.8	39	29.6	34.5	49.8	40
RAINFALL mm	76	58	52	86	55	29	33	58	134	87	97	169
RAINFALL in	3	2.3	2	3.4	2.1	1.1	1.3	2.3	5.3	3.4	3.8	6.7
DAYS OF RAINFALL	19	17	15	19	16	12	12	17	20	16	15	20

TUNDRA AND PERMAFROST

The higher parts of the interior of Iceland have an ecosystem known as the **tundra**. This is a result of the long, severe winters, a short growing season and precipitation which falls mainly as snow. The ground is permanently frozen, apart from the top 50cm (20in) or so which melts in summer. This condition is known as **permafrost**. Because of the permafrost, the surface of the land is often marshy and badly drained in the summer.

Above: *The mighty
Gullfoss waterfall is completely frozen in winter.*

LAND OF THE
MIDNIGHT SUN

This is a descriptive title
which is often applied to
Iceland, but it is only partly
true. It never really gets dark
anywhere in Iceland during
June, but to actually be able
to see the sun at midnight
means going to a location
within the Arctic Circle.
The only place where this is
possible is on the island of
Grimsey, about 41km
(25 miles) north of Akureyri.
Unfortunately for Grimsey, it
sees no sun at all during the
month of January.

The more eastern and
northern fringes of the
country, which are in the
rain shadow of the central
mountains and icecaps,
fare rather better from the
point of view of sunshine.
Akureyri, in the north, is
the warmest part of the
country and Egilsstaðir, in
the east, is the driest.
When the wind blows
from the Arctic, however,
the temperature can drop
alarmingly. Fogs are com-
mon on the eastern side of
the country, particularly
when cold ocean currents
from the north meet the
more temperate Gulf
Stream. Snowfall is heavy in the interior of the country,
especially on the high icecaps. Much of the interior is
only free enough of snow to allow transport during the
months of July and August. In the drier cold deserts and
sandur, windblown dust and gravel can seriously damage the paintwork of vehicles and make a misery of a
cycling holiday. Visitors, however, will also remember
Iceland for its clarity of light, largely thanks to the
unpolluted environment.

Iceland's position close to the Arctic Circle means
that its daylight hours vary considerably between summer and winter. During the winter months of December
and January, three to four hours of daylight are as much
as can be expected, and Icelanders can suffer from
'short-day despression', with suicide rates increasing at
this time of the year. One compensation, however, is
that this is the best season to see the *aurora borealis*,
or Northern Lights. The situation is reversed in the
summer, when in June and July daylight continues
throughout the night.

Wildlife

One of the main characteristics of the fauna and flora of Iceland is the small number of species to be seen. There are obvious reasons for this – until the end of the Ice Age some 20,000 years ago, Iceland was covered with snow and glaciers. With the climate improving only slowly, the recolonization of plants and animals has been a gradual process, and even today the inhospitable climate and the short growing season are limiting factors. A further reason is the fact that Iceland is an island in an isolated part of the North Atlantic Ocean, making the migration of species difficult.

The only **mammal** which is indigenous to Iceland is the **arctic fox**. Farmers have always blamed the fox for killing lambs, and large numbers have been shot. In fact, the arctic fox lives mainly on small birds and rodents, although it is also a scavenger and can be seen finishing off carcasses of sea birds or sheep. The arctic fox changes the colour of its coat in winter, and a small minority of the species turns completely white. Numbers of arctic foxes have dropped considerably and visitors will be lucky to see this wary animal.

There have been a number of mammals **introduced** inadvertantly, particularly rodents. **Reindeer** were brought in from Norway in the 18th century, but as Icelanders did not readily take to the idea of living as nomadic reindeer herders, the animals reverted to the wild. They were often hunted, both for meat and to prevent them grazing valuable sheep pastures, so that their numbers have frequently dropped to dangerously low levels. The reindeer is now a protected species in Iceland, and they live in scattered

FAILED INTRODUCTIONS

While there have been successful introductions of mammals to Iceland (such as the reindeer), in most cases the introductions have failed. Iceland would seem to be ideal countryside for the **mountain** or **snowshoe hare** and there were several attempts to introduce it as a game species in the 18th and 19th centuries. However, none survived to form a breeding colony. An attempt was made to release **ferrets**, with the object of keeping rat numbers down. This was also unsuccessful. There have been three attempts during the 20th century to introduce **musk ox**, but all the animals died of starvation or disease.

Below: *The arctic fox, Iceland's only indigenous mammal, is wary of man.*

KEIKO

Keiko was a **killer whale** or **orca** who was captured in Icelandic waters in the 1970s to be displayed in aquariums in Canada and Mexico. He became the centre of worldwide attention in the 1990s when he starred in the *Free Willy* film, after which a multimillion dollar campaign was set up to return Keiko to the wild. He was returned to Iceland, where he lived in a large acclimatising sea pen at Heimey in the Westmann Islands. Keiko, who was 35ft long and weighed six tons, was released in 2002. Mixing with several whale pods, he swam 850 miles to the Norwegian fjords, where he became a tourist attraction. Sadly, Keiko died in 2003.

Below: *Since the banning of whaling, orcas or killer whales have become increasingly common in Icelandic waters.*

groups, mainly in the east of the country. **American mink** were introduced for fur farming in the 1930s, and escaped mink can be found throughout the country in marine and freshwater sites. **Polar bears** from Greenland occasionally reach Iceland on ice flows. As this has been going on throughout history, it seems that polar bears could have established themselves in Iceland, but for the fact that they are usually shot on arrival.

Marine mammals are much more plentiful, with around 20 species regularly visiting Icelandic waters. Both common (or harbour) and grey **seals** breed around the coast, and Iceland has around half the world's total population of common seals – the best time to see them is at the end of June when they are pupping. **Walruses** also occasionally appear, mainly on the northwest coast. Spring and summer are the best times to see **whales**. Since the killing of whales has been banned, a number of Icelandic fishing ports have begun to specialize in whale-watching trips which have proved popular with visitors. The most commonly seen whales are sperm, minke, killer and fin, while common **porpoises** and white-beaked **dolphins** also turn up. Iceland's decision in late 2003 to resume a limited amount of whaling for 'scientific purposes' has roused huge international criticism.

There is no doubt that it is the **birds** which comprise the most spectacular part of Iceland's fauna. Although there are only around 70 resident breeding bird species, there are a large number of migrants and accidental visitors, making the Iceland list top well over 300 species. What attracts birders to the country is the rarity of the birds and the fact that they are a curious mixture of European, North American, Arctic and temperate species – three North American species (Barrow's goldeneye, the

great northern diver and the harlequin duck), for example, are found nowhere else in Europe. Sea birds breed in incredible numbers and include gulls, guillemots, skuas, puffins, razorbills, gannets, kittiwakes, fulmars, shags and cormorants. Iceland has an abundance of wetland sites which provide the ideal breeding habitat for geese, whooper swans and a wide variety of ducks. The most important breeding site is Lake Mývatn, where there are vast numbers of tufted duck, scaup, mallard, pintail, gadwall, wigeon and teal. Wading birds, too, are well represented, though birds of prey are limited to the merlin, the gyrfalcon, the threatened white-tailed sea eagle, and the rare snowy owl.

Iceland's freshwater areas abound with **fish**, but there are only five main varieties: Arctic char, eels, salmon, trout and sticklebacks. Visitors should be aware that licences for salmon fishing are cripplingly expensive. On the other hand, there is a rich variety of **oceanic fish**, including cod, haddock, whiting, plaice, ling, sole, redfish and herring. Of the larger fish, the Greenland shark is common in Iceland, and its meat is a popular delicacy.

Iceland's geographical isolation has meant that certain types of fauna are missing. No butterflies breed, although certain migrants, such as painted ladies, may appear in some years. Iceland has no amphibians, such as frogs, toads and newts. Nor, visitors will be pleased to know, are there any snakes!

Above left: *An eider duck's nest, showing the down that is collected for use in bedding.*
Above right: *The fulmar is Iceland's most common seabird, often nesting on inland cliffs.*

BIRDS YOU WILL NOT SEE

The climate and the natural vegetation of Iceland have a limiting effect on the range of birds to be seen. The lack of mature trees means that many of the **passerine** (perching) birds, such as **warblers**, are missing. So are hole-nesting species such as **woodpeckers**, **nuthatches** and **treecreepers**. The general lack of insect life cuts out **swallows**, **martins** and **swifts**. Furthermore, the often frozen water prohibits **kingfishers**. Nor will you find **penguins** – they are confined to the Antarctic!

Above: *Swathes of Alaskan lupins cover the lower hill slopes in early summer.*
Opposite: *Wild flowers are quick to colonize newly weathered soil on glacial moraine and lava flows.*

TUNDRA FLORA

Because of the permafrost conditions and the short growing season, plants on the tundra areas of Iceland have barely two months to complete their life cycles. Such plants must have a very high tolerance to cold and to lack of moisture (water is often unavailable as it is stored as snow or ice). Not surprisingly there are fewer species of plants on the tundra than on any other biome. Plants which do survive tend to be low-growing and rounded in order to gain protection from the wind. Flowering plants can be spectacular, with 'bloom mats' of anenomes, arctic poppies, saxifrages and gentians.

Flora

One of the first things that visitors notice about Iceland is the scarcity of **trees**. For much of the country, dwarf and scrubby willow and birch are the best that can be seen. It is claimed that early inhabitants felled the trees for building materials and fuel, and that sheep prevented regeneration by eating new shoots. Not everyone agrees with this opinion, however, as the Old Norse word for 'woods' is the same as the present-day word for 'willows'. Could it be that the widespread 'forests' were little more than the same scrub seen today? There are two areas of impressive woodland near Hallormsstaðarskógur in the east of the country and at Fnjóskadalur in the north. Many surburban gardens in Reykjavík, helped by a climatic 'heat island', also have a good collection of small trees.

The range of **flowering plants** is small but of considerable interest. It is largely of North European character. Early in the summer cushions of moss campion abound, particularly on the mature lava flows. Dandelions and Alaska lupins are also common at this time of the year, while later in the year vast swathes of white cotton grass cover the landscape. On the heathlands and moorlands, low-growing shrubs are dominant and include whortleberry, crowberry and bearberry. Mosses and lichens are found everywhere and are usually the first plants to colonize new lava flows. Geothermal regions develop their own assemblage of heat-loving plants.

HISTORICAL CALENDAR

700s Irish monks in Iceland.
800s Norse colonization of Iceland begins.
870 The first recognized settler, Ingólfur Arnarson, sets up home in the Reykjavík area.
930 The population reaches around 60,000. Immigrants are mainly people dissatisfied with life in Norway. The Alþing (National Assembly) is set up near Þingvellir Lake.
930–1230 The Saga Age.
990 Leifur Eiríksson discovers North America.
1106 Bishoprics are established at Skálholt and Hólar.
1220 Beginning of the Sturling Period, marked by feuds and violence.
1241 Sturluson is murdered.
1262 Iceland comes under the Norwegian crown.
1300s Period of disasters – earthquakes, volcanic eruptions, famines and diseases.
1397 Iceland and Norway under the Danish crown.
1550 Reformation imposed by the Danish king. The last

Catholic bishop is beheaded.
1700s More volcanic activity, including, in 1783, the Laki eruption. Poisonous gases kill over 10,000 people as well as thousands of animals.
1798 The Alþing moves from Þingvellir to Reykjavík.
1840s Campaign for self-rule led by Jón Sigurðsson.
1904 Home rule is achieved under Danish control.
1940 Denmark occupied by Germany. The Alþing decides that the union with Denmark is now void. Iceland is occupied by British troops as a strategic defence measure.
1941 The USA takes over the defence of Iceland and establishes a base at Keflavík.
1944 Iceland declared an independent republic at Þingvellir on 17 June.
1946 Iceland joins United Nations Organization.
1949 Iceland becomes a founding member of NATO.
1958 The first of the so-called 'Cod Wars' with

Britain over fishery rights.
1970 Iceland joins EFTA.
1974 Iceland's 1406km (874-mile) Ring Road is completed.
1980 Vigdís Finnbogadóttir becomes the world's first democratically elected woman President.
1986 Reagan–Gorbachov summit held at Reykjavík.
1989 Iceland ceases commercial whaling.
1990s Tourism begins to develop as a major foreign currency earner.
2003 Limited whaling resumed for 'scientific reasons'.
2008 World economic recession hits Iceland badly. Its stock market crashes and its three main banks go into receivership.
2009 Iceland applies for EU membership, hoping the Euro will stabilize the economy.
2010 An ash cloud from the volcano Eyjafjallajökull paralyses northern European air travel.

HISTORY IN BRIEF

Iceland's first recorded inhabitants were Irish monks who came to the area, probably by sea-going coracles, in the 700s. They had fled persecution in their own country and came to Iceland seeking a life of quiet contemplation. These hermits fled when the first Norse settlers came around the year 870. The first known Norseman to reach

Opposite: *The 19th-century wooden church at Þingvellir.*
Below: *Statue of Leifur Eiríksson, who is believed to have discovered North America in 990.*

Icelandic shores was a Viking called Naddodur. He found an unpromising snowy landscape. He called the country 'Snæland' and immediately sailed away. Later, a Swede called Garðar Svavarsson circumnavigated the land, confirming that it was an island. In 860, a third Viking called Flóki Vilgerðson navigated his way to the country with the aid of three ravens. He landed in the Breiðafjörður area, where his party spent the winter. He had neglected, however, to collect enough hay for winter food for his animals, which then perished. He named the island 'Iceland' and returned to Norway.

The settlement of Iceland now gathered pace. The immigrants were mainly from Norway where they were disenchanted with the tyrranical rule of King Harald Fair-hair. It is officially recognized that the first permanent settler was **Ingólfur Arnarson**, who arrived in 874. It is said that Arnarson selected the spot where they put ashore in the traditional Viking way by throwing his high seat pillar overboard and waiting to see where it landed. Arnarson named the area Reykjavík (smoky bay) after the vapours from the local hot springs.

Early Government

The period of settlement was over by 930, when the

population had reached asround 25,000. Arnarson's son, Þorsteinn Ingólfsson, founded the first 'þing', or local assembly, and in 930 he was one of the founder members of the **Alþing** or general assembly. The assembly was needed because a number of self-ruling groups had sprung up around the country and a code of law became necessary. The site of the Alþing was chosen to be on the shores of Lake Þingvellir, where delegates came from all over the country for two weeks every year. New laws were decreed, judgements were passed, criminals were punished and claims settled. The opportunity was also taken for marriages to be arranged and business deals to be concluded. For this purpose, a number of stone booths were erected and the remains of these can still be seen today. The Assembly also elected the influential law-speaker, whose task was to recite from memory one third of the country's laws each year. Around the year 1000, the Alþing decreed that Iceland should be a **Christian** rather than a pagan country. Although generally peaceful, there were times when the Alþing degenerated into chaos as armed groups took justice into their own hands and pitched battles resulted.

The Middle Ages

Violence escalated in the mid-13th century, which became known as the **Sturlung Period**. There were ferocious power struggles between the more influential families, the most significant of which were the descendants of Sturla. A key figure at this time was **Snorri Sturluson**, a writer and diplomat. He eventually fell foul of the Norwegian King Hákon the Old, who ordered Snorri's death. In the ensuing chaos, Hákon took over, and by 1262, the Icelanders were forced to surrender their independence to Norway.

The 14th century was an unhappy time for Icelanders, with social hardship and a string of natural catastrophes. Hekla erupted several times and the Black Death reached Iceland, killing two-thirds of the population. In 1380, both Norway and Iceland came under the rule of Denmark, following the Kalmar Union. The Danes imposed the Reformation and Lutheranism on the country and, when the Catholic Bishop of Hólar resisted the changes, he and his two sons were summarily beheaded. In 1602, Denmark introduced a trade monopoly granting exclusive trading rights in Iceland to Danish and Swedish firms. The woes of the Icelanders continued into the 18th century, when a smallpox outbreak killed a third of the population. There were also frequent natural disasters, with the eruptions of Hekla and Katla both leading to

THE SAGAS

The age of the Sagas was from the late 12th to the late 13th centuries. They were epic stories, written largely anonymously, about the early settlers and their struggle to survive. Human relationships were described in detail, so they contain much accurate historical information, including the violent battles and family feuds of the time. The Sagas were often recited by a member of the family while the others worked. They provided entertainment during the boredom of the cold winter nights. The Sagas were written in old Norse and because of the isolation of Iceland, the language has changed little over the centuries, enabling Icelanders today to read the transcribed accounts. Around 40 Sagas were written. The best known is the *Egils Saga*, the biography of Egill Skallagrísson, while the most popular, because of the sympathetic characters, is the *Njáls Saga*.

widespread famine. The most cataclysmic disaster, however, was the eruption, in 1783, of Laki. This went on for ten months, creating the largest lava field of historical times and producing a poisonous haze which destroyed pasture, crops and 75% of the country's livestock. The resulting famine killed nearly 20% of the population.

THE ICELANDIC MANUSCRIPTS

The Sagas and the other historical manuscripts of Iceland were originally written on vellum. When printing was developed in the 16th century, the old parchments lost their significance and many were lost. At the beginning of the 18th century, Árni Magnusson, a lecturer at Copenhagen University, made it his life's work to collect as many Icelandic manuscripts as he could find. Some were destroyed by fire in Copenhagen in 1728, but those that survivied were bequeathed to the University of Copenhagen. After independence in 1944, the people naturally wanted their manuscripts back. The Danish parliament authorized this in 1965 and the first batch arrived back in Iceland six years later. The complete collection is now housed in the Árni Magnusson Institute, which is part of the University of Reykjavík.

Towards Independence

From this low point in Iceland's history, things could only get better, and the 19th century saw the beginnings of the movement towards **independence**. The Alþing, which had been abolished by Denmark, was partially restored in Reykjavík. Denmark then lifted the trade restrictions in 1854 and the freedom of the press followed a year later. An important figure at this time was **Jón Sigurðsson**, a scholar and politician, who lobbied for the restoration of free trade and a return to the full powers of the Alþing. In 1874, Iceland was given its own constitution and was at last able to handle its own financial matters. In 1918, Denmark recognized Iceland as an independent state, although still within the Kingdom of Denmark, which retained responsibility for defence and foreign affairs. When Germany occupied Denmark in 1940, Iceland took control of its own affairs, requesting complete independence.

World War II was now raging and British troops occupied Iceland, which had no armed forces and would be vulnerable to German attack. In 1941, US forces took over and stayed on after the war, when the main threat came from Russia. On 17 June 1944, Iceland declared itself an **independent republic**. Thousands of Icelanders went to Þingvellir, the site of the original parliament, to celebrate the event.

The Modern Era

In the postwar years, Iceland's international participation grew apace when it joined the United Nations, and then in 1949 became one of the founder members of NATO. Iceland also maintained its traditional ties with its Nordic neighbours by becoming part of the Nordic Council.

In 1958 Iceland extended its fishery limits to 20km (12 miles), provoking the first of the **Cod Wars** with Britain. The second Cod War came in 1972, when the limit was extended to 75km (47 miles). The limit was then extended to 320km (200 miles) in 1975, leading to the third Cod War. When Iceland threatened to withdraw from NATO and break off diplomatic relations, Britain was forced to accept the limits. It was Iceland, however, which had to back down over the whaling issue, due to environmental pressure. At the moment the whaling industry in Iceland is dormant – being restricted to the culling of a number of minkes for 'scientific purposes'.

Iceland made considerable social advances in the postwar years. It was the first country in the world to have a woman president, and had a thriving Women's Party (which amalgamated with smaller parties in order to oppose the Independence Party). It has comprehensive health and education services, clean air and good housing. The unemployment rate is low and life expectancy is high. Today Iceland's living standards are amongst the highest in the world, but the country's stability was rocked in 2008, when the world economic crisis hit Iceland seriously, leading to the failure of the three main banks and the eventual collapse of the government. The incoming coalition administration immediately applied for membership of the EU, with the hope of stabilizing the economy (see panel, this page).

ECONOMIC COLLAPSE

With the world financial crisis in 2008, it became clear that Iceland's economy was built on unsustainable debt. Gordon Brown's anti-terrorist legislation froze the assets of Icesave, in which over 300,000 British people had invested. Despite help from the IMF, the standard of living in Iceland fell, leading to riots, protests and the fall of the government in January 2009. The replacement coalition led by Jóhanna Sigurðardóttir (the world's first openly gay prime minister) immediately applied for EU membership. It's hoped that the euro will replace the króna in 2011 when membership is confirmed and more stability will be brought to the Icelandic economy.

Opposite: *Crowds surround the statue of Jón Sigurðsson in Reykjavík on Iceland's National Day.* **Below:** *Iceland's fishing fleet has the benefit of a 330km exclusion zone.*

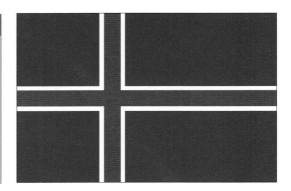

Above right: *Icelanders are exceedingly proud of their national flag, which is seen throughout the country, flying from prominent buildings as well as the most humble farmsteads.*
Below: *A man and toddler celebrate the Icelandic National Day, which is typified by various parades, music and folk dancing.*

GOVERNMENT AND ECONOMY

Iceland has been an independent democratic republic since 1944 (although it could be argued that it is the world's oldest parliamentary democracy). The parliament, or Alþing, has 63 members, of whom around a third are usually women. The parliament is elected from eight constituencies for a four-year term. A system of proportional representation is used and every citizen has the right to vote and to stand for parliament. The main **political parties** are, on the right, the Independence Party and the Progressive Party, and, on the left, the Social Democratic Alliance and the Left-Green Movement. The distribution of votes inevitably means that Iceland has a

coalition government, currently an alliance between the Social Democrats and the Left-Green Movement, led by Jóhanna Sigurdarðóttir. Presidential elections take place on a four-year basis. The president has a largely ceremonial and figurehead role. The fifth president of Iceland, who has held office since 1996, is Ólafur Grímsson. The next presidential elections will take place in 2012. Local government is run on the basis of 23 administrative counties, or *syslur*, subdivided into 200 rural districts, or *hreppur*.

Defence

Iceland has no armed forces of its own apart from a few armed fishery protection and coastguard vessels. Its security is guaranteed by its membership of NATO. The United States maintained a controversial naval air base at Keflavík from 1951 until September 2006, when it pulled out. The cessation of the Cold War with Russia made the base redundant (along with the 900 Icelanders who worked there). Communication equipment remains and the US has promised to continue to guarantee Iceland's security.

Above: *There have been successful experiments in farming salmon, such as in this fiord at Skjálfandi.*

The Economy

Iceland's economy relies heavily on **fishing**, which accounts for over 70% of the country's exports. There are over 900 vessels engaged in fishing, producing an annual catch of around 1.5 million tonnes. The fishing fleet, however, accounts for only 5% of the workforce, with a further 8% involved in fish processing. Fish are exported fresh, frozen, canned and salted. The main fish caught here are cod, redfish, capelin, haddock and saithe. Shellfish include prawns and lobster. Successful experiments have been carried out in salmon and trout farming. The traditional government opposition to joining the EU is primarily because of Icelanders' fear of losing control over their fishing resources.

Due to the short growing season and the brief, cool summer, only about 1% of the country is devoted to **farming**. Iceland is outside the northern limit of grain production, so the most important crop is hay, which is used as winter food for cattle and sheep. There are over half a million sheep in Iceland and lamb is an important export. In summer, the sheep graze in the highlands so that the better pastures can be used for hay. Farming has become increasingly mechanized and many of the boggy

Above: *Geothermal plants supply energy for homes, industry and horticulture.*

lowlands have been drained. Nevertheless, the number of farm workers has dropped and rural areas have been depopulated as Icelanders increasingly prefer an urban environment. The remaining farmers have been encouraged to diversify and many make a supplementary living out of tourism by offering farmhouse accommodation. Cheap geothermal electricity has led to the growth of a greenhouse industry, specializing in the production of tomatoes and other salad crops. Flowers and tropical fruits such as bananas are also grown. The industry is centred around Hveragerði in the southwest of Iceland. Many people are employed in the production of both geothermal and hydroelectric energy, the low cost of which has encouraged the development of aluminium smelting and diatom production (*see* page 86).

The largest growth industry is **tourism**. It is currently increasing both its income and the number of tourists who visit the country by 4–5% a year – around 200,000 visitors annually. Accurate statistics are difficult to obtain, however, since many visitors are transit passengers en route to North America or Europe, while others are Icelanders returning from working abroad. The majority of visitors come to Iceland in the brief summer season from July to August, when there is considerable pressure on accommodation. To overcome this, many boarding schools and colleges are turned into hotels for this period.

Inflation has often been a problem in Iceland, although in the early years of the present century it was largely under control. All this was to change in 2008 with the world finiancial crisis, when it reached nearly 14%. **Unemployment** has traditionally been low, with many Icelanders having more than one job in order to maintain a decent standard of living, but the economic meltdown has increased unemployment to 7.6% (July 2010). Over half of Iceland's **exports** go to the Eurozone, with 14% coming to the UK. The main exports are fish and fish products, aluminium and alloys, and animal products. The main **imports** are machinery and equipment, petroleum products, foodstuffs and textiles.

THE PEOPLE
It is frequently claimed that Icelanders are, in origin, the 'least Nordic' of the Scandinavian people, with research showing that there is a significant Celtic element in their genes. However, the country does not have a history of absorbing foreigners. Even today, immigration is strictly controlled. Visitors are likely to find that Icelanders are shy upon a first encounter, but this reserve usually gives way to warm hospitality.

Icelandic Names
Most Icelanders have a **patronymic** rather than a family surname, a system which was once common throughout Scandinavia. It is usual for a father, mother, daughter and son each to have a different last name. It works like this: a child takes his father's first name for a surname, to which is added 'son' if the child is a boy or 'dóttir' if a girl. Their own first name is then added. But there are further complications, because a woman retains her own name on marriage. This means that with a family comprising husband, wife, son and daughter, each family member will have a different last name. For example, the father might be called Magnus Jónsson, the son Sigurdur Magnusson, the daughter Gudrún Magnusdottír and the wife Vígdis Kristjándottír. For these reasons, Icelanders always refer to each other by their first name and will expect visiting foreigners to do likewise.

COPING WITH THE TELEPHONE DIRECTORY

Hotel guests paging through a telephone directory to ring a business colleague or friend are in for a shock. Firstly, Iceland is such a small place that the whole country can be covered in one directory. Secondly, everyone is listed by their first names, rather than their surnames. This means that there might be three pages of entries under the name of, say, Leifur. Thirdly, a husband and wife living at the same address and sharing a telephone will have separate entries – quite sensible really! Another useful feature is that many Icelanders also list their e-mail address in the directory.

Below: *Icelandic children in traditional woollen hats. In the remote rural areas, children attend boarding school from an early age.*

A LOVE OF BOOKS

Go into any house in Iceland and you'll find a well-stocked bookshelf. Icelanders are fiercely proud of their literary tradition, but also, because of their geographical isolation, see books about other parts of the world as a way of broadening their minds. Bookshops abound, not just in Reykjavík, but in many of the smaller settlements. There is a thriving publishing industry in Iceland and it is claimed that more books are published per head of the population than in any other country in the world. Furthermore, one in every ten Icelanders is said to write and publish a book during his or her lifetime.

Below: *A wedding in Akureyri. Many Icelanders, however, will live together rather than marry.*

Language

The geographical isolation of Iceland has enabled the country to maintain a language which is similar to Old Norse. The language is closely linked to the culture of the country so that its preservation is a matter of national pride and identity. It has changed so little over time that Icelanders are still able to read the Sagas written over 700 years ago. Sometimes called the 'Latin of the North', Icelandic is a highly complex language and very difficult for non-Nordic people to learn. After mastering their own tongue, Icelanders tend to find other languages easier to learn and many become excellent linguists. They are determined that Icelandic should not be corrupted and and a special academic committee has been formed to find Icelandic words for international terms such as 'computer' and 'mobile phone'.

Iceland has always produced accomplished writers and poets (*skalds*), from the writers of the Sagas and Eddic poems to the present day. In the 19th century, **Jónas Hallgrímsson** was a well-loved romantic poet who was at the forefront of the independence movement and the first Icelander to have a statue raised in his memory. The most important literary figure of the 20th century was undoubtedly **Hálldór Kiljan Laxness**, the winner

of the 1955 Nobel Prize for Literature. A one-time monk, communist and film writer, he spent much of his life living abroad, but his novels were largely about the harsh conditions of rural life in Iceland.

Not surprisingly, interest in **books** in Iceland is great. There are over 30 publishers in the country printing over 1000 new titles annually. This is the highest book per capita ratio in the world. There are numerous bookshops, particularly in Reykjavík. In addition, there are five national daily **newspapers**, plus regional papers and countless special-interest magazines. Furthermore there are four TV channels, a national theatre and opera house, many art galleries and numerous museums – not bad for a population of just over 300,000!

Religion

The established church in Iceland is the **Evangelical Lutheran Church**, which was made the national church after the Reformation in 1550. Some 96% of the population claim to be Protestants,

Above: *This turf church in Núpsstaður is the smallest church in Iceland.*

although only a small fraction attend churches on a regular basis. There are a small number of Roman Catholics, Jehovah's Witnesses and pagan followers of Thor.

Icelanders' attitude towards **marriage** has never been particularly serious. In fact, around 70% of first-born children are born to unmarried parents. Single mothers are not frowned upon (a recent president of the country was a single parent), and children are welcomed, whatever the circumstances of their birth.

The Role of Women

Women were given the right to vote in national elections in 1915. They marked the start of the United Nations Women's Decade in 1975 by holding a one-day strike, bringing the whole of Iceland to a standstill. As well as Iceland having a female president, a Women's Alliance political party was also formed and soon gained representation in parliament. This frightened the other political parties so much that they put forward a number of female candidates, which has resulted in the Icelandic parliament having some 22% female MPs. On the employment front, almost 90% of women in Iceland are employed outside the home, but their salaries are still little more than half those of men.

ELVES AND TROLLS

A recent survey found that 53% of Icelanders believed in fairies! Well, let us qualify that – 53% of Icelanders were not prepared to deny their existence. In fact, 5% of the population claim to have actually met a fairy, an elf, a troll or one of the 'hidden people'. In a country where the overwhelming majority claim to be Christians, these statistics are perhaps a little surprising. While ghosts were traditionally malevolent beings in Icelandic history, elves tended to be more welcome, and today modern Icelanders are happy to live alongside them – they consider the existence of elves to be a 'pleasant idea'.

POPULATION

Population: 320,000 (2009 census)
Ages: 0–14 years: 23.18%
15–64 years: 65.01%
65 and over: 11.81%
Population growth rate: 0.54%
Birth rate:
14.62 births/1000 people
Death rate: 6.3/1000 people
Sex ratio: (male:female)
at birth: 1.08
under 15 years: 1.07
15–64 years: 1.02
65 years and over: 0.81
life expectancy at birth:
male: 79.6 years
female: 83.0 years
Infant mortality: 2.4/1000 live births (2003 figures)

CHURCH ARCHITECTURE

The church architecture in Iceland ranges from small turf chapels built by local farmers, often no bigger than a garden shed, to large Lutheran cathedrals on which no expense has been spared. In between are village churches in typical Nordic style with red corrugated iron roofs, simple towers and plain interior fittings. The modern churches with a geological theme are memorable and everyone will want to see the **Hallgrímskirkja** in Reykjavík, with its basalt-like columns. The same architect produced a smaller version in **Akureyri**. Don't miss the church in **Blönduós**, which is designed like a volcano, complete with a crater.

Education

Iceland claims **100% literacy** and certainly education standards are very high. Because of the remoteness of the rural areas of Iceland, many children have to attend boarding school from an early age. Those students who go on to complete the secondary grammar stage will be nearly 20 years of age. There are over 5000 students at the University of Iceland in Rekjavík and at its outpost at Akureyri, and usually around 3000 Icelandic students at foreign universities.

Health

Iceland has an excellent National Health service, which is free to all. Icelanders have one of the greatest **life expectancy** figures in the world. Women can expect to live to 83.0 years, men 79.6 – a record which only the Japanese can better. Public health care is no doubt a contributing reason for this, but an unpolluted environment and a healthy fish-based diet are also important factors.

Arts and Crafts

Iceland has a long tradition of landscape **painting**, particularly since the beginning of the 20th century. Stalwarts include Ásgrímur Jónsson (1876–1959),

Jóhannes Kjarval (1885–1972) and Jón Stefánsson (1881–1962), whose work can be seen in numerous museums and galleries in Reykjavík. Visitors will soon appreciate Iceland's love of **sculpture**, starting at Keflavík airport, the environs of which have some striking modern pieces of work. Statues abound in Reykjavík and other towns, often representing poets and Icelandic heroes rather than politicians and generals. The best-known of the Icelandic sculptors are Ásmundur Sveinsson (1893–1982) and Sigurjón Ólafsson (1908–82), both of whom have museums devoted to their work in Reykjavík.

Icelandic **craft** work consists mainly of pottery and woollen goods. Many visitors take home woollen jumpers in traditional patterns, which are made from the fleece of the Icelandic sheep. The fleeces contain natural oils which keep out water and the soft inner wool makes a good insulation. The most popular line in ceramics is 'lavaware', which has pieces of lava fired into the clay, but discriminating buyers might consider it to be rather garish.

Food and Drink

Eating out is a major expense for the visitor to Iceland, largely because many food items have to be imported.

Icelandic food has traditionally been based on **lamb** and **fish**, which are the most commonly available products. In the past they were preserved for the winter in a variety of ways: smoked, pickled, dried and salted, methods which are reflected in the way in which they are served today. Many of the fish, which include cod, herring, halibut, haddock, salmon and trout, will be familiar to visitors. Other traditional foods include whale steaks, seal, and even sea birds such as puffins. The lack of fresh **vegetables** means that main courses are usually accompanied by such items as potatoes,

Opposite: *Modern sculpture at Keflavík Airport depicting, a bird emerging from its egg.* **Below:** *Drying fish at Flateyri, northwest Iceland.*

UNUSUAL FOOD SPECIALITIES

Early Icelanders needed to conserve food for winter. Not wishing to waste any part of the animal or fish, this led to some unusual food special- ities. The sheep, for instance, provides *Súrsaðir hrútspungar*, or pickled rams testicles; *svið*, singed sheep's head complete with eyes; and *slátur*, a collec- tion of sheep's leftovers boiled in a sheep's stomach, much like haggis. The most alien of all to foreigners is *hákari*, or putrefied shark meat. There are, however, more accept- able traditional dishes, such as Christmas meals of *Hanmgi- kjöt* (smoked lamb) and *rjúpa* (mature ptarmigan cooked in milk gravy). One result of the financial crisis in Iceland and the general tightening of belts has been a resurgence in the popularity of many of these traditional dishes.

pickled cabbage and tinned peas or carrots. The growth of the geothermally heated greenhouse industry has served to encourage the appearance of various **salads** on many an Icelandic menu in recent years. **Desserts** are usually in the form of cake or dairy produce.

Restaurants in Iceland are generally rather expensive, particularly those in hotels. Fortunately, some offer 'tourist menus' – usually consisting of soup, main course and coffee – at a fixed price, which is normally slightly lower at lunch time. American-style fast-food restaurants are common and popular in Reykjavík, but scarce in other parts of the country. A cheap option at kiosks and petrol stations is the **hot dog** (*pylsur*), which is enorm- ously popular with Icelanders.

The price of **alcoholic drinks** in Iceland is astro- nomical and visitors are advised to bring their own supplies into the country. Strong beer was prohibited until 1989. Now strong beers from abroad are on sale, and Icelandic beer is also excellent. Wines can be bought with meals but are extremely expensive. The local spirit is *brennivn*, a type of schnapps made from potatoes and flavoured with caraway seed. It is known as 'Black Death' after the name on the label.

Below: *Lounging in hot tubs is a popular activity throughout Iceland.*

Sport and Recreation

Iceland's most popular recreation is surely **swimming**. Although not great competitors, Icelanders love the social

activity of simply lolling around in hot, geothermally heated water, even when snow is falling around them. **Football** is very popular and the national team has embar- rassed some of the world's top countries in matches in recent years. There are a number of Icelandic profes- sionals who play for clubs overseas, particularly in the English premiership. **Golf** has

increased greatly in popularity through the years, and there are over 20 courses which allow visitors to play. The long winters restrict outdoor activities, so indoor sports are widely played, including **badminton** and **handball**, in which the Icelandic team is one of the best in the world. **Chess** is a national pastime and Iceland boasts no fewer than six grand masters, the highest per capita ratio in the world. **Bridge** is also keenly played, particularly since the national team won the world championship in Japan in 1991. There are **skiing** facilities near many towns in Iceland, although the short hours of daylight in winter are a restricting factor. **Horse riding** was once a necessity for the farming community, though nowadays farming is much more mechanized, and horse riding has become a popular pastime with Icelanders and visitors alike. Freshwater **fishing** is available throughout the country and there are several exclusive salmon fishing clubs. A licence for salmon fishing is extremely expensive, while trout fishing is more reasonably priced. Iceland has become one of the prime venues for **outdoor adventure activities**. Among the activities on offer are hiking and trekking, mountain biking, mountaineering and river rafting. Icelanders also have a fascination with cross-country touring on snowmobiles and in super jeeps.

Above: *Upskiing is one of the more unusual types of recreation in Iceland.*

THE GOLFING PHENOMENON

Considering Iceland's inhospitable climate and lack of daylight for much of the year, it is perhaps surprising that golf has become so popular. There are believed to be 40 courses in Iceland, ranging from five-hole tracts built by enthusiastic local farmers to 18-hole international standard courses on the outskirts of Reykjavík. Visitors are welcome at the 28 golf clubs in Iceland, but be prepared for some high green fees. The most novel competition is the Arctic Open at Akureyri, which takes place in midsummer, allowing players to tee off at midnight and play through the night.

2
Reykjavík

When **Ingólfur Arnarson**, Iceland's first recognized settler, threw his high seat pillars (*öndvegissúlur*) overboard, they washed ashore at a small peninsula in southwest Iceland. In the Viking tradition, he decided that this would be the place where he would settle. The year was 874. He called the place Reykjavík, which loosely translates as 'smoky bay', on account of the steam rising from the hot springs in the area. Today, 'smokeless bay' would be a more apt description, as Iceland's capital is one of the least polluted cities in the world. Despite this early settlement, Reykjavík was slow to grow. Two factors, however, accelerated the process. Firstly, in the mid-1700s, a businessman named **Skúli Magnusson** set up a number of local industries in an attempt to break the Danish trade barriers. His small factories attracted workers from the surrounding rural area. Secondly, the **Alþing** (the Icelandic parliament) was relocated, moving from Þingvellir to Reykjavík. Nevertheless, at the beginning of the 19th century, there were still only 300 inhabitants in the town. By the end of the century the population had grown to 2000. The steady growth continued and by Independence Day in 1944 the number of inhabitants stood at 45,000. Today that figure has quadrupled and stands at just under 200,000. Over half of Iceland's population now lives in the capital city.

Reykjavík is the world's most northerly capital and despite its small size it has a university, a National Theatre, a symphony orchestra and an opera house, plus all the other features one would expect to find in a

DON'T MISS

*** The Hallgrímskirkja: a modernistic church with great views from its tower over the city and harbour.
*** Tjörnin: city-centre lake full of wildfowl; City Hall stands in northwest corner.
** Öskjuhlið: a hilltop crowned by the city's water tanks and a revolving restaurant.
** Bernhöftstorfan: a group of old wooden buildings at the western end of Bankastræti.
** Austurvöllur: a pleasant city square, near parliament and the Lutheran Cathedral.

Opposite: *The distinctive Hallgrímskirkja, Reykjavik's most famous landmark.*

CLIMATE

Reykjavík, the capital city, is
located in the wettest and
windiest part of the country,
facing the full force of the
prevailing **southwesterly
winds**. In the dark winters, the
average temperatures fall to
just below freezing point.
Spring and autumn are cool,
but things improve in **summer**
with an average temperature
in July of 10.6°C (51°F).
Rainfall is moderate throughout the year, with a total of
799mm (31.5 in), peaking in
January and October.

Opposite: *Eider ducks are
among the many wildfowl
found on Tjörnin lake.*
Below: *A variety of buildings and architectural
styles on the shore of
the Tjörnin.*

capital city. Visitors to Reykjavík will find that Icelanders
are proud of their landscape and, both in the rural areas
and in the city, litter, thankfully, is not tolerated. Street
crime, too, is minimal and there is probably no safer city
in the world than Reykjavík.

THE OLD TOWN

The old town, where most of the important buildings in
Reykjavík are to be found, is a compact area which can
easily be covered on foot. The most readily recognizable
feature is the **Tjörnin**, or pond – a small lake which is a
haven for wildfowl. Built partly over the lake is the new
Town Hall, or **Ráðhús**. Just to the north is the pleasant
square known as the **Austurvöllur**, where Ingólfur
Arnarson originally had his hayfields. At the side of the
square is the **Alþingshúsið**, or parliament house, and
away to the east are the main shopping streets. Few
visitors will want to miss seeing the modern church
called the **Hallgrímskirkja**. From the top of its tower a
panoramic view stretches across the city's rooftops.
Another good view can be had from the **Perlan** (the
Pearl), a restaurant perched on top of the city's hot-water
storage tanks. Add the many museums and art galleries
and there is plenty to occupy the visitor for several days.

Around the Tjörnin ★★★

In the heart of the old town is the **Tourist Information Centre (TIC)**, located in the middle of a group of wooden buildings at Aðalstræti 2. A city map is available, along with a host of brochures, videos and maps of Iceland. The helpful staff can arrange accommodation and book tours. Particularly useful to visitors are the English-language publications *Around Iceland, Around Reykjavík, What's on in Reykjavík* and *Iceland Explorer*. The TIC is open daily, 08:30–18:00 in summer and 10:00–16:00 in winter; closed on Sundays (www.visitreykjavik.is).

From the TIC take the short walk to the **Tjörnin**. Warm springs keep this lake ice-free in winter so it is an all-year-round haven for birds. Identification boards help visitors to name the wildfowl, including the handsome eider ducks, which are found throughout Iceland. Arctic terns, which spend the winter in the Antarctic, breed on rafts in the centre of the lake, and whooper swans can usually be seen in the summer. Over 40 species of birds have been recorded at this lake. In the northwestern corner of the Tjörnin is the **Rádhús**, or Town Hall. It is ultramodern in

EIDER DUCKS

One of the first birds the visitor to Iceland will see is the eider duck, which breeds on the **Tjörnin Lake** in the centre of Reykjavík. The drake is handsome, with black, white and green plumage, while the female is a drab brown. They are essentially **marine ducks**, but will breed on lakes and rivers close to the coast. The female lines the nest with down from her own breast. The **down** has been used for centuries for stuffing pillows. The **eggs** are also eaten, and the eider duck has been semi-domesticated in Iceland. After hatching, the eider ducklings gather together in a crèche, often consisting of over 30 birds, looked after by one or two of the females.

Above: Reykjavík's modern Rádhús, or town hall, is built into the waters of Lake Tjörnin right in the centre of the city.

design and built partially on stilts over the lake. Completed in 1992, its design was controversial, because many people felt that it was out of place in the old part of the city. The entrance hall is well worth a look – there is an information desk and a huge relief map of Iceland. Away to the southwest of the lake are the modern buildings comprising the **University of Iceland**, which was established in 1911 and now has over 5000 students. Amongst the university buildings is the **Árni Magnússon Institute**, which was named after the man who, in the 18th century, did much to track down the original manuscripts of the Sagas and Eddas. The institute is open daily in summer from 13:00–17:00, with reduced hours in winter (www.arnastofnun.is). Also on the university site is the **Nordic House**, which acts as a cultural link between Iceland and the other Nordic countries. Documentary films are shown daily and there are information evenings for tourists. The Nordic House is open from 09:00–16:30 and has an excellent cafeteria.

Austurvöllur ★★★

Just to the north of the Tjörnin is the attractive square known as the **Austurvöllur**, occupying land which was once Ingólfur Arnarson's farm. In the centre of the square is a **Statue of Jón Sigurðsson** (1811–79), who led the 19th-century independence movement in Iceland. Built on the southern side of the Austurvöllur is the **Alþingishúsið**, or Parliament House. This dull, grey basalt building was constructed in 1881, before Iceland's independence from Denmark, which explains the Danish coat of arms on the front of the building. On the southeastern side of the Austurvöllur is the **Dómkirkjan**, or Lutheran Cathedral. It dates from 1796, when it was built on the orders of the Danish King. The inside is more interesting than the rather ordinary exterior. Look out for the modern font, made by the Danish sculptor Berthel Thorvaldsen. The Dómkirkjan is open on weekdays (except Wednesdays) from 10:00–17:00.

Around Arnarhöll ***

Located along Lækjargata is the **Stjórnarráðið**, or Government House. Built between 1765 and 1770, this whitewashed building was once a prison, but now contains the offices of the prime minister. A short distance to the north of Government House is a low, grassy hillock known as **Arnarhöll** (Eagle Hill). On the summit is a statue of Ingólfur Arnarson, Iceland's first official settler, shown looking out of his boat towards the land he was to make his home. The most interesting, and oldest, street in the area is **Aðalstræti**, which was where Skúli Magnusson set up his cottage industries in the mid-18th century. The oldest house is number 10, which dates back to 1752. It was once a small weaving workshop, but is now a popular restaurant.

> ### ICELAND'S NATIONAL DAY
>
> The **17th of June** is Iceland's National Day, celebrating the founding of the **Republic of Iceland** in 1944 and also the birthday of the independence leader **Jón Sigurðsson**. Although celebrations take place throughout the country, the place to be is **Reykjavík**. Celebrations start at 10:00 with the president laying a wreath at the statue of Jón Sigurðsson opposite the Alþing. Then follow the processions, bands playing national songs, and folk dancing. Vendors sell hats, flags, balloons and hotdogs. Between 30,000 and 40,000 people attend the celebrations each year.

Left: *Icelandic children wear traditional costumes on National Day.*

CITY OF SCULPTURES

Reykjavík probably has more sculptures per capita than any other major city in the world. The scene is set when the visitor arrives in the country at **Keflavík Airport**, which has a number of huge, eye-catching modern sculptures. Iceland has several important 20th-century sculptors, including **Einar Jónsson**, **Ásmundur Sveinsson** and **Sigurjón Ólafsson**. Their work, as well as that of contemporary artists, can be found through-out the city. A brochure, describing a **sculpture trail** around the old part of the city, can be obtained from the Tourist Information Centre.

Below: *The clarity of this panoramic view – from the top of the Hallgrímskirkja tower over Reykjavík – is due to the lack of pollution.*

Rooftop Views ★★★

There are two popular places to go for good views over the city: the Hallgrímskirkja and the Öskjuhlíð. **Hallgrímskirkja**, just to the east of the city centre, is often mistaken for the cathedral. Completed in 1974, it was built in memory of the Reverend Hallgrímur Pétursson, a noted composer of hymns. The church has one of the geological designs for which Iceland is noted, with its white-coloured west end built of basalt-like columns, which soar up to a graceful tower, some 75m (246ft) in height. The style of the austere interior is traditional Gothic, but most visitors come to take the lift to the top of the tower accompanied by taped choral music, for the superb view over Reykjavík. The church and tower are open from 10:00–18:00 (www.hallgrims kirkja.is). On the green in front of the Hallgrímskirkja is a statue of Leifur Eiríksson, a gift from the USA to celebrate the 1000th anniversary of the Alþing.

Öskjuhlíð, a hill which overlooks the domestic airport and the bay, is another good viewpoint. The summit has some old bunkers and gun emplacements, relics of World War II. Also perched on top of the hill is a group of hot-water storage tanks which supply the hot water to the city. A revolving restaurant called the **Perlan** (Pearl) is on top of the tanks. Also here is the Saga Museum (*see page 39*).

A path from the Öskjuhlíð leads down to the **Nauthólsvik Geothermal Beach**. Golden sand for the beach was imported from Morocco, and that, along with an artificial hot spring and numerous hot tubs, ensures that this is a popular venue for the locals during the summer months.

THE HARBOUR

Reykjavík's harbourside is full of interest. The shoreline here was once marked by **Hafnarstræti** (Harbour Street), but the waterfront was extended during World War II. The Customs House, on Hafnarstræti, has some excellent 19th-century houses on its southern side. The harbourside is the regular venue for the **Kolaportið flea market**, where great bargains

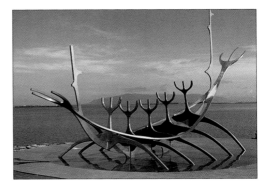

can be found, particularly home-made woollen goods. At the eastern end of the harbour, off Sæbraut, is probably the most remarkable of all the many sculptures in the city; the **Viking Ship**, by Jón Gunnar Árnason, is very photogenic. The harbour is the starting point for boat trips for whale watching and bird observation.

Above: *Of all the artworks in Reykjavík, this harbourside sculpture of a Viking boat, the work of Jón Gunnar Árnason, is the most distinctive.*

MUSEUMS AND GALLERIES
The National Museum ★★

Founded in 1863, the National Museum moved to its present location on Hringbraut (entrance in Suðurgata) in 1950. It has over 16,000 artefacts from Viking times to the present, including costumes, agricultural implements, nautical equipment, furniture and boats. The most famous item is the wooden church door from Valpjófsstaður. This door was carved in the 13th century and depicts a Norse battle scene. Open 10:00–17:00 (summer), 11:00–17:00 (winter); closed on Mondays. Suðurgata 41, tel: 530 2200, www.natmus.is

Listasafn Íslands (National Gallery of Iceland) ★

Located just behind the Fríkirkjan (or Free Church) at Fríkirkjuvegur 7, this building has a chequered history. Originally a storage space for ice cut from Lake Tjörnin, it later became a nightclub, before a fire reduced it to a shell in 1971. It was then renovated to house the picture collection from the National Museum. There are

IN PURSUIT OF SALMON

Reykjavík is unique as a capital city in having a first-class salmon river running within its boundaries. But visitors beware! Any salmon caught in Iceland is likely to be one of the most pricey caught anywhere in the world! A licence to catch salmon is extremely **expensive**. Add the price of a guide, equipment and transportation and you have some of the most costly angling imaginable. Fortunately there is the cheaper option of fishing for char and trout. Contact the **Angling Club of Reykjavík**, tel: 568 6050.

Above: *The city's hot water storage tanks are the unusual location for the Pearl Restaurant.*

A MAN-MADE GEYSER

Visitors to the revolving **Pearl Restaurant** on Öskjuhlíð hill are now treated to an additional attraction besides the view. An automatic geyser has been installed. It is not mechanical, but designed on the same principle which causes natural geysers to spout. Superheated geothermal water enters a tapering tube under pressure. Eventually the pressure builds up to such an extent that an eruption of water occurs every five minutes or so. The pipe then refills and the cycle is repeated.

---

also some visiting exhibitions. Open 11:00–17:00, Tuesday–Sunday, tel: 515 9600, www.listasafn.is Admission is free, except for special exhibitions.

Ásmundur Sveinsson Museum ★

Located on Sigtun, in the east of the city, this museum is in a remarkable igloo-shaped building, designed by the sculptor himself. Although he spent a great part of his life abroad, the themes of Sveinsson's work come from Icelandic folklore. The museum's garden is full of the sculptor's abstract concrete figures. Open 10:00–16:00 (summer), 13:00–16:00 (winter). Ásmundur Sveinsson's house is at Freyjugata 41, opposite the Hallgrímskirkja, and also houses the Iceland Labour Union's Art Gallery. Open daily, 14:00–19:00; tel: 553 2155.

Einar Jónsson Museum ★

This cube-shaped building, designed by the sculptor, is also near the Hallgrímskirkja. The most mystic of all the Icelandic sculptors, Jónsson's only traditional work is the statue of Jón Sigurðsson in the Austurvöllur Njarðargata. Open June–September, 14:00–17:00 but closed on Mondays; tel: 551 3797, www.skulptur.is

Kjarvalsstaðir ★

Located in Miklatún Park, the Kjarvalsstaðir (Municipal Art Gallery) displays the works of Iceland's best-known artist, the surrealist painter Jóhannes Kjarval (1885–1972). His work is displayed in two large rooms, but there are also numerous exhibitions by other painters, both Icelandic and international. Open 10:00–18:00, daily.

Numismatic Museum ★

This museum at Kalkofnsvegur 1, near the Kjarvalsstaðir, houses collection of coins, medals, military decorations and related books. Open weekdays only, 13:30–15:30.

Natural History Museum ★

Situated at Hverfisgata 116, near Hlemmur bus station, this museum has a large collection of rocks, minerals and indigenous flora and fauna. Open Tuesday, Thursday, Saturday and Sunday, 13:30–16:00. Admission fee.

Sigurjón Ólafsson Museum ★

This museum, located at Laugarnestangi 70 between Laugardalur and the harbour, displays a collection of this sculptor's work. Opening times vary according to the season; tel: 553 2906

Museum of Photography ★

A collection of ancient and modern photographs as well as photographic equipment, at Borgartún 1. Open weekdays, 12:00–15:30.

Saga Museum ★★

Realistic dioramas of important moments in Iceland's history; in the Perlan complex and hot water tanks on Öskjuhlíð hill. Open 10:00–18:00, June–August; tel: 511 1517, website: www.sagamuseum.is

Below: *The Natural History Museum has some fine geological specimens.*

Árbæjarsafn (Open Air Museum) ★

Based on a mid-15th-century farm on the eastern outskirts of the city, Árbæjarsafn is a collection of ancient farm buildings and homes from around the country, and reassembled on the site. They include a turf church (1842) from the Skagafjörður area, numerous barns and a sheep hut. There are also transport items, including the only locomotive to run in Iceland (used to construct Reykjavík harbour). Open in summer only, daily except Monday, 10:00–18:00. Admission fee.

Reykjavík 871 +/-2

This fascinating museum is based around a Viking longhouse dated at around 871, which was discovered when the Hotel Centrum was built. Artefacts recovered show that the inhabitants were farmers, hunters and fishermen, who knew how to smelt metals. Located at Adelstræt 16; tel: 411 6370, website: www. reykjavík871.is

OTHER PLACES OF INTEREST
Höfði House ★

This building in Borgartún, close to the shore, is used for civic receptions and functions. Its main claim to

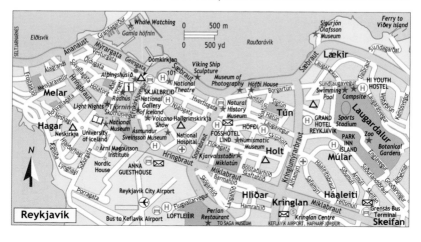

fame is that it was the venue for the Reagan–Gorbachev summit in 1986. There is a superb sculpture in the front of the building by Sigurjón Ólafsson.

Botanical Gardens ★

Approximately 65% of Iceland's plants are found in the Botanical gardens, located in the Laugardalur area in the east of the city. The collection was started by an enterprising local citizen

and bought by the city authorities in 1955. Open on weekdays in summer from 08:00–22:00, and weekends from 10:00–22:00. During winter the gardens are open from sunrise to sunset .

Above: *Children enjoy a puppet show on the shores of Lake Tjörnin.*

Laugadalur ★

This open space located in the east of the city is the main sport and recreation area. It has Reykjavík's largest open-air geothermally heated swimming pool, a football stadium, ski slopes, the Botanical Gardens, a zoo and an ice-skating rink. Don't miss the curious Old Wash House (where, in times past, washerwomen scrubbed the city's laundry), and the Family Fun Park and Zoo.

Ellidaár River ★

Reykjavík is probably the only capital city in the world with a salmon fishing river within its boundaries. The Ellidaár River is in the eastern suburbs and is fed from Lake Ellidaár (which is excellent for trout fishing). The best time to watch the salmon leaping their way up-stream is during late July and early August.

WHERE ARE ALL THE CATS AND DOGS?

It slowly dawns on visitors that Icelanders keep few pets. Cats are rarely seen and any dogs noticed are likely to be working animals on farms. In fact, the Iceland government decided that it was unhygenic to keep dogs in city apartments and for years they were banned in Reykjavík. The law has recently been repealed, but dogs are still rare in the city.

Above: *Traditional wooden houses in the inner suburbs of Reykjavík, with the spire of the Hallgrímskirkja in the distance.*

DOMESTIC ARCHITECTURE

Builders in Iceland have always had a shortage of timber. Even driftwood found on the beach was a valuable commodity. Wealthy people could import wood from Norway. Stone was impractical for building as volcanic rock, particularly lava, can rarely be cut to suitable shapes. For the ordinary person turf was the common building material, so it is not surprising that few buildings have survived from before the 18th century. During the 20th century, materials such as concrete and corrugated iron became available and these are dominant today. Most Icelanders live in detached houses, but in Reykjavík there are some low-rise apartment blocks of imaginative design.

ENTERTAINMENT IN REYKJAVÍK

Reykjavík's **National Theatre** is located at Hverfisgata 19. It does perform operas and ballets, but concentrates mainly on plays. The building itself is of interest, with the interior said to be inspired by the basaltic columns of the Svartifoss waterfall in Southern Iceland. Reykjavík also has a **Symphony Orchestra** and an **Opera Company**; the main tourist office will have details of performances; tel: 551 1200, website: www.leikhusid.is There are seven **cinemas** in the city. Films are screened in their original language and have Icelandic subtitles. There are two **shows** which will appeal to tourists. The **Volcano Show** is based in a small film theatre at Hellusund 6a near Tjörnin Lake. The films are the work of two Icelandic photographers who have recorded all the eruptions in the country for the last 40 years, and include the award-winning *Birth of an Island*, describing the growth of Surtsey in the Westmann Islands. The Volcano Show is essential viewing for all visitors going on to the volcanic parts of the country. There are three performances a day in English, and also programmes in French and German. **Light Nights**, which is shown at Tjarnargata 10e, is performed in English and is an interesting account of the settlement of Iceland and of the Sagas. Performances, which last about two hours, run nightly (except on Sundays) during the summer. There are a vast number of **pubs** and **discos** in Reykjavík, but none are cheap. They are crowded at weekends, but rarely start to liven up until around 23:00.

GREATER REYKJAVÍK

Stretching away from the city centre are very pleasant suburbs of detached houses and low-rise apartment blocks. As more and more Icelanders move from the rural areas to the capital city, the suburbs of Reykjavík advance across the lava plains. The skill of Iceland's architects ensures that even the apartments have a certain flair and the design is never dull. Gardens are attractive and there are probably more mature trees in Reykjavík than in the rest of the island. Amongst the suburbs is the occasional shopping mall, such as the modern **Kringlan Centre** in the east of the city. Further out is Greater Reykjavík, with its rather characterless settlements. An exception is **Hafnarfjörður**, which is an interesting town in its own right.

Located at the end of the Reykjavík Peninsula is the pleasant suburb of **Seltjarnes**, from where there are often good views across the sea northwards to the icecap of Snæfellsjökull. The National Medical Museum, or Nesstofa, is housed in an 18th-century stone building in Seltjarnes. It is open daily in summer from 13:00–17:00. Immediately to the south of the city is the suburb of **Kópavogur**. Its main claim to fame is that, with 20,000 residents, it is Iceland's second largest community. Kópavogur's Smáralina Centre is the largest shopping mall in Iceland. Further south is **Garðabær**, which is considered to be Reykjavík's most elite suburb. Away to the southwest is **Hafnarfjörður** which, although part of Greater Reykjavík, is a town in its own right and is therefore described in Chapter 3, which deals with the Reykjanes Peninsula. East of Reykjavík, and immediately outside its boundary, is the fast-growing town of **Mosfellsbær**, with a population approaching 5000.

A very popular excursion from Reykjavík is a trip to **Viðey Island**, located a few kilometres north of the mainland. During summer, ferries run hourly from Sundahöfn harbour to Viðey. The island, which is situated on an extinct volcano, has been a religious centre since the 12th century and the second oldest church in Iceland is found here. There are some pleasant walks, fine basalt cliffs and an up-market restaurant.

OVERTURNING THE BAN ON BEER

Iceland has a long history of alcohol controls and even today, wines and spirits can only be bought at state monopoly shops. In 1912, full prohibition was introduced and only in 1933 were wine and spirits legalized. Beer was weak, watery stuff. For the next 50 years, strong beer was only brewed illegally at home – little wonder that pubs began to add a shot of vodka to the existing watery brew. On 1 March 1989, known as '**Beer Day**', the government legalized the sale of beer with an alcohol content of over 2.2%. Beer still costs three times as much here as it does in most of Europe and North America.

Below: *A lift takes visitors to the top of Hallgrímskirkja, from which there are stunning views over the city and the harbour.*

Reykjavík at a Glance

BEST TIMES TO VISIT

Because of the climate and relative hours of daylight and darkness, most tourists visit during the **summer** peak season of June–August. Tourist authorities want to extend the season into spring and autumn with 'city breaks' to Reykjavík, where the lively nightlife attracts visitors at times such as New Year.

GETTING THERE

The majority of visitors arrive by plane via Keflavík Airport, some 48km (30 miles) from Reykjavík. Buses meet every incoming flight, departing 45 minutes after arrival and taking travellers to Icelandair's terminal, which is at the Hotel Lofteiðir. Visitors using the car ferry will arrive at Seyðisfjörður on the east coast and have a long car or coach journey of around 740km (460 miles) to Reykjavík using the Ring Road.

GETTING AROUND

Reykjavík's **taxis** are cheaper than one might expect and tipping is not required. **Bicycles** can be hired economically, but the constant wind in Reykjavík makes cycling difficult. **Buses** offer cheap and convenient transport and the two main terminals are at Lækjartorg and Hlemmur (which has a tourist information desk). A free map of the bus routes is provided by the TIC. There is a standard fare for all routes and distances. Drivers do not give change. The **Reykjavík Tourist Card** (obtained from the City Hall)

provides unlimited use of the city's buses and free admission to some museums and swimming pools. Kids will enjoy the hop-on hop-off bus which connects all the major places of interest and has recorded commentaries in six languages.

WHERE TO STAY

A range from luxury international **hotels** to **guesthouses** and **hostels**. A significant number close during winter. **Camp sites** only open in summer.

LUXURY

101 Hótel, Hverifisgata 10, 101, tel: 580 0101, www.101 hotel.is Contempary boutique hotel; popular restaurant/bar, spa and art gallery.
Hótel Borg, Pósthússtræti 11, 101, tel: 551 1440, fax: 551 1420, www.hotelborg.is Art Deco hotel located on Austurvöllur Square.
Hótel Reykjavík Centrum, Aðalstræti 16, 101, tel: 514 6000, website: www.hotel centrum.is This hotel spreads over three ancient buildings. Built over a museum containing a Viking longhouse.
Grand Hótel Reykjavík, Sigtún 38, 105, tel: 514 8000, fax: 514 8030, website: www. grand.is Business hotel; quiet location near Kringlan Centre.

MID-RANGE

Guesthouse Aurora, Freyjugata 24, 101, tel: 552 5515, fax: 551 4894, e-mail: aurora@ simi.is Attractive traditional house in downtown Reykjavík.

Anna Guesthouse, Smáragötu 16, 101, tel: 562 1618, fax: 562 1656, website: www. guesthouseanna.is Beautifully decorated guesthouse; in former Czechoslovakian embassy.
Hótel Skjaldbreið, Langavegur 16, 101, tel: 595 8510, fax: 895 8511, website: www. centerhotels.is Well-equipped rooms on main shopping street.

BUDGET

Guesthouse Baldursbrá, Laufásvegur 41, 101, tel: 552 6646, fax: 562 6647, website: http://notendur.centrum.is/ ~heijfis Simple, basic rooms and shared bathrooms and hot tub. Generous buffet breakfast.
HI Youth Hostel, Sundlaugavegur 34, 105, tel: 553 8110, fax: 588 9201. Next to camp site in Laugardalur. Closed 20 December–5 January. Booking essential in summer.
Salvation Army Guesthouse, Kirkjustræti 2, 101, tel: 561 3203, fax: 561 3315, website: www.herinn.is Simple rooms in the heart of the city.

CAMPING

The camp site at **Laugardalur** is open 15 May to 15 September. It can be crowded in July and August. Showers, laundry and cooking facilities. Daily morning Flybus to Keflavík Airport.

WHERE TO EAT

There is a range of restaurants in central Reykjavík and the suburbs. Though food is a big expense for visitors, bargains

Reykjavík at a Glance

can be found, particularly with lunchtime tourist menus.

LUXURY

Perlan (The Pearl), Öskjuhlið hill, tel: 562 0200, website: www.perlan.is Spectacularly sited on top of city's water tanks; revolves to give views over Reykjavík. Expensive.
Lækjarbrekka, Bankastræti 2, tel: 551 4430, www.laekjar brekka.is Gourmet seafood and lamb, traditional building.
Tveir Fiskar (Two Fishes), Geirsgata 9, tel: 511 3474. Specialist harbour-side fish restaurant. Fresh fish daily.

MID-RANGE

Á Næstu Grösum (One Woman Restaurant), Laugavegur 20b, tel: 552 8410, www.anaestu grosum.is Vegetarian meals and organic wine.
Asia, Laugavegur 10, tel: 562 6210. Oriental cooking.
Fógetinn, Aðalstræti 10, tel: 551 6323. Reykjavík's oldest house; Skúli Magnusson had a weaving shed here. Traditional Icelandic food; live music.
Naust, Vesturgata 6–8, close to the harbour, tel: 551 7759. Offers a range of seafood.

BUDGET

Fast-food outlets include **Pizza Hut** (Hotel Esja), **McDonalds** (Austurstræti and Suðurlands-braut), **Kentucky Fried Chicken** (Faxafen 2), and **Hard Rock Café** (Kringlan Centre). **Kaffi**, Austurstræti, Reykjavík, tel: 552 2615. Student-style café, good value, hearty meals.

Reykjavík's main downtown shopping streets are Banka-stræti, Laugavegur, and Austurstræti. Skólavoðustígur, which connects Laugavegur with the Hallgrímskirkja, has chic boutiques and craft shops. Many larger shops have moved from the city centre to the **Kringlan Mall**, which has over 100 shops, plus cinemas, pubs, restaurants and banks, making it an 'alternative city centre'. There is also the massive **Smáralind Mall** in Kópavogur. Despite its reputation as an expensive city, you can find bargains in **woollen goods** at the Hand-knitting Association of Iceland (Skólavöðustígur 19) and the Icelandic Crafts Centre (Hafnarstræti 3). Home-made woollen goods can be bought cheaply at the Kolaportið Flea Market near the harbour. For various **crafts**, visit the Icelandic Craft House at Lækjargata 4, near the Tourist Information Centre. Last-minute shopping at Keflavík Airport's duty-free includes Iclandic products such as vacuum-packed fish.

A popular excursion for visitors to Reykjavík is a relaxing trip to the **Blue Lagoon** in the Reykanes Peninsula, usually combined with a visit to the Hafnir aquarium or local bird cliffs. Airport transfers also stop here. More demanding is the **Golden Circle Tour**, stopping at the greenhouse town of Hveragerði, the volcanic crater of Kerið, Skálholt Cathedral, Gullfoss, Geysir and Þingvellir – more than enough for a day. Most travel agencies also offer a **City Tour of Reykjavík**.

Tourist Information Centre, Bankastræti 2, tel: 562 3045, fax: 562 4749, www.visit reykjavik.is
Iceland Tourist Bureau, Skógarhlið 18, tel: 562 3300.
BSÍ Travel, Umferðarmið-stödin, Vatnsmýrarvegi 10. A consortium of bus operators, tours throughout the country.
Farm Holidays, Hotel Saga, Reykjavík, tel: 568 3640.
Reykjavík Excursions, Vatnsmýrarvegi 10, tel: 562 1011, website: www.re.is Widely used agency for day trips from the capital.
Guðmundar Jónasson Travel, Borgartún 34, tel: 511 1515, website: www.gjtravel.is Organizes coach and camping tours.

REYKJAVÍK	J	F	M	A	M	J	J	A	S	O	N	D
AVE. TEMP. °C	-0.4	-1.6	-1.5	0.4	7.2	9.8	11.6	11.1	6.6	5.0	3.7	-0.3
AVE. TEMP. °F	30.9	29.9	30.4	37.7	44.9	49.6	52.8	51.9	43.8	41.0	38.6	31.4
AVE. RAINFALL mm	75.6	71.8	81.8	58.3	43.8	50	51.8	61.8	66.5	85.6	72.5	78.7
AVE. RAINFALL in	2.97	2.83	3.22	2.29	1.73	1.97	2.04	2.43	2.62	3.37	2.86	3.1

3
Around Reykjavík

The area to the east and south of Reykjavík is the only part of Iceland which some short-term visitors see. Fortunately it boasts many of the essential historical and geological features which make the country so fascinating. The **Mid-Atlantic Ridge** runs through the area from northeast to southwest. Frequent volcanic eruptions over recent geological time have left extensive lava flows on the Reykjanes Peninsula – a desolate scene for travellers arriving at Keflavík Airport. Further inland, there are volcanoes such as **Hekla** and explosion craters such as **Kerið**, but the star attractions are the geothermal features in the **Geysir** region – where the geyser **Strokkur** performs reliably every three minutes or so – along with the amazing **Gullfoss** waterfall.

The area to the east of Reykjavík is one of the most fertile in Iceland and the two main market towns are **Selfoss** and **Hveragerði**. At the latter, the local geothermal heat is harnessed for electricity, which is the basis for a significant greenhouse agriculture, while the lovely lakeside resort of **Laugarvatn** is popular with weekenders from Reykjavík.

This part of Iceland is steeped in history. Most tours visit the religious centre of **Skálholt**, with its small modern cathedral. Away to the northwest is Iceland's largest lake – **Þingvallavatn**. At its northern end is the **Þingvellir** historical area, which was the site of the annual Alþing, an outdoor parliamentary assembly, which first functioned in 930 and witnessed the birth of the modern Icelandic Republic in 1944.

DON'T MISS

★★★ **Gullfoss:** Iceland's most visited waterfall.
★★★ **The Great Geysir Area:** fumeroles, mud springs, hot springs and Strokkur geyser.
★★★ **Þingvellir Historical Site:** location of Iceland's ancient outdoor parliament
★★★ **The Blue Lagoon:** bathe in the healthy, warm lake, surrounded by lava flows.
★ **Krýsuvíkurberg and Hafnaberg:** sea-bird cliffs on the Reykjanes Peninsula.
★ **Kerið:** explosion crater near Selfoss, with the volcano Hekla in the background.

Opposite: *The geyser Strokkur erupts regularly every three to five minutes.*

Most historic sites are usually visited in the whirlwind day trip known as the **Grand Circle Tour**. It gives a good insight into the scenery and history of Iceland, but it can be rather exhausting and the sites crammed with tourists and coaches. It is far better to take two days and travel independently out of season. Tourist coaches are less obvious in the Reykjanes Peninsula, except at the **Blue Lagoon**, where the waters are known to cure a variety of skin diseases.

Above: *Four-wheel-drive coaches take tourists on the popular Grand Circle Tour from Reykjavík.*
Opposite: *A 'sea-bird city' on the basalt cliffs of Krýsuvíkurberg, located on the southern part of the Reykjanes Peninsula.*

THE REYKJANES PENINSULA

The low peninsula of Reykjanes, just to the south of Reykjavík, juts out into the Atlantic Ocean, facing the full force of the prevailing southwesterly winds. Sitting right on the Mid-Atlantic Ridge, the peninsula is composed largely of lava fields, which are covered with Iceland's ubiquitous grey-green moss. Because of the porous nature of the lava, there are no surface streams and only one lake of any substantial size.

CLIMATE

The weather to the east and south of Reykjavík is quite similar to that in the capital, but the upland in the east attracts higher amounts of both **rain** and **snow**. The Reykjanes Peninsula in the south juts out into the Atlantic Ocean and therefore receives the full force of the prevailing **westerly winds**.

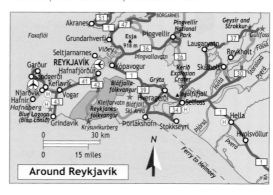

Around Reykjavík

Hafnarfjörður ★

Known as the 'gateway to the Reykjanes Peninsula', Hafnarfjörður, with its population of some 25,000 people, has lately been swallowed up by Greater Reykjavík. However, it is a town in its own right in an administrative sense, having a long history as a trading port, with English merchants controlling the town in the early 15th century, until they were thrown out by the Germans. They, in turn, succumbed to the Danish Trade Monopoly in 1602. The port and fishing industries are still thriving and the town has developed a reputation as a cultural centre. There are a number of museums in Hafnarfjörður, the best being the **Maritime Museum of Iceland**, which is combined with **Hafnarfjörður Folk Museum**, situated at Vesturgata 6–8. It is housed in a 19th-century warehouse appropriately close to the harbour. 220 Hafnarfjörður, tel: 585 5780. Open 11:00–17:00 daily, with reduced opening hours in winter. The **Institute of Culture and Fine Art** at Strandgata 34 stages concerts and exhibitions. It has a pleasant coffee shop with fine harbour views. The highlight in Hafnarfjörður is the annual **Viking Festival** held on the longest day of the year in June. It attracts visitors from all over the world and features strong man competitions, combat exhibitions, folk dancing, longboat trips and traditional Viking foods.

Located immediately to the north of Hafnarfjörður, at the end of the Álftanes Peninsula, is the historic estate of **Bessastaðahreppur**, which is now the official residence of the Icelandic head of state.

To the southeast of Hafnarfjörður, in the centre of the peninsula, is the skiing area of **Bláfjöll** (Blue Mountains). The hills here rise to 702m (2300ft). There are a number of downhill runs and cross-country ski trails, together with chair and rope lifts.

THE LAST GREAT AUK

It is believed that the last pair of great auks were clubbed to death on the island of **Eldey** in 1844. These large, flightless sea birds were very cumbersome on land and therefore easily caught. Their flesh was tasty and for centuries they were an important part of Icelanders' diet. The **Museum of Natural History** in Reykjavík has on display a stuffed great auk, which was obtained at an auction in London in 1971. Meanwhile the great auk's relative, the little auk, survives in small numbers. There are just two pairs left breeding on the island of **Grímsey**. They are closely protected.

Reykjanesfólkvangur ★

South of Hafnarfjörður, situated in the centre of the peninsula, is the national nature reserve of Reykjanesfólkvangur which covers some 775km² (300 sq miles). In amongst the hiking tracks are some amazing lava formations and, in the south of the reserve, a geothermal area known as Krýsuvík with impressive mud springs, solfataras and steaming vents. In the middle of the reserve is **Lake Kleifavatn**. Its blue waters cover some 10km² (6 sq miles) and it is reputed to be nearly 100m (328ft) deep. Inevitably there are tales of a resident monster. A recent earthquake partially drained the lake and where the water went, nobody knows. Trout fishing is possible here. At the extreme south of the reserve are the sea-bird cliffs of **Krýsuvíkurberg**. Look for three species of guillemot, kittiwakes, razorbills and, at the top of the cliffs, puffins. The island of **Eldey**, 14km (9 miles) offshore, is reputed to be the place where the last great auk was killed. Today Eldey has one of the world's largest gannet colonies.

Opposite: *One of several modern sculptures at Leifur Eiríksson International Airport. Made of aluminium and coloured glass, it represents a rainbow.*
Right: *Visitors stroll towards the fumeroles, hot springs and geysers of the Krýsuvík geothermal area.*

The Western Towns ★

The town of Keflavík is a long-established trading port and still has one of the largest fishing fleets in Iceland. It has merged with the neighbouring village of **Njarðvík** to form a settlement of around 10,000 people. Keflavík is best known for being the site of the US-operated NATO military base. American troops came here in 1941 during World War II, replacing British soldiers, with the aim of preventing a German occupation of Iceland. They finally pulled out in September 2006. Keflavík is also the site of the **Leifur Eiríksson International Air Terminal**. The ultramodern building was built with US help and opened in 1987. The air-

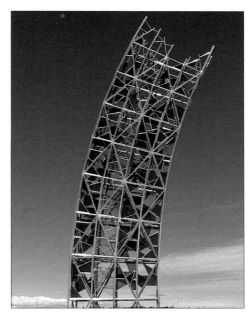

port grounds are noted for their large modern sculptures, which were the result of a competition. Particularly impressive are sculptures of a rainbow and a bird breaking out of an egg.

In the 'toe' of the peninsula are the two somewhat unremarkable fishing villages of **Garður** and **Sandgerði**. Here, some fish processing takes place. Further south is the deserted village of **Bátsendar**, destroyed by a freak wave in 1798. More picturesque is the fishing village of **Hafnir**, midway down the west coast. It has a fine 19th-century wooden church and some restored houses. A 10-minute walk along the cliffs southwards leads to the sea-bird cliffs of **Hafnaberg**.

The only settlement of any size on the south coast of the peninsula is the fishing port of **Grindavík**, which has around 2300 inhabitants. The port has a long trading history and was used by English and German merchants in the late middle ages. One astonishing

THE NATO BASE

Some 5000 US servicemen were stationed at the Keflavík NATO base, arousing strong opinions among Icelanders. The country has no armed services of its own. Many saw the US troops as an occupying army, particularly since the thawing of the Cold War. But the base provided considerable employment. Over 900 Icelanders worked at Keflavík and many more gained an indirect living from the US troops. The base closed in 2006, with the perhaps unsurprising result that the town of Keflavík has the highest unemployment rate in Iceland.

historical fact is that it was raided in 1627 by Algerian pirates, who took away a large number of the local people as slaves. Fish processing and exporting take place here today. Look out for the moving fishermen's monument, called *Hope*, that shows a fisherman's family looking hopefully out to sea.

Above: *Bathing in the medicinal waters of the Blue Lagoon.*
Opposite: *Tomatoes for sale at the roadside. They are grown in geothermally heated greenhouses.*

HEALTH TREATMENT AT THE BLUE LAGOON

The silvery-blue opaque waters of the Blue Lagoon and the white silica mud on its bed have been proven to have great health properties. The cocktail of **minerals** in the water, which comes from up to 1830m (6000ft) below the ground, has eased skin conditions such as psoriasis and eczema. A range of products has been developed, including mineral bath salts, lagoon mud for the face and body, moisturizing cream, and shampoo. Not surprisingly, a complex of facilities opened in 1999 to cope with the 200,000 annual visitors.

The Blue Lagoon (Bláa Lónið) ★★★

Midway between Grindavík and Keflavík amongst the black lava fields is the popular tourist venue known as the Blue Lagoon. The pale blue waters of the Lagoon are in fact the effluent from the Svartsengi power station. Sea water is heated and then filtered as it passes through the lava. The run-off water, which is rich in minerals, has a temperature of 70°C (158°F), but bathing is restricted to one area of the lagoon where temperatures are a more bearable 40°C (104°F). Algae thrive in the hot water, but die as the water cools, adding to the white silica mud on the lake bottom. It sounds unpleasant, but the lagoon water has been shown to relieve the effects of psoriasis, eczema and other skin ailments. There are basic changing rooms, a restaurant and a guesthouse, plus a luxurious touch – swimmers can be served cocktails on floating tables! With steam rising all around and the space-age power equipment and lava fields in the background, a 'swim' in the lagoon can be one of the great tourist experiences of Iceland. The Flybus airport service to and from Reykjavík stops at the Blue Lagoon; tel: 420 8800, website: www.bluelagoon.com

Þorlákshöfn ★

In the southeastern corner of the Reykjanes Peninsula, the **ferry port** of Þorlákshöfn is located, where regular ferries leave for the **Westman Islands**. This is the only suitable port in the area between Grindavík and Höfn, which accounts for the long, and often rough, voyage. The ferry boat *Herjólfur* makes a daily return trip to the Westman Islands, weather permitting. The port is named after Saint Þorlákur, who was a bishop of Skálholt during the 12th century and, incidentally, the only Icelander ever to have been canonized by the Roman Catholic Church.

EAST OF REYKJAVÍK

The Ring Road (or Route 1) leaves Reykjavík eastwards, running through lava fields and over a mountain pass, before dropping down to the fertile lowland which is one of the country's richest agricultural areas. The first town of any size is **Hveragerði**, with around 1700 inhabitants, many of whom commute daily to the capital. Hveragerði is located on an active geothermal area and several hot springs and steaming vents are readily seen. The geothermal power has been used to heat numerous greenhouses in which crops such as tomatoes, lettuces, cucumbers and flowers are grown. Bananas and other tropical fruits are also produced, but not in a commercial way – just to prove that it can be done! Not surprisingly, Hveragerði is the site of Iceland's National College of Horticulture. There is a small geyser known as Gryta (or Ogress), which erupts several times daily.

On the outskirts of the town is a health clinic, with mineral and mud baths, physiotherapy and a health-food shop. Coach tours stop at a tourist trap by the name of **Eden**, based on an old geothermal greenhouse and selling locally grown potted plants, fruits, souvenirs, woollen goods and postcards. The next town along the Ring Road is **Selfoss**, a pleasant market town on the banks of the Ólfusá River. Although it has little of

ICELANDIC PLACE NAMES

The majority of Icelandic place names refer to physical or man-made features. If a few of these are understood, it is possible to know something about a place simply by looking at its name on a map. Some of the most common elements are shown below:

á • river
borg • rock outcrop
brekka • hillside
dalur • valley
ey • island
fell • hill
fjall • mountain
fjörður • fiord
foss • waterfall
gil • gorge or ravine
höfn • harbour
jökull • icecap or glacier
jökulsá • glacial river
mýri • marsh
nes • peninsula
skögur • woods
vatn • lake
vík • bay

TURF AS BUILDING MATERIAL

Turf was a commonly used building material in rural Iceland until 1900. Largely used because of the shortage of timber; ideal for the climatic conditions. Icelandic grass grows very thickly, so turf is a strong combination of roots and soil which can last as a building material for up to a century. Most farm buildings were composed of thin shells of wood separated from each other by a thick wall of turf. This also acted as an **insulation** layer. The turf roofs had to be sloped at the correct angle, so that rain water drained off. If the roof was too flat, the water would seep through. If the roof was too steep, the turf would crack in dry weather, leading to further leaks.

Below: *Turf buildings were largely a response to the lack of timber available.*

historical interest, Selfoss makes a good centre for exploring the area to the north. Just to the northwest is a hill called **Ingólfsfjall** which rises to a height of 551m (1808ft). The mound on the top is claimed to be the burial site of Ingólfur Arnason, but the summit is solid rock, so this is a doubtful assertion.

From Selfoss, Route 35 leads inland to some of Iceland's most popular tourist locations. After a short distance, on the right-hand side of the road, is the explosion crater of **Kerið**. Some 55m (180ft) deep and enclosing a rather menacing green lake, it was one of a crater swarm formed around 3000 years ago. From here there are distant views of the volcano **Hekla**, its summit usually swathed with cloud. Hekla has erupted at least 20 times since the settlement of Iceland, most recently in 1991.

Skálholt **

The route then leads to the **religious centre** of Skálholt, marked today by a simple, modern church. Its history goes back to the 11th century, when Gissur the White established the first wooden church here. His son, Ísleifur Gissurason, after an education in Germany, became the **first bishop** of Iceland. Skálholt became an important educational centre and an elaborate wooden cathedral replaced the original church. Dark deeds were to come in the 16th century, when the country converted from Catholicism to the Danish Lutheran religion. Bishop **Jón Arason** (who opposed the reformation) and his two sons were beheaded at Skálholt without trial. Today, there is a memorial to Arason on the road leading to the church. The site was destroyed during an earthquake in 1784 and shortly afterwards the bishopric was moved to Reykjavík. The present memorial church on the site was built in the 1950s. When the foundations were laid, the remains of the original cathedral were discovered, showing that it was twice the size of the new building. The simple church is worth a visit and is distinguished by some excellent modern stained glass as well as a superb altar mosaic by Nina Tryggvadóttir.

Great Geysir ★★★

From Skálholt, the road leads northeast to the Great Geysir area of **Haukadalur**. Plumes of steam and the sulphurous smell can be noted from some distance away. The Great Geysir is probably the most famous geyser in the world and gave its name to all phenomena of this type. Geysers are spouting hot springs, and the Icelandic word means 'gusher'. The Geysir area covers around 3km² (1.2 sq miles) and consists of geysers, hot springs, mud springs and fumeroles. All have been given Icelandic names. Unfortunately, Great Geysir no longer erupts (although eruptions can be induced by throwing soap powder into the crater!), but luckily its neighbour **Strokkur** ('a churn') is very active, erupting every three to five minutes to a height of around 20m (66ft). The silica crater of Geysir can be inspected, and also some superb blue hot springs nearby. Redeposited silica and travertine surround the spring, and when this material weathers, a wealth of plants and orchids appear. The Great Geysir area has belonged to a number of landowners, including several Englishmen, one of whom used to charge for admission. In 1935, the land was bought by an Icelandic doctor who then gave it to the nation. There is a convenient hotel nearby, plus a petrol station, cafeteria and

Above: *Unusual religious sculptures carved in stone outside Skálholt's cathedral.*

GEOTHERMAL TERMINOLOGY

Geothermal activity is found in areas of active vulcanicity. The main features are:
Geysers: an explosive spout of hot water
Fumeroles: superheated water turns to steam when the pressure drops as it emerges from the ground.
Solfataras: sulphurous gases escape at the surface, giving the typical 'rotten eggs' smell.
Hot springs: water is heated underground and emerges at the surface.
Mud springs: Hot water mixes with volcanic material and bubbles at the surface.

Above right: *The geyser Strokkur begins to erupt. Every three to five minutes, clouds of steam and water burst up to 20m (65ft) in height.*
Right: *Gullfoss is Iceland's best-known waterfall. The name means 'golden falls', named after the rainbow formed by the sun and spray.*

camping facilities. At the side of the cafe is the Geysirtofa, an audiovisual exhibition explaining the workings of volcanoes and geysers. The highlight is a platform on which you can stand to experience an earthquake measuring 5.1 on the Richter Scale.

Gullfoss ★★★

Route 35 continues briefly until Iceland's most famous **waterfall**, Gullfoss, is reached. The name means 'golden falls', after the persistent rainbows which are formed by the spray on sunny days. The **River Hvítá**, swollen by melting snow and ice in the interior, drops some 32m (105ft) over two falls. Above and below Gullfoss is a 2.5km (1.5-mile) gorge up to 70m (230ft) deep.

Last century the falls were under threat of hydro-electric development and a local farmer's wife, Sigrídur Tómasdóttir, walked all the way to Reykjavík to protest against this, threatening to throw herself down the falls if the plan went ahead. A memorial to Sigrídur stands high above the falls. A footpath from the car park leads down to a viewing platform between the two falls – be sure to take waterproofs as the spray is penetrating.

Laugarvatn *

Southwest of Geysir and Gullfoss is the **spa resort** of Laugarvatn, situated on the shores of a lake of the same name. The name means 'warm lake', and a hot spring nearby called **Vígdalaug** was the traditional place for Christian baptisms by the early bishops of Skálholt. Today, Laugarvatn is an **educational centre**, with a number of colleges which convert to hotels during the summer. The area is a very popular weekend retreat for the inhabitants of Reykjavík, who come for camping, sailboarding and the steam baths.

Þingvellir ***

The Golden Circle Tour's last stop is at Þingvellir, the site of the ancient outdoor parliament, or Alþing. The setting is very dramatic, being at the northern end of Þing-vallavatn, Iceland's largest lake. It is also right on the Mid-Atlantic Ridge, where the European and North American plates are moving apart. The site is bordered by parallel fissures, namely **Hrafnagjá** in the east and **Almannagjá** in the west. In the early days, the Öxará river was diverted along the Almannagjá to form some rather impressive falls. Just above the bridge over the Öxará is a 'drowning pool' where adulteresses and witches were thrown (delinquent men were usually decapitated). There are numerous historical

> ### RIVER RAFTING
>
> Iceland is the ideal location for many types of adventure activities. One of the most popular is river rafting. The level can vary from fairly gentle family-style fun to whitewater rafting on rather fearsome glacial rivers and canyons. Strict **safety** is observed with the issue of flotation suits, and with training sessions in basic safety and paddling skills. The main sites for rafting are on the river Hvita near Geysir in southern Iceland, near Varmalið in Skagafjörður, and near Egilsstaðir in eastern Iceland. Contact local tourist offices for details.

Below: *Þingvellir is situated on the edge of the 5km-wide fault that divides the American Plate from the European Plate.*

Right: Þingvellir
Historical Site, where the
39 chieftains would meet
annually to review the
laws of the country.

THE DROWNING POOL

Icelandic history is full of
grisly stories of murder and
dastardly deeds. Its system of
justice was often swift and
brutal, particularly when it
came to the punishment of
women. At Þingvellir, the
Great Edict of 1564 proclaimed that women found
guilty of adultery, infanticide,
perjury or, indeed, any other
criminal act, would be
executed by drowning. At
Þingvellir a special pond,
the **Drekkingarhylur**, was
used for this purpose. The
guilty women were tied in a
sack before being thrown
into the deep 'drowning
pond'. This practice con-
tinued until as late as 1838.

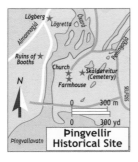

sites here. The **Lögberg** or 'law rock' on the western side of
the river was where the law-speaker was obliged annually
to recite the laws of the land from memory. The spot is
marked today by a flagpole and plaque. Just east of the
Lögberg, on lower ground, was the **Lögretta**, which was
the meeting place of the Law Council of 39 chieftains
who would discuss new laws. Scattered around the site
are the remains of stone *búdir* or **booths** set up by each
chieftain for the two-week duration of the Alþing. They
were used for shelter and as business premises. There are
a number of buildings on the site. The **Church** was built
in 1859 and is the last of many to have occupied the
Alþing area. It has a number of relics from past buildings.
The cemetery, or **Skáldareitur**, just behind the church, is
usually referred to as the 'Poets' Graveyard', although no
contemporary poets seem to have selected this as their
last resting place. The long **farmhouse** nearby is used as a
summer home for the prime minister of Iceland and also
contains the offices of the National Park Warden. There
are a number of water-filled chasms in the area and one
of these, the **Peningagjá**, has developed into a wishing
well. The unobtrusive wooden **Hotel Valhöll** on the eastern side of the river occupied the site of Snorri Sturluson's
old booth. Sadly, the hotel burnt down in July 2009 and
in the present economic climate there is unlikely to be
any haste to rebuild it. The region around Þingvellir is
excellent hiking country, with a number of well-marked
trails. It is also possible to drive around the lake on the
narrow gravel roads, but traffic can get busy during the
summer months.

Around Reykyavík at a Glance

The Blue Lagoon is popular all year, and the rest of the area is a **summer** destination from May–September. Be prepared for crowds at major sites, particularly Gullfoss, Geysir and Þingvellir in July and August.

Tour coaches and BSÍ buses connect the major sites from June to September, but can be infrequent. The BSÍ Omnibus Pass is available at the BSÍ bus terminal in Reykjavík or at airline offices and travel agents.

Reykjanes Peninsula
LUXURY

Hótel Keflavík, Vatnsnesvegi 12, 230 Keflavík, tel: 420 7000, fax: 420 7002, www.hotelkeflavik.is Everything for the air traveller; pool, jacuzzi and sauna; elegant dining room.

MID-RANGE

Northern Light Inn, Blue Lagoon, tel: 426 8650, www.northernlightinn.is Bungalow type hotel, walking distance to the Blue Lagoon, and free shuttle to the airport.

BUDGET

Youth Hostel Strönd, Njarðvíkurbraut 48–50, tel: 421 6211. Both hostels have airport transfers available.
Camp site Keflavík-Njarðvík, tel: 421 1460. Good camp site, open June to mid-September.

East of Reykjavík
LUXURY

Hótel Ranga, 851 Hella, South Iceland, tel: 487 5700, www.hotelranga.is Countryside resort in rustic log cabin style. Gourmet restaurant and many facilities. Celebrities and royalty have stayed here.
Hótel Örk, Breidumork 1c, 810 Hveragerði, tel: 483 4700, www.hotel-ork.is Health resort with pool and sauna complex, nine-hole golf course and other outdoor activities. Gourmet restaurant using locally grown organic ingredients.

MID-RANGE

Lykilhótel Valhöll, Þingvöllum, 801 Selfoss, tel: 486 1777, fax: 486 1778, e-mail: booking@keyhotel.is Wooden hotel, boats for hire.
Hótel Geysir, Haukadal, 801 Selfoss, tel: 480 6800, www.geysircenter.com Geothermal pool and hotpots, restaurant.

BUDGET

Gistiheimilið Geysir, Haukadal 111, 801 Selfoss, tel: 486 8733, fax: 872 1573. Basic guesthouse, good value.
HI Youth Hostel, Reykholt, tel: 486 8831, fax: 486 8709. Access to pool and saunas.

CAMPING

Camp sites at Geysir, Laugarvatn, Hveragerði, Reyholt, Þingvellir.

The best (but most expensive) restaurants are in hotels.

The restaurants at Keflavík Hotel and Flughótel in Keflavík offer good menus.

Reykjanes Peninsula
MID-RANGE

Jenny by the Blue Lagoon, tel: 426 8650. Restaurant and bistro overlooking the lagoon.
Olsen Olsen, Hafnargata, Keflavík, tel: 421 4457. American 50s-style theme.
BUDGET
Sjómannastofan Vör, Grindavík, tel: 426 8570. Snack bar overlooking the harbour.

East of Reykjavík
MID-RANGE

Lindin, Laugarvatni, tel:486 1262. Restaurant and pizzeria overlooking the lake. Local ingredients used, including reindeer and sea birds.
BUDGET
There are good **snack bars** attached to petrol stations at Selfoss and Geysir. Also worth trying are branches of **Pizza 67** in Selfoss and Hveragerði.

Regional Tourist Information Centres: Keflavík Bus Station, tel: 421 5575; Leifur Eiríksson Air Terminal, tel: 421 4608; Selfoss, tel: 482 1704; Hveragerði, tel: 483 4280.
Þingvellir National Park Information Service Centre, tel: 482 2660. Information on weather and road conditions in Þingvellir, tel: 482 2677.
Þorlákshöfn–Westmann Islands Ferry, tel: 483 3413 (this may change; *see* ch. 8).

4
West and Northwest Iceland

This chapter covers the region immediately to the north of Reykjavík as far as the Northwest Fiords. This is a region of wide contrasts, both physically and socially. In the south of the area are the two scenically attractive fiords of **Hvalfjörður**, once the centre of Iceland's whaling operations, and **Borgarfjörður**, which is associated with the *Egils Saga*, and the main towns of **Akranes** and **Borganes**, site of the new **Settlement Centre**. Inland, the village of **Reykholt** has strong links with the 13th-century statesman and writer **Snorri Sturluson**.

The **Snæfellsnes Peninsula** juts out into the ocean and has a number of small fishing settlements scattered around its coastline. At the western end is the icecap of **Snæfellsjökull**, which, on a clear day, can be seen all the way from Reykjavík, 100km (60 miles) away.

The **Northwest Fiords** area is one of the remotest parts of the country. Here, most forms of communication between the small, scattered fishing and farming communities are so difficult that light aircraft are commonly used. The region has suffered badly from **depopulation** in recent years, as many of its people have now given up the battle to eke out a living from the harsh landscape and have migrated to Reykjavík. Nevertheless, the wild, uninhabited country of the Northwest Fiords is attractive to hikers in the summer months. Bird-watchers also like to visit the teeming sea-bird cliffs at **Látrabjarg**, the most westerly point in Europe, and **Hornstradir** in the north. The inhospitable climate, however, ensures that tourists are rare birds themselves!

TOP ATTRACTIONS

** Reykholt: associated with 13th-century statesman and writer Snorri Sturluson.
** Sea-bird cliffs: at Látrabjarg and Hornstradir in the Northwest Fiords.
** Ísafjörður: town with good fiord location and Iceland's best maritime museum.
** Hraunfossar and Barnafoss Falls: waterfalls in the upper reaches of the Hvítá valley.
** Settlement Centre: newly opened museum at Borganes, tracing the history of Icelandic settlement.

Opposite: *Sugandafjörður, in the Northwest Fiords area of Iceland.*

CLIMATE

The weather in the southern part of the area differs little from that in Reykjavík, but the climate deteriorates to the north. The Snæfellsnes Peninsula juts out into the Atlantic and attracts a lot of wind and rain. Stykkishólmur has an annual **rainfall** total of 756mm (29.6in), a **January** average temperature of 1.8°C (29°F) and a **July** average of 10°C (50°F). The Northwest Fiord area experiences cold **Arctic winds** and heavy **snowfall** in winter, with Ísafjörður having an average temperature below freezing point for three months of the year.

HVALFJÖRÐUR AND BORGARFJÖRÐUR

North of Reykjavík, the Ring Road runs seaward around **Mount Esja**, some 918m (3012ft) high, before swinging around into **Hvalfjörður**. The name means 'whale fiord' and this was the centre of Icelandic whaling operations until the country's withdrawal from the industry in 1992. Whales are frequently seen in the fiord today and some 17 species have been recorded here. The deep waters of Hvalfjörður were ideal for British and American warships in World War II, and the remains of the base can be seen on the north side of the fiord. Equally unattractive is the ferro silicon smelter at Grundartangi, near the mouth of the fiord. On the north side is the delightful little church at **Saurbær**, built in memory of Hallgrímur Pétursson, who in the 17th century composed Iceland's best-known religious work, *50 Passion Hymns*.

Akranes ★★★

One of Iceland's largest fishing ports (population of just over 5500), Akranes is located right on the very tip of the peninsula which separates Hvalfjörður and Borgarfjörður. The town is dominated by the chimneys of its cement works, which uses local basalt and shell sand. Akranes can be reached by the new road tunnel across the mouth of Hvalfjörður, which has cut the journey from Reykjavík by about 60km (37 miles), or alternatively by regular ferry services from the capital. The main attraction at Akranes is the **Regional Folk and Maritime Museum** (tel: 431 5566, open 10:00–17:00 daily, reduced hours in winter), just east of the town, at Garðar. There are indoor and outdoor exhibits, including *Sigurfari*, an old 19th-century decked cutter, and also numerous whaling artefacts. Outside the museum is a stone tower with inscriptions in both Icelandic and Gaelic.

Below: *Inshore fishing boats. Most of the coastal villages in the northwest of Iceland depend on fishing for their income.*

It was a gift from Ireland in 1974, commemorating the 1100th anniversary of the Settlement and Akranes's original Irish immigrants who founded the town around AD880.

Borganes ★★★

Situated halfway along the northern side of Borgarfjörður, Borganes is quite unusual in that it is perhaps the only coastal town in Iceland that doesn't specialize in fishing. Instead, it is a service centre for the inland area. Borganes has a small folk museum (open daily in summer, 14:00–18:00), but most visitors head for the small park. Here is a burial mound, said to be that of Skallagrímmur Kveldúlfsson, the father of Egill Skallagrímsson of

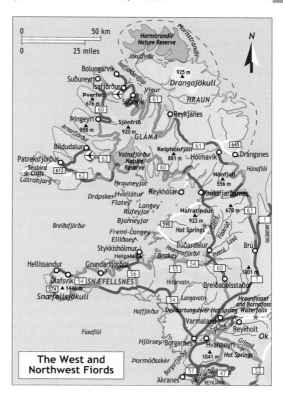

The West and Northwest Fiords

Egils Saga fame. It is said that Egill carried the body of his drowned son to be buried next to his grandfather – a touching tale that is depicted on a relief plaque made by the Danish artist Annemarie Brodersen. In 2006, the **Settlement Centre** was opened in some converted shoreside warehouses. It has two major exhibitions – The Settlement of Iceland and Egils saga, with full audiovisual support (open 10:00–19:00 Jun–Aug, 11:00–17:00 Sep–May; tel: 437 1600, www.landnam.is).

Near to the Settlement Centre is **Puppet World** (tel: 551 1620, www.figurentheatre.is). Located in a line of restored 18th-century houses, the museum features puppets that bring to life the various Icelandic sagas.

THE UBIQUITOUS LUPIN

In mid-June the countryside is covered with wild flowers. One of the most noticeable is the **Alaskan Lupin** (*Lupinus nootkatensis*) which grows in blue swathes. This is no ordinary wild flower, for being a leguminous plant, it adds nitrogen to the soil. Its root system binds the soil together and helps to prevent erosion, which has proved useful on the *sandur* in south Iceland.

Reykholt ★★★

This small hamlet to the west of Borganes is one of Iceland's most important historical sites. It was the home of **Snorri Sturluson**, the famous 13th-century Saga writer and statesman. Snorri lived at Reykholt from 1206–1241 and wrote many of his best works here. Today, we can see the thermal pool where Snorri bathed and the nearby tunnel which connected with the farm where he lived. The tunnel probably led to the cellar where he was murdered by his enemies in 1241 at the age of 62. The modern church has a cultural centre where some of his work is on display. In front of the school is a statue of the writer by Norwegian sculptor Gustav Vigeland. It was a gift from Norway in gratitude for one of Snorri's most famous works, *Heimskringla*, a Saga featuring the kings of medieval Norway. In the cemetery of the older church is a gravestone marked *Sturlingareitur*, and it is possible that this might be Storri's last resting place. Also of interest in the Reykholt valley is the country's most powerful hot spring, known as **Deildartunguhver**. It spurts out water at 200 litres (352 pints) per second at a temperature of 100°C (212°F). Not surprisingly, a greenhouse industry has developed here and fresh produce is often on sale at the roadside. The hot water is piped some 60km (37 miles) to supply both Borganes and Akranes.

Inland from Reykholt ★

To the east of the Ring Road and to the west of the Langjökull icecap is an area, full of geological interest, which is known as **Húsafell**. It can also be approached by a scenic road from Þingvellir, though this route is only likely to be open during July and August. To the east of Husafell are extensive lava sheets which include the **Hallmundarhraun Caves**. These feature a series of tubes within the lava; the longest, known as Surtshellir, is

---

THE FORMIDABLE SNORRI

The life of the 13th-century Icelandic writer and diplomat Snorri Sturluson was as full of intrigue and violence as any of the Sagas. Born in 1179, he married an heiress at the age of 21, and liaisons with other wealthy women ensured that he became the richest man in Iceland. He mainly lived and worked on a large estate at Reykholt where he wrote his greatest works. He became law-speaker of the Alþing at the age of 36. He developed a close relationship with the King of Norway. Later that relationship soured and the King demanded Snorri's return to Norway. Snorri ignored his request and in 1241 he was assassinated at Reykholt by Gissur Þorvaldsson, a rival chieftain hoping to impress the King of Norway. Snorri left behind a formidable collection of literature, including the *Prose Edda*, *Heimskringla* and, in all probability, *Egils Saga*.

some 4km (2½ miles) in length. The caves have the usual stalactites and stalagmites, and occasional large caverns. Visitors should bring a torch, as there is no artificial lighting. West of Husafell are the **Hraunfossar Falls**, where the glacial River Hvítá has created a gorge over 1km (0.6 mile) in length. The sides of the gorge have a long string of springs which emerge from the junction of porous rock and basalt. A track leads upstream to **Barnafoss** ('children's waterfall'), named after children who, while on their way to church, fell from a natural rock arch over the falls and were drowned.

THE SNÆFELLSNES PENINSULA

Running east–west and jutting out into the ocean, the Snæfellsnes Peninsula receives the full force of Atlantic gales. The population, not surprisingly, is sparse here. The south coast of the peninsula has a broad coastal plain, but lacks good harbours. Consequently there are no townships of any size, just a scattering of farmsteads. A mountain chain runs along the centre of the peninsula, rising to approximately 930m (3051ft) at **Tröllatindar**. The highest mountain, however, is **Snæfellsjökull**, at 1446m (4744ft), at the western end of the peninsula. It is a conically shaped dormant volcano with three distinct peaks, covered by a small icecap which can frequently be seen from Reykjavík, some 100km (60 miles) to the south. In Jules Verne's story *Journey to the Centre of the Earth*, the explorers began their journey at Snæfellsjökull, emerging sometime later at Stromboli volcano in Italy! Snæfellsjökull can be climbed by three different routes, which each take about four to five hours to complete and which demand the use of equipment such as crampons and ice axes. There are also snowmobile routes to the summit. Always be prepared for the worst possible weather.

GRAVEL ROADS

The surface of many roads in Iceland (even parts of the Ring Road) is composed of gravel. This brings great hazards to the motorist. When two cars are passing, drivers are advised to **slow down**, as projectile stones may shatter windscreens. The shoulders of gravel roads can be quite soft and drivers must be careful not to allow their outside wheels to skid in this material. There are not always road signs to indicate the change from an asphalted road to a gravel road. Take care in summer, when the dust raised by a passing car can obscure visibility for some time.

Opposite: *Snorri's Pool, Reykholt. Here the statesman and Saga writer Snorri Sturluson lived and died.*
Below: *At Hraunfossar, a line of waterfalls emerges from a rock junction in the side of the gorge.*

Below: *Sunset across Breiðafjörður, a lovely wide island-studded bay marking the start of the Northwest Fiord area. Ferries from Stykkishólmur regularly cross the bay.*

Stykkishólmur ★★★

The largest town on Snæfellnes Peninsula, Stykkishólmur has a long history and many connections with the Sagas. In the early days it was a religious centre. The nearby hill of **Helgafell** (or Holy Mountain) has always been considered to have supernatural powers and also figures strongly in local folklore. Today Stykkishólmur is a trading and fishing port, specializing in shellfish. Close to the harbour is a folk museum called the **Norwegian House**, which was brought from Norway in 1828 by Árni Þorlacius (who also made Iceland's first meteorological measurements at Stykkishólmur in 1845). The museum is open from 15:00–18:00 on weekdays and 11:00–18:00 on weekends. Stykkishólmur's most striking building, however, is its new **Roman Catholic Church**. Built on a headland and made of concrete, it soars skywards in gentle curves.

Also worth a visit is the new **Volcano Museum** in Eldfjallasafn (tel: 433 8154, open 11:00–17:00 June to mid-September). Located in an old cinema, the museum is largely the work of retired vulcanologist Haraldur Sigurðsson. The museum also organizes local field trips.

The car ferry *Baldur* makes regular trips from Stykkishólmur across Breiðafjörður to Brjánslækur

in the Northwest Fiords. Breiðafjörður is littered with over 2000 small islands, and the ferry stops at one of these, named **Flatey**. Once a religious and cultural centre, few people live on Flatey today, although many city dwellers have holiday homes here. The island houses Iceland's smallest and oldest library.

Left: *Looking towards the Drangajökull icecap, showing a typical U-shaped glaciated valley.*

Elsewhere on the Snæfellsnes Peninsula ★★★

There are a number of other fishing settlements along the north coast of the peninsula. The most westerly is **Ólafsvík**, Iceland's longest established trading port, having been given its charter in 1687. There is a small folk museum based in an old packing house and an amazing church built without a single right angle. Further east is **Grundarfjörður**, surrounded by forbidding mountains. In the early 19th century it was used as a base by French fishermen, who built a church here. The northeastern part of the peninsula is marked by the broad **Hvammsfjörður**. The coastal village of **Búðardalur** is the main service centre for the region. Inland is the narrow **Laxárdalur Valley**, famous as the site of the *Laxdæla Saga*, a popular Icelandic love story. Several famous Icelanders were born in Laxádalur, including the writer Snorri Sturluson, the discoverer of America, Leifur Eiríksson, and the heroine of the *Laxdæla Saga*, Guðrún Ösvífursdóttir.

THE NORTHWEST FIORDS

Northwest Iceland is one of the most inhospitable parts of the country. Geologically, this is the oldest part of Iceland, with basalt rocks some 50 million years old. It was one of the most recent areas to be glaciated and has a large surviving icecap, called **Drangajökull**, which covers about 175km² (68 sq miles). The high interior, known as **Gláma**, is a tundra plateau, with thin rocky soil,

Above: *The small settle-ment of Mýrar, which nestles on the north side of Dýrafjörður.*
Below: *The rugged scenery of the northwest highlands is formed by some of the oldest rocks in the country.*

FEATHERED NOMADS

One of the world's most remarkable nomadic birds, the **Arctic Tern** (*Sterna paradisæa*) is, in fact, very common in Iceland. The bird summers in northern sub-Arctic regions where it breeds, but in the northern winter it flies over 17,000km (10,500 miles) to the Antarctic. Arctic terns are regarded with special affection by the Icelanders, as their arrival is seen as the harbinger of spring. The birds can be less affectionate at their nesting sites, and will 'dive bomb' any intruders, including human beings, who are well advised to wear head protection.

moraines and lakes. The ice, which has only recently left, has carved out deep, steep-sided coastal fiords, making this region the most scenically attractive in Iceland. The climate, though, is harsh, with piercing Arctic winds and heavy snowfalls in winter. Farming is extremely difficult and many parts have become abandoned. Communications are problematic too. Remote from the Ring Road, northwest coastal roads are badly surfaced and wind around fiords, making journeys long and arduous. Public transport by road is infrequent, but there are a few ferries, particularly in Ísafjarðardjúp. The only sustainable work in the area is **fishing**. The warm Gulf Stream and cold Greenland Current meet offshore, providing good spawning conditions for fish. There are also sheltered harbours aplenty. Unfortunately, Govern-ment quotas on the fish caught have resulted in many fishermen leaving. There are, however, many attractions for the tourist in summer. For hikers, there are numerous marked trails amongst wilderness scenery, while for bird watchers, the northwest holds some of the finest sea-bird cliffs in the world.

Ísafjörður ★★★

The largest settlement in the Northwest Fiords area is Ísafjörður, which has around 4000 inhabitants. It has one

of the most dramatic locations of any town in Iceland, situated on a narrow sand spit jutting out into the fiord, its steep sides cloaked with scree slopes and, at upper levels, hanging valleys left by glaciers. Ísafjörður has a long history as a trading port and today has an important fishing industry. It also acts as the cultural and commercial centre of the Northwest Fiords. Regular flights to Ísafjörður from Reykjavík have helped develop a modest tourist trade, but due to its remoteness and poor infrastructure, it will never be swamped with visitors.

A number of 18th-century wooden houses have survived on the end of the sand spit. Today these house the **Westfjörds Maritime Museum** which is full of old photographs, nautical artefacts and fishing implements. The star exhibit is a reproduction of an early six-oared sailing ship. Open from 13:00–17:00 during summer.

There are several ferries which double as fiord sightseeing boats, including the *Fagranes*, which cruises the Ísafjarðardjúp, stopping on request. Its ports of call include the islands of Vigur and Ædey (Eider Island), both of which are noted for their bird life. *Fagranes* also visits **Hornstrandir**, in the northernmost tip of the Northwest Fiords. This wilderness area is now uninhabited and is designated as a nature reserve, typified by sheer sea cliffs, glaciated valleys and rugged mountains. The arctic fox thrives here, and whales and seals are often seen offshore. In the absence of grazing sheep, the wild flowers are spectacular. Most impressive of all are the sea-bird

ICELANDIC ICON

At the mention of Iceland, most people's thoughts turn to the haunting and original voice of the singer, songwriter and artist **Björk**. She was born Björk Guðmundsdóttir in 1965 in Reykjavík and came from a musical family. After completing music school, she developed punk music into new and exciting directions. Later, she performed with the rock band Sugarcubes, putting Icelandic music on the world map. She launched her solo career in 1993 with the album *Debut*. This was followed up with *Post*, *Homogenic*, *Vespertine*, *Medúlla* and in 2007 *Volta*, establishing her as a musical legend. Björk has performed worldwide and won a vast number of awards both for singing and acting.

Left: *An eider duck sits on her nest in the remote Dýrafjörður area of northwest Iceland.*

Above: *The reflections of Dvergarsternsofell in the waters of Álftafjördur in northwest Iceland.*

THE LAST HAUNTS OF THE WHITE-TAILED SEA EAGLE

The majestic white-tailed sea eagle once occurred all round the coast of Iceland and along its lakes and rivers. During the 19th century, however, numbers declined drastically as the eagle was persecuted by farmers who blamed it for killing lambs and taking eiders. Many of the birds were shot and others died after taking poisoned bait meant for foxes. In fact, the white-tailed sea eagle mainly takes dead lambs and can make little impression on the half a million eider ducks in the country. In 1913 a law was passed protecting the sea eagle, but it had little effect and by 1959 there were only 11 pairs in the country. There has been a gradual recovery in numbers, and there are now 30–40 breeding pairs, mainly in the Northwest Fiords.

cliffs, which rise vertically in places to over 500m (1650ft). Guillemots, puffins, razorbills, kittiwakes and fulmars breed in profusion, while there is always the possibility of seeing the rare white-tailed sea eagle. Note that there is no accommodation in the Hornstrandir area apart from mountain huts.

An hour's excursion by boat from Ísafjördur leads to **Vigur Island**. In this pristine environment there are only 11 inhabitants, but thousands of tame seabirds nesting on the grassy slopes. There is a tea room, post office and the only eider duck feather factory in Iceland.

Around the Northwest Fiords ★★★

Other coastal settlements of note include **Suðavík**, once a Norwegian whaling station, the geothermal centre of **Reykjanes**, and **Suðureyri**, which is in the unenviable position of having no direct sunlight for four months of the year. The most westerly point in Europe is marked by the lighthouse at **Látrabjarg**. To the south of this are the **Látrabjarg Cliffs**, which are 12km (7½ miles) long and rise to over 500m (1650ft). In summer the ledges of the cliffs teem with breeding sea birds, including puffins, guillemots, fulmars and cormorants. There is also an estimated one-third of the world's razorbills nesting here. The local people are accomplished at abseiling down the cliffs to collect birds' eggs, a skill that came in useful in 1947, when a British trawler ran aground at the foot of the cliffs. The local farmers casually saved the entire crew by hauling them up the 200m (650ft) cliffs by rope, even stopping halfway up, it is said, to give them soup!

West and Northwest Iceland at a Glance

BEST TIMES TO VISIT

The south of this region can be visited for most of the year. The further north you go, however, the more hostile the winter climate becomes. The chilling Arctic winds and the poor surfaces of most of the roads in the Northwest Fiords area make this a **summer** venue.

GETTING THERE

The Ring Road goes through the southern part of this area, which is also well served by a number of scheduled bus routes. However, access is more difficult in the region of the Snæfellsnes Peninsula, and particularly in the Northwest Fiords. The ferry *Akraborg* runs at least four times a day between Reykjavík and Akranes. The ferry *Baldur* plies the route between Stykkishólmur on the Snæfellsnes Peninsula and Brjánslækur on the south side of the Northwest Fiords. From there it is a circuitous drive to anywhere else in the area. Air Iceland flights run from Reykjavík to Stykkishólmur and Ísafjörður.

GETTING AROUND

Travelling in the Snæfellsnes Peninsula and the Northwest Fiords is difficult in winter when heavy snowfall can cause problems on the road. Many of the bus services in the region only run in summer, and even then careful planning is essential.

WHERE TO STAY

In the remoter areas of the west, few hotels are open all year, and in summer they can quickly become booked up. Forward planning is advisable.

LUXURY

Hótel Búðir, 365 Snæfellsnes Peninsula, tel: 435 6700, www.budir.is Claims to be the only boutique hotel outside Reykjavík. A favourite haunt of Nobel prize winning author Halldór Laxness. Good views. Open all year round.

MID-RANGE

Hótel Borgarnes, Egilsgata 14–16, 310 Borgarnes, tel: 437 1119, fax: 437 1443, website: www.hotelborgarnes.com Open all year; good restaurant.
Hótel Stykkishólmur, Vatnsás, 340 Stykkishólmur, tel: 430 2100, fax: 430 2101, website: www.hringhotels.is Has a restaurant, and there are bikes for hire. Free golf.
Hótel Ísafjörður, Silfurtorg 2, 400 Ísafjörður, tel: 456 4111, www.hotelisafjordur.is Good restaurant. Cheaper annexe nearby. Open all year.

BUDGET

Budget accommodation available in hostels and camp sites.

There are a number of **HI hostels** in the area, namely at Patreksfjörður, Borganes, Reykholt and Stykkishólmur. There are several excellent **camp sites**, including those at Borganes, Ólafsvík and Ísafjörður.

WHERE TO EAT

High-class restaurants are somewhat few and far between in this part of the country, and frequently the restaurants in the hotels are the only available choice for dining. Particularly well recommended are the restaurant at the **Hótel Ísafjörður**, which has a very good tourist menu, and the one at the **Hótel Borganes**.

USEFUL CONTACTS

There are **Tourist Information Centres** at these places:
Akranes: Skólabraut 31, tel: 431 3327.
Borganes: Hyrnan at Bruartorg, tel: 437 2214.
Stykkishólmur: Aðalgata 2, tel: 438 1150.
Ísafjörður: Aðelstræti 7, tel: 450 8060.
Vesturfirðir: the tourist office is at Ísafjörður, tel: 456 5121, and offers a variety of boat cruises and hiking excursions in the vicinity.

STYKKISHÓLMUR	J	F	M	A	M	J	J	A	S	O	N	D
AVE. TEMP. °C	-1.8	-0.7	-0.8	1.6	4.9	8.1	9.9	9.6	6.7	3.9	0.9	-0.8
AVE. TEMP. °F	28.7	30.7	30.5	34.9	40.8	46.6	49.8	49.3	44	39	33.6	30.5
AVE. RAINFALL mm	67.5	68.9	71.7	52.9	33.7	40.2	42.1	51.7	56.6	80.3	66.8	71.6
AVE. RAINFALL in	2.66	2.71	2.82	2.08	1.33	1.58	1.62	2.04	2.23	3.16	2.63	2.82

5
Northern Iceland

After the Reykjavík area, Northern Iceland is the part of the country which is most popular among tourists. It has many attractions, not the least of which is the weather. Despite being only a stone's throw away from the Arctic Circle (which straddles the offshore island of Grímsey), summers can be pleasantly warm and much drier than in the south of the country. Pastoral farming thrives in the lowland areas.

The coastline is marked by a series of rugged peninsulas protruding into the Arctic Ocean, with fiords, bays and occasional river deltas. Some of the inland areas have been heavily glaciated, leaving spectacular mountain scenery. The eastern part of the area lies on the plate boundary, and in the **Lake Mývatn** area there are numerous volcanic features, such as **Krafla** volcano, lava flows, pseudo craters and mud springs. In the extreme east is a largely unpopulated, gravel-strewn, cold desert, almost totally devoid of vegetation. Hikers head for the attractive **Jökulsárgljúfur National Park**, where a long gorge has been formed by glacial meltwaters. Numerous waterfalls can be seen here, including the imposing **Dettifoss**, said to be the most powerful falls in Europe. Bird-watchers are in their element in this part of Iceland, with Lake Mývatn a major attraction. Huge numbers of duck breed in this shallow lake, which is fed by warm underground springs.

The Ring Road bisects Northern Iceland and most of the important settlements can be found along its route. Dominating the area is **Akureyri**, the country's second

DON'T MISS

★★★ Jökulsárgljúfur National Park: Iceland's own version of the Grand Canyon, with the powerful Dettifoss waterfall.
★★★ Lake Mývatn Area: teeming bird life and the country's most spectacular volcanic features.
★★★ Glaumbær Folk Museum: take a look inside a turf farm complex.
★★ Húsavík: superb whale-watching from this northern fishing port.
★★ Goðafoss: the accessible 'Waterfall of the Gods'.

Opposite: *Turf huts at the Glaumbær Folk Museum to the south of Sauðárkrókur.*

Above: *Whale-watching tours from Húsavík are likely to be rewarded with photographs such as this tail fin of a breaching sperm whale.*

largest town and the regional and service centre for the whole of Northern Iceland. It has an outpost of Reykjavík university, a clutch of interesting museums and some fine botanical gardens. It is also the main air and sea port of the area. A number of small fishing ports are scattered around the coastline, including **Húsavík**, which has become quite well known for its whale-watching tours.

The West of the Region

The Ring Road joins the area at the small settlement of **Brú** at the head of the narrow **Hrútafjörður**. This leads out into the wide bay of **Húnaflói**. The word translates as 'Bear Bay', named, no doubt, after the many Greenland bears which have washed ashore here on ice floes. The Ring Road now heads to the northeast, with distant views of the moraine-dammed salt-water lagoon of **Hóp**, where seals can often be seen basking on the sand at low tide.

The first settlement of any size is **Blönduós**, situated on both banks of the River Blandaá, a popular (and expensive) salmon river. Blönduós is dominated by its church – a modern concrete affair clearly designed in the shape of a volcanic crater. The only other features to detain visitors are a small **Textile Museum** exhibiting local handicrafts and costumes, and the **Sea Ice Exhibition Centre**, which looks at the effects that the weather had on early settlers. Don't miss the stuffed polar bear, who made a nuisance of himself when he washed up in the summer of 2008.

North of Blönduós is the rugged and remote **Skagi Peninsula**. The only settlement of importance here is the old trading centre and current fishing port of **Skagaströnd**. A gravel road runs around the perimeter of the peninsula. The northerly point is marked by an unmanned lighthouse, and nearby are some remarkable ledges of horizontal basalt.

CLIMATE

The north of Iceland has a more continental climate than the south, with drier, sunnier summers, but colder winters and more snowfall. Rainfall is light, but northerly winds can bring very cold conditions. This is the most sunny part of the country, but the wind-chill factor is high. The temperature in Akureyri averages 2.4°C (27.5°F) in **January** and 10.7°C (51°F) in **July**, with an average total **rainfall** of 470mm (18.5 in).

From here the Ring Road heads inland over some superb glacial scenery, before dropping right down into the Héradsvötn valley and the little settlement of **Varmahlíð**, which is currently growing as a service centre for the surrounding area.

Sauðárkrókur ★★★
Located at the head of Skagafjörður, Sauðárkrókur, with a population of around 2600, is the second largest town in the north of Iceland. Its position 25km (15.5 miles) north of the Ring Road means it doesn't see as many tourists as it deserves. The town developed on the site of an old trading post, and its industries include fish processing and the making of fibreglass. The small **Art and Folk Museum** (tel: 453 6870, open 13:00–18:00 Jun–Aug) includes one of the few blacksmith's forges in Iceland. There are hiking possibilities in the mountains behind the town. Boat trips are offered to the island of **Drangey** in Skagafjörður, where the steep cliffs house thousands of breeding sea birds. Both the birds and their eggs have been a rich source of food for local people in the past.

THE ARCTIC FOX

Iceland's only native land mammal is the **arctic fox** (*Alopex lagopus*). Greyish brown in summer, in winter it grows a thick, furry coat that turns much lighter, almost white. It is well insulated and may even grow fur on its paws. The arctic fox was common throughout the country, but because farmers thought it killed lambs, it has been persecuted and has retreated to less habited areas. In fact, it poses little threat to healthy sheep and largely exists on small birds, eggs, fish and shellfish, though it will feed on carcasses of sheep and dead sea birds. There have been attempts to **breed** foxes on fur farms, but these animals have been brought in from abroad.

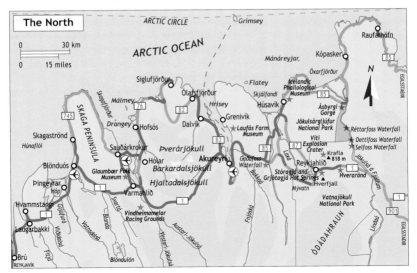

South of Sauðárkrókur ★★★

The Héradsvötn River has built up a sizeable delta at the head of Skagafjörður. Although it is rich farmland, it is prone to flooding when snows melt in early summer. Above the flood plain to the west is the **Glaumbær Folk Museum** (tel: 453 6173), based on an 18th-century turf farm. It consists of a complex of small separate buildings linked by a central passageway. The buildings include guest rooms, a dairy, a pantry, a kitchen and living rooms (or *baðstofa*). It was in the latter that the work of the farmhouse took place. The women of the house would weave and spin, while the men combed wool and made ropes. A member of the household would usually read a Saga or recite poetry while the others worked. The *baðstofa* also contained beds, and many people would sleep together for warmth. The rooms are full of fascinating artefacts from previous centuries. Glaumbær is also the burial place of Snorri Þorfinnasson, who is believed to have been the first European to be born in North America. This was in the year 1003, when his parents went on an expedition to Vinland. The museum, which is open daily, 09:00–18:00 from June to September, is highly recommended. There is a small café in a nearby building.

Iceland horse enthusiasts will certainly wish to visit the **Vindheimamelar Racing Grounds**, approximately 10km (6 miles) south of Varmahlíð. An audiovisual presentation is followed by a demonstration of the five gaits of this hardy breed. Refreshments are provided, but reservations are necessary.

Hólar ★★★

Another diversion to the north of Varmahlíð along the eastern side of the Heraðsvötn valley eventually leads to the **religious centre** of Hólar. This was the northern bishopric in Iceland from 1106 until the Reformation. The first

Left: *Icelandic horses show their paces at the Vindheimamelar Racing Grounds.*
Opposite: *The Glaumbær Folk Museum is on an 18th-century turf farm.*

wooden cathedral here was built from Norwegian timber, and for a century it was the world's largest wooden church. In 1798, the bishop's seat was abolished, and the site later became an **agricultural college**. The present church at Hólar dates from 1757 and is made of the local red sandstone. The bell tower contains the remains of the first Bishop, Jón Ögmundarson who, together with his son, was executed at Skálholt for his opposition to Danish reforms. The interior of the church is full of interest and well worth a visit. Climb the tower for spectacular views. There are guided tours between 14:00 and 18:00 daily.

AKUREYRI

Located at the head of Eyjafjörður, the fast-growing town of Akureyri is the 'capital' of Northern Iceland and one of the country's most pleasant urban areas. Akureyri became a trading centre in the early 17th century, but it was over 100 years later that the first people lived here. Its main growth has taken place during the 20th century. It now has a population of around 17,000. Akureyri has always specialized in fish products, and herring salting was initially important. After the stocks declined, the emphasis turned to the canning and freezing of larger fish such as cod. Other industries include food processing, brewing and, increasingly, tourism. A number of old wooden buildings have been preserved in the town, and its residents take great pride in their gardens, which means that the town has a pleasant cared-for feel. There is an attract-

THE REMARKABLE ICELANDIC HORSE

Despite the small size of the Icelandic horse, please don't ever call it a pony! It is a **purebred** horse, found in a variety of colours, and unique in having **five gaits**. In addition to the usual walk, trot and gallop, it has the tölt and the pace, the latter two giving a smooth, comfortable ride for the equestrian. This singular horse is a valuable animal and is exported throughout the world. A hardy animal, it is also a good **workhorse**, and up to the start of the 20th century it was essential for transport and farm work. Furthermore, its toughness meant that it was quite happy to spend the winter outdoors. Today, the Icelandic horse is largely used for **sport** and **recreation**.

Above: *The harbour at Akureyri, where there is an important fish canning and freezing industry.*

ive central shopping mall and numerous bookshops, libraries, churches and museums. The riverside is full of interest, with fishing and cargo boats, families of harlequin and eider ducks, and planes flying low down the fiord to land at the airport.

Akureyrarkirkja ★

The parish church sits high on the hill overlooking the town centre and is well worth the climb. This modern church has rather a 'geological' appearance, and it is not really surprising to learn that it was designed by the same architect who was responsible for the Hallgrímskirkja in Reykjavík. It is worth looking at the interior – the central chancel window came from the old Coventry Cathedral in the UK, somehow surviving the blitz. The ship hanging from the ceiling is an old Norse tradition meant to protect seafarers.

Museums ★★★

Akureyri has an extraordinary number of museums. Many of these are small affairs celebrating former sons of the town and will be of minimal interest to the foreign visitor, but others are well worth a visit.

The **Natural History Museum** at Hafnarstræti 81 contains a comprehensive collection of eggs, mammals, insects, flora and stuffed birds. The star exhibit is a mock-up of the extinct Great Auk, the parts having been put together from other birds. Open 10:00–17:00, June–September.

The fascinating **Akureyri Folk Museum** displays a collection of household and workplace artefacts dating back to the time of the Settlement. Situated at Aðalstræti 58, this museum is open 11:00–17:00 daily, June–September; in winter it is open on Sundays from 14:00–16:00.

Nonnahús, located at Aðalstræti 54, is the childhood home of the Reverend Jón Sveinnsson (1857–1944), who was nicknamed 'Nonni'. He wrote a number of works for children, based on his own youthful experiences. The building is a revealing example of the cramped conditions people lived in during the 19th century in Iceland. Sveinnsson's statue dominates the garden. The house is open from 11:00–17:00 daily, June–September.

Laxdalshús, at Hafnarstræti 11, is the oldest building in Akureyri, dating from 1795. It functioned originally as a Danish trading house. An excellent audiovisual display traces the history of the town. It is open from 11:00–17:00 daily, June–September.

There are also small museums celebrating the work of Davíð Stefánsson and Matthías Jochumsson, both of whom became Icelandic poets laureate.

Visitors arriving by air could check out the **Icelandic Aviation Museum** at Akureyri Airport (tel: 461 4400, open 13:00–17:00 Jun–Aug). Icelandic aviation history is detailed and there are a number of restored aircraft.

Visitors should not leave Akureyri without visiting the **Botanical Gardens**. The gardens were founded in 1912 by the local townswomen and were then taken over by the local authority in 1955. There is a comprehensive collection of Icelandic plants, all carefully labelled, plus a number of different plants from all around the world. It is amazing to find Mediterranean plants surviving at this high latitude. The Botanical Gardens are open from 08:00–22:00, June to September; tel: 462 7487.

Below: *Akureyri Church, designed by the architect responsible for the Hallgrímskirkja in Reykjavík.*

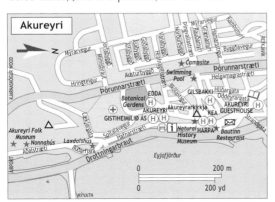

THE BIG WHALING DEBATE

In 1986 the International Whaling Commission banned commercial whaling. It took a further three years and much international pressure for Iceland to comply. A large whale-watching industry developed, based at former whaling ports such as Húsavík. By 2002, whale-watchers numbered over 60,000 annually, bringing more than US$16 million to the Icelandic economy. In 2003 Iceland decided to resume commercial whaling for 'scientific reasons'. A recent survey has shown that over 70% of Icelanders support the resumption of whaling. However, the decision to resume whaling has backfired on Iceland. There is little demand for whale meat in the country and the plan to export it to Japan has not materialized, as Japan fears that the Icelandic-caught whale meat may be contaminated with heavy metals and, in any case, is stockpiling its own 'scientifically' caught meat. Moreover, environmentalists were clearly boycotting whale-watching trips, as revenue was greatly reduced. Clearly, whales are worth more to Iceland alive than dead, and in late 2007, the Icelandic minister in charge announced the he would no longer be issuing further whale-catching quotas until a market could be secured. For news updates visit: www.greenpeace.org/whales or www.iwoffice.org

NORTH OF AKUREYRI

There are a number of small ports north of Akureyri. On the eastern side of Eyjafjörður is **Grenivík**, which has a large fish-freezing plant. Just to the south is the **Laufás Farm Museum**, based on an old turf farmhouse dating from 1850. On the opposite side of the fiord is the ferry port of **Dalvík**. Its main claim to fame is the 1934 earthquake which measured 6.3 on the Richter Scale and destroyed half the town. Ferries leave Dalvík for Grímsey, calling en route at the island of Hrísey in the middle of the fiord. Further north is the port of **Ólafsfjörður**, which is considered to have one of the most attractive settings in the country. It is now reached by a 3.5km (2-mile) tunnel through the surrounding peaks. At the northern end of the peninsula lies the fishing port of **Siglfjörður**, located in a short but spectacular fiord. It was originally named Thormóðseyri after Thormóður the Strong, who was the first settler. Siglfjörður was the third largest town in Iceland during the years of the herring boom. The town declined with the herring, but the golden years are remembered in the harbourside Herring Museum. Open 10:00–18:00, daily.

Goðafoss ★★★

The Ring Road leaves Akureyri eastwards and follows the far shore of the fiord, giving superb views across to the town. It then climbs the mountains through superb glacial

Left: *Goðafoss is Iceland's most accessible waterfall.*
Opposite: *The northern fishing port of Húsavík is the whale-watching capital of Iceland.*

scenery before dropping down into the next valley, that of the River Skjálfandaflót. Just a short stroll from the road is Goðafoss, Iceland's most accessible **waterfall**, formed as the river cuts into a lava field. The name means 'Waterfall of the Gods', a title which dates back to AD1000 when the law-speaker, Þorgeir, was returning from the Alþing. The parliament had just decided to adopt the Christian religion, and Þorgeir decided that the falls would be a good place to dispose of his pagan idols.

Húsavík ★★★

From the road junction at nearby Laugar, Route 845 leads northwards to the busy **fishing port** of Húsavík. Situated on an attractive harbour and backed by snow-capped mountains, Húsavík has a population of around 2500 and is the main service centre for northeast Iceland. Húsavík's first inhabitant was a Viking named Garðar Svavarsson. He gave up and left after the first winter, but two of his slaves were unfortunately left behind. In reality, these were Iceland's very first settlers, but they are never credited as such. Today Húsavík makes its living mainly from fish processing, sulphur exports and tourism. In recent years the town has become Iceland's most important **whale-watching centre**. Over 90% of trips record minke whales, while other cetaceans commonly seen are humpbacks, fins, sei and orcas, plus harbour porpoises and dolphins. Before you go on a whale-watching trip, it is worth paying a visit

THE GOÐAR AND THE FALLS

Way back in the year 1000, the 'goðar', or pagan chieftains, had a heated debate at the **Alþing** about whether to abandon paganism and adopt Christianity. The decision was finally left to the **law-speaker**, Þorgeir Þorkelsson. He is said to have curled up under his sheepskin in a booth at Þingvellir for three days and nights while he considered the problem. He finally came up with a classic compromise, deciding in favour of Christianity, but allowing the people to practice paganism in the privacy of their homes if they so wished. To set a good example, Þorgeir, on his way home, threw his pagan effigies into the waterfalls – thereafter to be known as the 'Waterfall of the Gods', or **Goðafoss**.

Above: *Húsavík's distinctive church, built with timber brought from Norway.*

GRÍMSEY'S AMERICAN BENEFACTOR

One of the most remarkable stories of 19th-century Iceland was the strange tale of an American millionaire named **Daniel Willard Fiske**, who befriended the people of Grímsey, largely, it seems, because of their enthusiasm for playing chess. Although he never set foot on the island, he poured in resources such as money and firewood. He also arranged for a school and a library to be built. Fiske, who was the American **chess champion**, sent over 11 marble chess sets – one for each farm on the island. Ironically, few people on Grímsey are interested in the game today.

to the **Whale Museum** (tel: 414 2800, open 09:00–19:00 Jun–Aug, 10:00–17:00 May and September, www.whalemuseum.is). Located in an old harbourside slaughterhouse, the museum charts the history of whaling and more recent conservation measures. It is difficult not to be impressed by the huge whale skeletons.

The **Icelandic Phallological Museum** (tel: 561 6663, www.phallus.is) is surely one of the most bizarre museums anywhere in the world. Relocated from Reykjavík, it contains a collection of over 300 species of penises from a variety of animals. Although there are no human contributions, it is said that a number of men have bequeathed their private parts on their death!

The town museum, the **Safnahúsið**, is also worth a visit. As well as the usual social memorabilia, there is also a stuffed polar bear, which was washed up on the island of Grímsey and greeted with a bullet.

There are two islands in Skjálfandi Bay, namely **Flatey** and **Lundey**, which are easily reached by boat from Húsavík. The latter is particularly noted for its large colony of puffins.

GRÍMSEY

Some 41km (25 miles) north of the mainland is the island of Grímsey. Covering an area of 5.3km² (2 sq miles), it straddles the Arctic Circle (visitors can obtain documents certifying that they have crossed over into the Arctic). Only 120 people live on the island, mainly around the harbour at Sandvík. Ferries and planes connect Grímsey to the mainland, especially in the summer months. Most visitors are bird-watchers. The cliffs teem with sea birds during the breeding season, with guillemots, puffins, razorbills, fulmars and even a few pairs of the rare little auk.

LAKE MÝVATN AREA

This is one of the most important tourist locations in Iceland, currently receiving an estimated 100,000 visitors a year. Apart from the lake itself, which attracts bird-watchers from all over the world, there are a host of volcanic features to observe. The climate, too, is agreeable as the area is in the rain shadow of the Vatnajökull icecap, making it one of the driest parts of the country.

Lake Mývatn ★★★

The lake, which sits on the Mid-Atlantic Ridge, covers around 37km² (14 sq miles). It is essentially a shallow lake, with an average depth of 2.5m (8ft). This means that light can penetrate right to the bottom, making it rich in vegetation and nutrients, which in turn prove attractive to wildfowl. The numbers of ducks present in the summer are staggering, with probably around 50,000 pairs and 15 species represented. These include tufted duck, wigeon, mergansers, long-tailed duck, teal, gadwall and goosanders. Add to this list whooper swans, slavonian grebe, red-necked phalarope, skuas, terns, snow buntings and snowy owl, and it is clear why birders flock here in huge numbers. European bird-watchers in particular are keen to see American species such as Barrow's goldeneye and harlequin duck (which breeds along the River Laxa).

A metalled road runs along the east of the lake and a dirt track follows the western side. A large area in the northwest of the lake is a protected nesting area and out of bounds for much of the summer. Although much of Mývatn ices over in winter, part of the northern

PSEUDO CRATERS

A feature of the Mývatn area is the large number of **islands** in the lake (about 50) and the numerous small hills in the vicinity. On inspection they are seen to have concave summits and are described by geologists as **pseudo craters**, largely because no lava ever flowed out of them. They were formed when lava flowed across the lake. The trapped water boiled and exploded through the lava, building up cones and craters. They vary in size from 3m (9ft) to 250m (820ft) across.

Below: *The shallow waters of Lake Mývatn teem with a variety of wildfowl.*

Opposite: *Remnants of winter ice in the Viti explosion crater and lake situated on the slopes of the frequently active Krafla.*

section is fed by hot springs and remains ice-free, so that there are wildfowl present throughout the year. Bird-watchers and other visitors should beware of insects. Mývatn means 'lake of the midges' and there are swarms of these little pests, especially on calm days in the summer. Net head covers are recommended.

The lake contains over 50 islands, most of which are **pseudo craters**. They look like mini volcanoes, but were in fact formed by gas explosions. This gives a hint of the **volcanic features** which abound in the area, particularly to the northeast of the lake. There has been continual volcanic activity since the end of the Ice Age. Particularly significant were the '**Mývatn fires**' which flowed from the Krafla area between 1724 and 1729 along a fissure which is still occasionally active. More recent were the '**Krafla fires**' in the early 1980s. Subterranean rumblings suggest that more volcanic activity is imminent. Many of the volcanic features can be viewed at first hand.

Dimmuborgir ★★

Dimmuborgir, which can be translated as 'black castles', is an area of lava located on the eastern side of the lake. Thought to be around 2000 years old, the lava here is believed to have been dammed by older material and then forced up into a wide variety of contorted shapes. It is possible for visitors to wander around among the lava pillars, caves and holes, which are now developing some interesting vegetation. To save the area from human erosion, set walking routes have been roped off – but it is still quite possible for people to get lost!

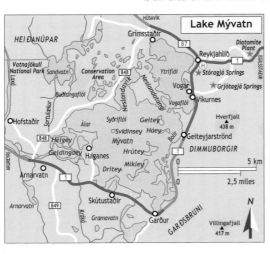

Lake Mývatn

Hverfjall ★

Just north of Dimmuborgir stands the cinder cone of Hverfjall which rises to 163m (534ft). It was formed during a cataclysmic eruption around 2500 years ago. It is possible to walk up the steep path to the rim of the large crater, though hikers are no longer allowed to descend to the crater floor.

Hot Springs ★

Situated between Hverfjall and the village of Reykjahíð are a couple of popular hot springs which give visitors an opportunity for bathing. The first, **Stóragjá**, is hidden in a crevice and has to be reached by means of a rope ladder, but the second, **Grjótagjá**, is much more accessible and is divided into separate sections for men and women. The water temperatures are generally around 47°C (116°F), but are cooling annually.

Krafla ★★★

To the northeast of the lake is the impressive Krafla volcanic complex. It is readily accessible, with visitors able to drive there directly from the Ring Road, passing the Krafla Geothermal Power Station en route. Krafla itself does not resemble the archetypal cone-shaped volcano, but is in fact a reasonably level system of fissures, along which the surface occasionally swells and erupts. Nearby, however, is the dramatic **Viti explosion crater**. Viti is the Icelandic name for 'hell' and the 320m (1050ft) wide crater, which often fills with ice floes in the winter, certainly fits the description.

Hverarönd ★★★

About 6km (3.7 miles) to the east of the lake, at the side of the Ring Road and situated on the Mid-Atlantic Ridge, is the hill known as **Námafjall**. Among its cracks and fissures are bands of yellow sulphur. The mineral was once mined

---

COPING WITH THE MIDGES

One of the less appealing aspects of Lake Mývatn is the swarms of midges which gave the lake its name. They hatch between June and August and can make life very unpleasant. They seem particularly attracted to the **carbon dioxide** on people's breath and seem intent on entering the nose, eyes, ears and mouth. They are particularly active on **calm days** and reduce in number the further you are from the lake. Insect repellent and net headware are strongly recommended. The good news is that the midges do not bite (although the blackfly certainly does – it can be readily identified by its buzzing noise). Midges are eagerly devoured by wildfowl and fish. In fact, the Laxa River is reputed to have the country's biggest salmon as a result of this.

here, but was not commercially successful. Beneath the hill is the remarkable area of **Hverarönd**, undoubtly one of Iceland's most unforgettable sights. There are bubbling mud pools, steam vents, hot boiling springs, fumeroles and the distinctive stench of sulphur everywhere. Visitors are advised to stick to the roped-off paths as some of the surface material is fragile.

Above: *Part of the lava flow that threatened the church at Reykjalið in 1929.*
Opposite: *Dettifoss is claimed to be Europe's most powerful waterfall in terms of water volume.*

DIATOMS

The bed of Lake Mývatn has a layer of diatomaceous ooze which is up to 15m (49ft) thick. Diatomite is the skeletal remains of diatoms, which are microscopic single-cell **algae**. The fossil shells are one tenthousandth the size of a grain of sand and consist largely of silica. The diatomite is sucked up from a barge and pumped by pipeline to the processing plant, where it is dried using steam from the nearby Bjarnaflag geothermal power station. The result is a white powder which is packed and transported to Húsavík, from whence it is **exported** to Europe for use as a filler in a variety of industries.

Reykjahlíð ★★★

This is the only settlement of any size in the Mývatn area. Though originally merely a farmhouse, it has grown in size with the development of tourism and is now an important service centre for the surrounding region. There is a church, hotel, supermarket, tourist office, bank and small museum. The original church was threatened by the 1929 lava flow which completely destroyed many of the buildings in the village, but miraculously the flow passed by a few metres from the church. A modern church was built on the site in 1972 and is well worth a visit.

The Reykjahlíð area has seen a number of industrial ventures, some of which have been successful, others spectacular failures. The main employer at the moment is the Bjarnarflag **diatomite plant**, which is fortunately well away from the lake. Diatoms are microfossils which are dredged up from the lake bed. After treatment they are used as a filler in such products as paint and toothpaste. The diatomaceous ooze is moved by pipeline to the refining plant just north of the Ring Road. There are environmental questions about the effect the dredging is having on the ecology of the lake, and naturalists are particularly worried about operations moving to other parts of the lake. Though diatomite mining is highly successful, the **Krafla Geothermal Power Station** has been a dubious operation and its drilling is believed to have set off the Krafla eruptions in the mid-70s. Before leaving the area, take a look at the land on the opposite side of the road to the diatom plant. This is marked by a pipe with steam bursting out of it and was the site of a drill hole to ascertain the feasibility of locating a geo-thermal power station here. Just by its side is an underground bread oven. Peer through the glass doors to see the *hverabrauð* taking 24 hours to bake.

JÖKULSÁRGLJÚFUR NATIONAL PARK ★★★

Jökulsárgljúfur was given its national park status in 1978. It is essentially a 30km (19-mile) canyon formed by *jökulhlaup*, or glacial meltwater floods. The canyon is drained by the River **Jökulsá á Fjöllum**, which rises on the Vatnjökull icecap and then flows north for 206km (128 miles) to the Arctic Ocean. Jökulsárgljúfur is often described as 'Iceland's Grand Canyon' and although its measurements cannot compare with the American giant, it is certainly an impressive sight. The main part of the canyon averages 100m (328ft) in depth and has a width of 500m (547yd). There is a series of impressive waterfalls, including Hafragilsfoss, Dettifoss and Selfoss. Of these, **Dettifoss** should not be missed, as it is claimed to be Europe's most powerful waterfall. Although only 45m (148ft) in height, it dispatches some 500m³ (17,658ft³) of water per second – a truly awe-some sight. Downstream from here is another extraordinary landform, detached from the main canyon and known as **Ásbyrgi**. It is a dry, horseshoe-shaped

THE SNOWY OWL

Few sights are more evoc-ative of Iceland than the flight of the white, ghostly snowy owl. This magnificent bird is **diurnal** and largely solitary. It can often be seen sitting upright on a low eminence, surveying the surrounding land for prey. It is resident in Iceland, but has become **extremely rare**, being largely confined to the more inaccessible areas – although some have been seen in the Mývatn area in recent years. Snowy owls usually prey on ptarmigan, but will take young ducks and goslings in the breeding season.

gorge, which the Vikings believed was the hoofprint of Odin's horse. The geographical explanation is that it is an incised abandoned meander, left high and dry when the Jökulsá á Fjöllum changed its course during a *jökulhlaup*. Fulmars breed on the walls of the gorge in summer. The national park is wonderful for hiking, but there is no formal accommodation within the park, and just two official camp sites. The national park brochure in-dicates the main walking trails.

Northern Iceland at a Glance

As with most parts of the country, the **summer** months from June to September are the most convenient times to visit the north of Iceland. At this period the area is drier than it is in the south, and it also has more sunny days. At this northerly latitude there is scarcely any night at all during the summer. The **winter** months are not recommended for visitors, due to the heavy snowfall, the cold blasts of wind from the Arctic, and the lack of daylight, particularly during the months of December, January and February.

GETTING THERE

The Ring Road is usually kept open during winter, but may be temporarily closed from time to time during heavy snowfalls until the snow can be cleared from the surface. Akureyri is approximately 390km (242 miles) by road from Reykjavík. BSÍ coaches take the better part of a day to cover this distance. It is much quicker to reach the northern parts of the country by air. Air Iceland operates daily flights from Reykjavík to Akureyri, and less regular flights from Akureyri to Egilsstaðir, Grímsey, Ísafjörður and the Westman Islands.

GETTING AROUND

The Ring Road is very well surfaced throughout the north of Iceland, and cars have no problems during summer. However, four-wheel-drive vehicles are generally recommended for travelling here in winter. The main settlements in the area are all linked by bus, but away from the Ring Road bus services may be confined to one or two services a day. Cars and four-wheel-drive vehicles may be hired in Akureyri and in Sauðárkrókur.

WHERE TO STAY

There is no accommodation in the international luxury range in northern Iceland. There are, however, several comfortable hotels in the mid-range.

MID-RANGE
Hotel Kea, Hafnarstræti 87–89, 600 Akureyri, tel: 460 2000, fax: 460 2060; website: www.keahotels.is Situated in the shadow of the church, this hotel has all the facilities, but on a busy road. **Hotel Reynihlíð**, 660 Reykjahlíð, Mývatn, tel: 464 4170, www.myvatnhotel.is The accommodation price includes a continental buffet breakfast. **The Edda Group** runs a number of hotels in the area, some are summer hotels. They are found at Laugarbakka, Blönduós and Akureyri; website: www.hoteledda.is **The Foss Group** have hotels at Laugar, Fosshóll, near Goðafoss, Sauðárkrókur and two in Akureyri. Some are summer hotels; website: www.fosshotel.is

Hotel Harpa, Hafnarstræti 83–85, Akureyri, tel: 460 2000, www.keahotels.is Recently renovated with modern styling. Shares restaurant with the nearby Hotel Kea. **Hotel Varmahlið**, 560 Varmahlið, tel: 453 8170, www.hotelvarmahlid.is Modern hotel right on the Ring Road. Best restaurant in the area.

BUDGET
Akureyri Guesthouse, Brekkugata 4, Akureyri, tel: 661 9050, www.akureyriguesthouse.is Basic, good value rooms on pedestrianized street. **Árból Guesthouse**, Asgarðsvegur 2, 640 Húsavik, tel: 464 2220. Plain bedrooms and shared bathrooms. Friendly owners. Open all year. **Gistiheimilið Hraunbrún**, Reykjahlíð, tel: 464 4103. This is a good centre for the Mývatn area. Next to the campground. **Gistiheimilið Ás**, Skipagata 4, 600 Akureyri, tel: 461 2248, fax: 461 3810. Centrally located near bus station. Self-catering units are available. **Youth Hostels** can be found at Akureyri, at Ósar (near Hvammstangi in the west of the region), and at Sæberg, near Brú. For booking, tel: 533 8110, fax: 588 9201.

CAMPING
Two camp sites in the Jökulsá National Park, others at Mývatn, others at Akureyri, Blönduós, Goðafoss, Húsavik, Sauðárkrókur and Ólafsfjörður. These are all official seasonal sites.

Northern Iceland at a Glance

The best restaurants in the north of the country are invariably those in hotel dining rooms, and in the more remote areas these are often the only option in the evenings. Hotel restaurants, however, are usually rather expensive. There are a few other restaurants in the larger settlements which can be recommended:

Sauðárkrókur
MID-RANGE
Kaffi Krókur, Aðalgata 16, Sauðárkrókur, tel: 453 6299. This is a cosy restaurant in the heart of the town, serving Icelandic food in a cosmopolitan setting.

Akureyri
MID-RANGE
Bautinn, Hafnarstræti 92, tel: 462 1818, website: www.bautinn.is Here, mountains of food are to be had at bargain prices, served in an atrium-like setting.
Greifinn, Glerágata 20, tel: 460 1600. This restaurant serves moderately priced Icelandic food as well as a selection of burgers, pizzas and pasta.

Mývatn
MID-RANGE
Gamli Bærinn, Reykjalið, tel: 464 4170. This restaurant serves an excellent meal of the day packed with local specialities, including the cake-like *hverabrauð*.

Húsavík
MID-RANGE
Gamli Baukur, tel: 464 2442. Well-cooked fresh fish in a popular wooden harbourside restaurant.

BUDGET
Cheaper options are found at **snack bars** attached to service stations, which usually have a filling tourist menu.

Many tours and excursions around the popular venues in the north can be booked in Reykjavík, but a number of local firms can arrange tours for small groups, particularly for adventure trips.
Hestasport, located at the Vindheimamelar racing grounds 20km (12 miles) south of Varmalið. Raftahlið 20, 550 Sauðárkrókur, tel: 453 5066. Arranges riding tours as well as trips to experience the autumn *rettir* (sheep round-ups).
Activity Tours, tel: 453 5066. This firm specializes in whitewater rafting trips.
Nonni Travel, Ráðhúsplads, Akureyri, tel: 461 1841, arranges excursions to Hólar and Grimsey by ferry and by air. This company also offers excursions in the Mývatn

area amongst many others. For whale-watching tours from Húsavík, contact **North Sailing**, on the harbourside, tel: 464 2350. They use traditional Icelandic oak boats. Alternatively try **Sjóferðir-Arnar**, tel: 464 1748.

Tourist Information Centres are situated at all the major settlements in the north. The most important one is in **Akureyri** at the bus terminal, Hafnarstræti 82, tel: 553 5999, website: www.visit akureyri.is It is open Jun–Aug, weekdays from 09:00–21:00, weekends from 12:00–20:00. Also Sep–May, weekdays from 08:30–17:00. The office is planning to move to the new Culture House by the harbour in 2010.
Other Tourist Information Centres can be found at:
Blönduós, situated at the campground, tel: 452 4520;
Varmahlið, at the Shell petrol station, tel: 455 6161;
Sauðárkrókur, at the Fosshotel Áning, tel: 453 6717;
Mývatn, at Reykjahliðar school, tel: 464 4390; and
Húsavík, Garðarsbraut 5, tel: 464 4300 (but planning to move to the Whale Museum).

AKUREYRI	J	F	M	A	M	J	J	A	S	O	N	D
AVE. TEMP. °C	-2.2	-2.6	-2.6	0.7	7.2	9.9	12.5	10.5	6.3	3.7	1.7	-0.5
AVE. TEMP. °F	28	27.3	27.3	33.3	44.9	49.8	54.5	50.9	43.3	38.6	35	31.1
AVE. RAINFALL mm	55.2	42.5	43.3	29.2	19.3	28.2	33	34.1	39.1	58	54.2	52.8
AVE. RAINFALL in	2.17	1.67	1.7	1.15	0.76	1.11	1.3	1.34	1.54	2.29	2.14	2.08

6
East Iceland

Remote from the Mid-Atlantic Ridge, East Iceland is the country's geologically most stable and oldest area. It consists largely of basalt, a rock which flowed large distances from long-lost volcanoes. The whole area was later **glaciated**. Moving down from corries high in the mountains, the glaciers gouged out deep, U-shaped valleys, which were later flooded – in the post-glacial rise in sea level – to form today's impressive **fiords**. The Ring Road from Mývatn in the north to Egilsstaðir passes through one of Iceland's most majestic features: a **cold desert**, which is almost completely devoid of vegetation. The southwest boundary of the region is marked by the edge of **Vatnajökull**, Europe's largest icecap, from which numerous **glaciers** run down to the coastal plain.

The main service and transportation centre for the area is the rather unremarkable town of **Egilsstaðir**, which is located in the **Largafljót Valley**. The river here flows through **Lake Lögurinn**, which is 100m (330ft) deep. It is also Iceland's longest lake and reputedly has a resident monster. The slopes of the valley are clothed with the country's largest and most mature forest, which has a network of footpaths for exploring the woods. Each fiord has a small fishing port, the most important of these being **Seyðisfjörður**, **Djúpivogur** and **Reyðarfjörður**. Further to the south is the sheltered port and communications centre of **Höfn**, the first major settlement on the Ring Road since Selfoss, approximately 400km (250 miles) away to the west.

DON'T MISS

*** The Cold Desert: the fascinating mountain desert in the rain shadow of the Vatnajökull icecap.
** The Eastern Fiords: a region of fishing villages and lovely Scandinavian-style wooden buildings.
** Lake Lögurinn: a deep ribbon lake, reputedly with its own resident monster.
** Petra's Rock Museum: Petra Sveinsdóttir's private collection of rocks, minerals and fossils, displayed in her house and garden.

Opposite: *The ptarmigan, Iceland's most common game bird. Many are taken annually by gyrfalcons.*

Seyðisfjörður is Iceland's only car ferry link with Europe. From the ferry port, drivers once had to take the northerly route to Reykjavík via Mývatn, but in 1974 the Ring Road was completed. This allowed cars to take the southerly option, cutting both time and distance considerably. Few motorists stop for long in the eastern fiords region, with the result that it has none of the usual trappings of tourism, thus adding to its attractions for the discriminating visitor.

CROSSING THE DESERT

The route between Mývatn and Egilsstaðir crosses an interior cold desert which is one of the most fascinating parts of the country. The Ring Road, which is largely surfaced by gravel in this region, passes bare plains covered with volcanic ash and the glacial deposits of occasional meltwater floods. It climbs remote rocky passes and bridges rushing streams, with hardly a single item of vegetation to be seen. On a fine day, the journey is full of interest, but in the mist and rain, it can have a brooding, rather sinister atmosphere. Surprisingly there are two small isolated areas of farming here. At the northern end of the road, close to the Jökulsá á Fjöllum

Right: *The tiny church at Möðrudalur, built by a local farmer in memory of his wife.*

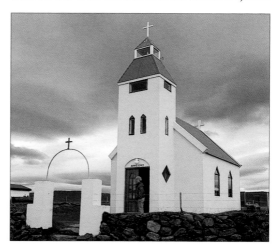

River, is the remote farm of **Grímsstaðir**. The road here was once crossed by ferry, and the old ferry-man's hut, reputed to be haunted, can still be seen in the distance. Further south is the little oasis of **Möðrudalur**. At 469m (1539ft), this is almost certainly the highest farm in the country. Buses stop here for half an hour or so, to allow passengers to use the snack bar and toilets. It is worth strolling over the road to see a small church, built by the local farmer in 1949 in memory of his wife. Note its unconventional altarpiece. This particular stretch of the Ring Road gives excellent views of **Herðubreið** (the name means 'broad-shouldered'), a plateau-like mountain capped with a volcanic cone. Composed of palagonite, it rises to a height of 1060m (3478ft) and dominates the surrounding area. The Ring Road then crosses a high pass capped with cairns, which are said to mark the boundary of the bishoprics of Hólar and Skálholt, before dropping down into the valley of the **Jökulsa á Dal**.

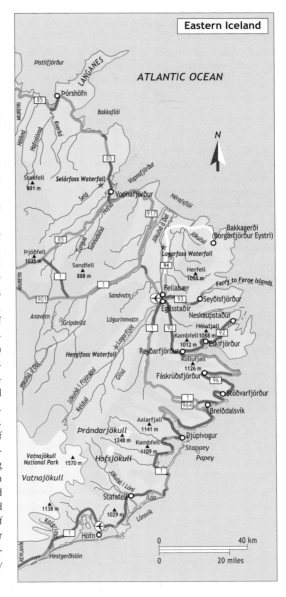

Eastern Iceland

Above: *East Iceland is the most likely part of the country to spot small herds of wild reindeer.*

THE MONSTER OF THE DEEP

Many of the deep glaciated ribbon lakes of the world, probably not coincidentally, have stories of resident monsters. Despite state-of-the-art, high technology research at many sites, nowhere has the presence of a 'monster' been conclusively proven. Lake Lögurinn, to the south of Egilsstaðir, is no exception. Despite centuries of rumours of the existence of a dragon-like creature, there is no hard evidence available. Nevertheless, in a country in which a survey of over 50% of the population showed a lack of denial over the existence of elves, anything is possible!

EGILSSTAÐIR

Originally just a farmstead on the eastern bank of the Lagarfljót river, Egilsstaðir has grown rapidly with the completion of the Ring Road and the development of air travel, so that it is now the transportation and service centre for the whole of eastern Iceland. It has a population of around 1600 and, despite its rather sterile look, it makes a good centre for exploring the surrounding area. There is little to see in the town itself, apart from the modern geological theme **church** and a **folk museum** which also includes a restored farmhouse. The River Lagafljót, which is about 140km (87 miles) long, is Iceland's second longest river. Its murky glacial floodwaters are crossed by one of the country's longest bridges, some 310m (339yd) in length, which links Egilsstaðir with the altogether more attractive village of **Fellabær** on the western bank.

Around Egilsstaðir ★★★

To the north of the town, Route 94 leads to the bay of **Héraðsflói**, where the Jökulsa á Dal and Lagaflót rivers form a delta, with marshes and coastal sand dunes. At the farmstead of **Húsey** there is a youth hostel. This is an excellent bird-watching area, particularly for waders and geese.

South of Egilsstaðir, the river flows through **Lake Lögurinn** (or **Lagarfljót**). This long, deep ribbon lake is reputed to have a resident monster (Lagarfljótsormurinn or Lagarfljót Worm). It is possible to circumnavigate the lake by road, although some of the surface is composed of gravel. The eastern shores of the lake are clothed with some of Iceland's most mature trees, one rising to the princely height of 15m (50ft)! This is excellent walking country, with its many hiking trails and picnic sites. Further trails to the south of the lake lead to the water-falls of **Hengifoss** (Iceland's third highest) and **Lagarfoss**, the latter of which has a small power plant and a fish ladder for migrating salmon. A further track, accessible by four-wheel-drive vehicles, leads to a boggy moorland and the extinct volcano of **Snæfell**. At 1833m (6014ft), it is the highest mountain in the country outside the icecaps. It is also as good a place as any in Iceland for seeing wild reindeer.

THE EASTERN FIORDS

Though lacking the rugged grandeur of their counterparts in the northwest of Iceland, the Eastern Fiords are scenic-ally one of the most pleasant areas of the country. The fiords are generally aligned east–west, so that the settle-ments are usually on the north (south-facing) sides of the water, to receive the maximum benefit of the sun. There is a string of small fishing ports, which gained considerable prosperity in the days of the herring boom, so that their wooden houses have a wealthy Scandinavian feel about them. Despite having a reputation for the best weather in Iceland, few tourists stay in this area for long. Those that do stay have the benefit of missing the crowds.

REFORESTATION

On the eastern bank of Lake Lögurinn lies the **Hallorms-staðarskógur**, Iceland's largest area of forest. Over 50 varieties of trees are seen here, mainly types of conifer, birch and poplar. This has been the headquarters of the **State Forestry Service** since 1907. They have searched the world for species which will survive in Iceland's harsh climate. It is quite probable that Iceland was covered with trees in the days of the Viking settle-ment, but that they were quickly removed for fuel and building material, and re-generation was prevented by sheep grazing. Today, there are a number of organiza-tions throughout the country, in both rural and urban areas, engaged in planting trees, using the advice of the State Forestry Service.

Left: *Trees on the State Forestry Service's land on the eastern bank of Lake Lögurinn, near Egilsstaðir.*

Below: *The garden of Petra's Stone Museum at Stöðvarfjörður.*

Borgarfjörður Eystri ★★★

Due north of Egilsstaðir, and reached by way of Route 94 and the stunning mountain range of **Dyrfjöll**, is the small village of Borgarfjörður Eystri (shown on some maps as Bakkagerði). This was the home of Iceland's best-known landscape artist, **Jóhannes S Karvel**. The village church has an altarpiece painted by Karvel, representing the Sermon on the Mount.

Seyðisfjörður ★

Due east of Egilsstaðir and connected by Route 93 is the **ferry port** of Seyðisfjörður. For many people this will be their first glimpse of Iceland – and they are rarely disappointed. It sits at the head of a narrow curving fiord backed by snow-capped mountains. The attractive harbourside buildings are made of wood, all mainly constructed by a Norwegian entrepreneur in the middle of the 19th century, when it was an important trading port. The *Norröna* ferry, operated by Smyril Line, runs a scheduled service throughout the year, connecting Seyðisfjörður with the Faroe Islands, Shetland, Norway and Denmark.

Neskaupstaður ★

The next settlement is **Neskaupstaður** which, with a population of over 1600, is the largest town in East Iceland. Owing to its remote position, it is bypassed by most tourists. In fact, it was not linked to the rest of

the country by road until 1947. Today, its economy is largely involved in fish-related industries. Just to the southwest is the fishing and trading port of **Eskifjörður**, backed by the attractive mountain Hólmatindur which rises to some 985m (3231ft). The town is mainly noted for its **Maritime Museum** (tel: 470 9063, open 13:00–17:00 Jun–Aug). Housed in a 19th-century warehouse, it is filled with fishing and whaling artefacts. In the hills behind the town is an old Iceland Spar mine which, although it is now closed down, was once the world's biggest producer of this mineral which was a vital component of early microscopes.

Reyðarfjörður ★★★

This town is located at the head of the fiord of the same name, in the midst of rich farmland. Reyðarfjörður was an important Allied base during World War II, and a **Museum of War Memorabilia** opened here in 1995. The Ring Road reaches the coast near Breiðalsvík. Reyðarfjörður is the site of a controversial aluminium smelting works which opened in 2005, stretching for 2km (1¼ miles) along the shores of the fiord. It is worth visiting the small fishing village of **Stöðvarfjörður** just to see the amazing **Rock Museum** (tel: 475 8834, www.steinpetra.com). Situated in a private house, it is the personal collection of Petra Sveinsdóttir. Rocks, fossils and minerals seem to fill every corner, along with the odd stuffed bird and ancient household artefact.

Above: *The harbour at Djúpivogur. An old warehouse in the port has been converted into an interesting folk museum.*

Djúpivogur ★

Of the remaining fishing villages, only Djúpivogur is of interest. It is located on a headland on the southern side of Berufjörður and backed by the pyramid-shaped Búlandstindur, which rises to 1090m (3576ft). Djúpivogur was an important **Danish trading station** as far back as the 16th century, and some of the oldest houses in the town today were built by Danish merchants. The *Löngubúð* warehouse on the harbourside has been restored and is now the **local museum and art gallery**. Just offshore is the island of **Papey**, which was once a hermitage for Irish monks, until they fled at the arrival of the Norsemen. Today the island is uninhabited, apart from its seals and sea birds. Cruises run from Djúpivogur to Papey during the summer months.

THE YULETIDE LADS

As Christmas approaches, Iceland's version of Santa Claus puts in an appearance. These are the **Yuletide Lads**, or *jólasveinar*. In the country's folklore they were child-eating ogres who descended from the mountains in groups of 13, in homespun clothes, to play pranks on people. Nowadays, influenced by the commercial Father Christmas image from other parts of the world, the Yuletide Lads have adopted the red garments and long white beards of the traditional Santa Claus. An Icelandic horse, however, is more likely to pull their sledge than a red-nosed reindeer.

Above: *Numerous glacier tongues run down from the Vatnajökull icecap.*

Höfn ★★★

The Ring Road skirts the first of the *sandur* which mark the southern side of the Vatnajökull icecap. The main town and **port** of this stretch of the coast is Höfn. The name means 'harbour', and its pronunciation can best be described as a 'hiccup'. Located on Hornafjörður, which is in fact a bay that is almost completely enclosed by two spits, the narrow entrance calling for skilful navigation.

The completion of the Ring Road has boosted Höfn's **population**, which is fast approaching 2000. Fishing, farming and tourism are the main sources of employment.

The **Regional Folk Museum** in the town is worth a look. Based in an old warehouse, it has displays on local fishing, farming and wildlife. Open 10:00–12:00 and 14:00–17:00, June–August.

Don't miss the **Glacier Exhibition** in Hafnabraut (open 10:00–18:00 Jun–Aug, reduced hours in winter, www.joklasyning.is). It is full of information about glacial action and jökulhlaups, including a 10-minute video on glaciers and volcanoes .

Höfn is also the main centre for arranging tours to the **Vatnajökull icecap** and to the **Jökulsárlón Glacial Lagoon** (*see* chapter 7 for information on both). There are icecap tours available by snowmobile, and also by glacier buggy, skiddoo and by ski. However, visitors are warned not to venture out on to the icecap independently, but to use the expert guides that are available and take their advice regarding equipment and clothing.

East Iceland at a Glance

BEST TIMES TO VISIT

The **summer**, June–August, is the best time, particularly if arriving by car ferry from the Faroes, Scandinavia and Scotland. The eastern fiords have the most favourable climate, and here the visiting season can be extended into May and September.

GETTING THERE

This is the only part of Iceland that can be approached by **ship** from abroad. The ferry *Norröna*, run by the Faeroese Smyril Line (tel: 298 345 900, website: www.smyril-line.com) operates a weekly service all year linking Seyðisfjörður with Esbjerg in Denmark, Bergen in Norway, Tórshavn in the Faroe Islands, and Shetland. The **road** route to the area is via the Ring Road; the southern route is quicker and shorter than the northern. Bus services connect the main towns on the Ring Road. **Air Iceland** runs services to Egilsstaðir from Reykjavík, Akureyri and Ísafjörður.

GETTING AROUND

Apart from a private **car**, the only option for getting around the region is by **bus**. There are services daily around the Ring Road, but routes linking the fiord ports are less regular. Be prepared for a reduced time-table in winter.

WHERE TO STAY

There are no hotels in the luxury range, but plenty of choice in the other categories.

MID-RANGE

Hotel Höfn, 780 Hornafjörður, tel: 478 1240, fax: 478 1996, website: www.hotelhofn.is Also has a cheaper annexe.
Hotel Snæfell, Austarvegur 3, 710 Seyðisfjörður, tel: 472 1460, fax: 472 1570. Harbour-side hotel convenient for ferry.
Hotel Egilsbuð, Egilsbraut 1, Neskaupstaður, tel: 477 1321, fax: 477 1322. Near harbour.
Hotel Framtíð, Vogaland 4, 765 Djúpivogur, tel: 478 8887, fax: 478 8187, website: www.simnet.is Overlooks the harbour; good restaurant. The **Edda Group** has hotels at Egilsstaðir, Hallormsstaður and Höfn, tel: 505 0910; and the **Foss Group** at Vatnajökull and Hallormsstaður, tel: 471 1705.

BUDGET

Guesthouse Skipalækur, Fellabær, tel: 471 1324. Sleeping bag accommodation and some lakeside chalets.
Youth Hostels at Höfn, Reyðarfjörður and Seyðisfjörður, tel: 553 8110.

CAMPING

Camp sites at Borgafjörður, Egilsstaðir, Neskaupstaður, Eskifjörður, Reyðarfjörður, Breiðdalsvík and Höfn.

WHERE TO EAT

Good restaurants are scarce outside hotel dining rooms, but most service station snack bars serve a good tourist menu.

BUDGET

Ormurinn, Kaupvangur 2, Egilsstaðir, tel: 471 2321. Chicken and pasta dishes.

TOURS AND EXCURSIONS

In Egilsstaðir, **Austurlands Travel**, tel: 471 2000, and **Lagarfljótsormurinn**, tel: 471 2900, offer boat trips on Lake Lörgurinn, while **Tanni Travel**, tel: 476 1399, arranges hikes around the Snæfell area and buggy trips on Vatnajökull.
Papeyjarferðir, tel: 478 8183, runs cruises in summer from Djúpivogur to the island of Papey.
In Höfn, **Glacier Tours**, tel: 478 1000, run snowmobile and jeep tours on and around Vatnajökull.

USEFUL CONTACTS

Major **Tourist Information Centres** are at: Egilsstaðir, tel: 471 2320; at Seyðisfjörður (in the Smyril Line building), tel: 472 1551; and at Höfn, tel: 478 1500.

EGILSSTAÐIR	J	F	M	A	M	J	J	A	S	O	N	D
AVE. TEMP. °C	0.3	0.6	0.1	1.4	3.3	6.2	8	8.3	6.6	4.5	1.8	0.6
AVE. TEMP. °F	32.5	33	32.2	34.5	37.9	43.2	46.4	46.9	43.9	40.1	35.2	33
AVE. RAINFALL mm	134	103	116	87	93	87	97	114	180	169	129	121
AVE. RAINFALL in	5.28	4.05	4.57	3.42	3.66	3.42	3.82	4.49	7.09	6.66	5.08	4.77

7
South Iceland

The central part of South Iceland is dominated by the huge mass of the **Vatnajökull icecap**, which is Europe's largest ice sheet and the third largest in the world. Iceland's highest mountain, **Hvannadalshnjúkur** at 2119m (6952ft), pokes its head above the ice. Vatnajökull National Park has now been extended and claims to be the largest in Europe. **Glaciers** snake their way down from the icecap, most prominently in a southerly direction. Lurking under the ice are several **volcanoes**, such as **Grimsvötn**, which periodically erupt and melt large quantities of ice, causing glacial floods or *jökulhlaups*. As well as causing widespread damage, these *jökulhlaups* have built up huge spreads of sand and gravel known as **sandur**. It was these *sandur* which prevented the completion of the Ring Road until 1974. Only after this date was the south central part of Iceland opened up for tourism.

Just to the southwest of Vatnajökull is a smaller icecap, **Mýrdalsjökull**, which also has a subglacial volcano, **Katla**. Here, again, there is a *sandur* to the south. The area around the icecaps has a wealth of places for tourists to visit and few fail to be impressed with **Jökulsárlón**, a glacial lagoon where calving icebergs can be viewed from a boat. **Skaftafell**, Iceland's largest national park and the second to be proclaimed, is also popular with visitors and offers good hiking possibilities amongst stunning scenery. Snowmobile and ice-buggy trips on the two ice-caps are another favourite tourist activity. Waterfalls abound, including the impressive **Svartifoss** (named after

DON'T MISS

*** The Icecaps: try a snow-mobile or glacier buggy ride on Vatnajökull or Mydalsjökull.
*** Jökulsárlón Lagoon: take a boat trip among the icebergs.
*** The Interior: cross the wild and uninhabited interior by four-wheel-drive vehicle.
*** Skaftafell National Park: attractive area with a variety of scenery and wildlife.
** The Coast around Vík: cliffs, stacks and beaches, full of breeding sea birds.
* The Sandur: huge sand and gravel plains deposited by glacial floods.

Opposite: *Skógafoss, one of Iceland's most impressive waterfalls.*

Above: *Svínafellsjökull, in the Skaftafell National Park.*

CLIMATE

The climate of south Iceland differs little from that of the Reykjavík area to the west, except that there is heavier snowfall on the higher land, the icecaps and the interior. The snow ensures that the tracks through the interior are only open for around two months of the year. On the coastal plain the rainfall is moderate to heavy for much of the year. The Skaftafell area, situated in the shelter of Vatnajökull, has a sunnier microclimate. Vík receives an annual rainfall of around 2300mm (91in), with an average **January** temperature of 0.9°C (33.6°F) and an average **July** temperature of 9.7°C (49.5°F).

its black lava columns) and **Skógafoss**. There are several places of interest for bird-watchers. The *sandur* contain Iceland's largest concentration of skuas, while the cliffs and stacks at **Dyrhólaey** have a good selection of breeding sea birds, including puffins and guillemots.

The coastline of this region is somewhat featureless, and it is one of the few parts of the Icelandic coast with no fishing ports. There are few settlements of any size at all. The only coastal town in the area is **Vík**, while the sole settlement between Mýrdalsjökull and Vatnajökull is the former religious site of **Kirkjubæjarklaustur**. In the western part of the region are the largely modern towns of **Hvolsvöllur** and **Hella**, located in the middle of an area that is rich in associations with the *Njáls Saga*.

THE VATNAJÖKULL AREA ★★★

The facts and figures applied to the Vatnajökull icecap are impressive in themselves. It is Europe's largest ice-sheet and the third largest in the world (after Antarctica and Greenland). It covers an area of 8538km² (3296 sq miles), which is approximately 8% of Iceland. Its central plateau lies around 1500m (4922ft) above sea level, with fringing *nunataks* (mountain peaks protruding above the ice) such as **Barðarbunga**, at 2009m (6592ft), and **Hvannadalshnjúkur**, which at 2119m (6952ft) is Iceland's highest mountain. It is estimated that the icecap is over 1000m (3281ft) thick in places. Whereas the Ice Age ended around 8000BC in most parts of Europe, the base of the ice on Vatnajökull dates from the start of the 1st century AD. Because of the high precipitation in the area and the fact that the accumulation of snow in winter is greater than the rate of melting in summer, the ice has built up rapidly. On the other hand, global warming has led to the retreat of the glacier snouts over the last two decades, leaving meltwater lakes between terminal moraines and the ice front. These features can easily be seen on **Kvíájökull**, **Fjallsjökull** and **Svínafellsjökull**, three glacial tongues just to the northwest of Höfn. Vatnajökull National Park takes up 13% of the country's landmass and now incorporates Deltifoss and the entire Vatnajökull icecap.

Owing to the dangerous conditions on Vatnajökull, excursions are best confined to organized tours. The usual route to the icecap is from the Ring Road up a track to the Skálafellsjökull mountain hut. Here, opportunity to sample glacier buggies and snowmobiles abounds. There are also cross-country ski options.

> ### THE VATNAJÖKULL GLACIER BURST
>
> In September 1996, the **Grímsvötn** subglacial volcano on Vatnajökull erupted, sending a column of steam over 10,000m (33,000ft) into the sky. The magma melted the ice, forming a huge subglacial lake. Just over a month later the waters of the lake rose and drained in a massive glacial burst, or *jökulhlaup*, causing an estimated 3000 billion cubic litres of water to pour down onto the coastal plain within a few hours. The protective dykes proved useless and some 1200m (3500ft) of Ring Road bridges were destroyed. Believed to have been Iceland's fourth largest volcanic eruption this century, it was seen on television screens throughout the world.

Jökulsárlón ★★★

Many visitors vote Jökulsárlón to be the highlight of their Icelandic experiences. It is an impressive glacial lagoon located at the snout of Breiðamerkurjökull glacier, which calves off icebergs into the lake. These icebergs are varied in colour – some white, some blue, others black or striped with volcanic ash. As they melt, they crack and crash around. The whole lagoon is incredibly

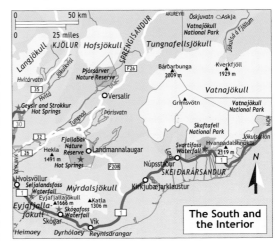

The South and the Interior

MORAINES

The Vatnajökull glaciers have some fine examples of moraines. These are ridges of boulders and rock 'flour' which have been eroded by glaciers on their slow passage downslope and eventually re-deposited. **Terminal moraines** are found across the snout of a glacier. If the glacier then retreats, a **moraine-dammed lake** may result. **Lateral moraines** are found along the sides of glaciers, while **medial moraines** are seen on the ice in the centre of the glacier (usually formed from lateral moraines after two glaciers have merged). Both lateral and medial moraines are temporary features, as they are destroyed by meltwater.

beautiful and the icebergs can be viewed at close hand from an amphibious boat. Seals occasionally pop up their heads as the boat drifts past. The lagoon was used for several scenes in the James Bond film *A View to a Kill*. All the service buses that travel along the Ring Road stop at the lake, where there are toilets, a restaurant and a camp site. It is well worth walking from the lagoon to the sea. The lagoon is drained by the **River Jökulsá** (almost certainly Iceland's shortest glacial river), which runs under the suspension bridge carrying the Ring Road before reaching the sea about 200m (220yd) or so away. Icebergs are quite frequently washed down the river and many of them become stranded on the beach, where they gradually melt away, forming curious shapes in the process.

Sandur Country ★★

A few kilometres west of Jökulsárlón, the first of the *sandurs* are encountered. These desert-like areas are plains of gravel and sand interspersed with a host of ever-changing braided streams. Much of the material is deposited during glacial bursts, or *jökulhlaups*. The largest of the *sandur* is **Skeiðarársandur**, which is fed

Left: *Svartifoss (Black Falls), named after the dark columns of basalt that occur on either side.* **Opposite:** *Melting ice-bergs assume these strange shapes in the Jökulsárlón glacial lake.*

from the Skeiðarárjökull glacier. The *sandurs* have always presented problems for transport, and it was not until 1974 that the Ring Road was completed in this area. Even so, the road can be temporarily put out of use after a *jökulhlaup*, such as the one which occurred in 1996.

SKAFTAFELL NATIONAL PARK ★★★

Tucked into a sheltered south-facing lobe of the Vatnajökull icecap is Iceland's largest National Park, Skaftafell. In terms of visitor numbers it is one of the most popular locations in the country. Founded in 1967 (as a joint venture between the government and the World Wildlife Fund), the park covers 1600km² (618 sq miles). It includes such diverse landscapes as ice sheet, glaciers, tumbling glacial rivers, waterfalls, luxuriant vegetation and moorland. Add a variety of bird life and abundant wild flowers and Skaftafell's popularity is understandable. It also has the benefit of a superb microclimate, situated as it is in a sheltered sunny position.

Skaftafell has a number of good hiking trails, the most popular of which is to the **Skaftafellsjökull glacier**, the snout of which is black with rubble and volcanic material. This takes around two hours return, but there are many hikes of longer duration with marvellous views of the glacial features. Another attraction is the **Svartifoss** waterfall, named after the black basalt columns along the lip of

---

CROSSING THE SANDUR

One of the most formidable tasks for travellers in Iceland has always been crossing the *sandurs* – the outwash plains of sand and gravel deposited in glacial bursts. It was not until 1974 that the Ring Road was completed by bridging some of the larger streams on the *sandur* to the south of Vatnajökull. During the summer months, storms can be caused by the descending movement of cold air from the icecap. The resulting wind-blown sand can do considerable damage to the bodywork of cars. At such times, motoring organizations suggest putting a cardboard sheet across the radiator grill to protect the engine. Attempting to cycle across the *sandur* in these conditions can be sheer misery.

Above: *Iceland's most popular camp site, in the Skaftafell National Park.*

the falls and the valley sides, which are said to be the inspiration for many public buildings around the country. Svartifoss is reached by the path from the campground. Allow 1½ hours for the return walk. It is also worth continuing along the track to the west of the falls to **Sjónarsker**, a prominent rock with a viewing disc, giving panoramas towards the sandur and the coast. Skaftafell is of great interest to wildlife enthusiasts. Over 200 species of plant have been recorded here, while trees include rowan, birch and willow, some of which are quite tall (in Icelandic terms). Many of the typical highland bird species are found here, including golden plovers, redwings, ptarmigan, snipe and meadow pipits, all of which breed in the park.

Park Practicalities

Skaftafell is very accessible, being so close to the Ring Road, and the BSI Reykjavík–Höfn buses also stop here. The park's facilities include a car park, camp site, service area with restaurant, coffee shop, supermarket and an information centre. Detailed maps of the park are available in the shop. Skaftafell's popularity, however, comes with a price. On summer weekends it can become extremely crowded, and the noisy camp site has been likened to a 'tented refugee site'.

WEST OF SKAFTAFELL

The Ring Road at this point crosses the northern side of Skeiðarársandur. After about 35km (22 miles), the little hamlet of **Núpsstaður** is reached. Backed by the steep cliffs of Lómagnúpur, which rise to 767m (2550ft), the

---

SAFETY ON THE ICECAPS

Nature rules on the Icelandic icecaps, and the country's history is full of examples of accidents and tragedies which have befallen foolhardy travellers. Heavy snow, strong winds and whiteouts can occur at any time, even in summer, and crevasses can be deep and treacherous. Experts suggest that no climbing should take place at all in winter. Visitors in summer should be well equipped, know the routes, check the prevailing conditions and be aware of how to contact the rescue services in case of an emergency. Better still, go on a professionally led tour.

settlement of Núpsstaður was once an ecclesiastical centre. All that remains today is a collection of working farm buildings plus a delightful turf-roofed church. Made of stone and wood, the church dates from 1756 and is probably the smallest place of worship in Iceland. It was restored in the 1930s, and services are still held annually on the first Sunday in August. The key can be obtained from the farmhouse.

Klaustur ★★★

The only settlement of any size between Vík and Höfn is the unpronounceable **Kirkjubæjarklaustur**, generally known as 'Klaustur'. The modern appearance of this village belies its fascinating history. It was first inhabited by Irish monks before they were driven away by the Vikings. Later, in 1186, a Benedictine convent was established here, but it was disbanded in the mid-16th century during the Reformation. This may not have been a bad thing, as two of the nuns are said to have been burnt at the stake – one for criticizing the Pope and the other for sleeping with the Devil! In 1783 Kirkjubæjarklaustur was threatened by lava from the Laki eruptions (a series of fissures to the north of the village). The local priest, Jon Steingrímsson, is reported to have assembled all the inhabitants in the church and delivered a 'fire and brimstone sermon'. When the service was over, the congregation went outside only to find that the lava had miracu-lously been diverted past the village. A modern **Steingrímsson Memorial Chapel** was built in 1974, on the site of the original church, to commemorate the priest's *eldmessa*, or 'fire sermon'. One strange feature which should not be missed is the **Kirkjugólf**, a more or less flat rock

---

AVIAN PIRATES

Skuas are large hawk-like sea birds with generally dark plumage and angled wings when in flight. Their behaviour is often described as 'piratical', as they will chase and harass other birds until they disgorge their food. **Arctic skuas** are common throughout Iceland and will chase, in particular, Arctic terns. The **Great skua** is the largest of the skua family and will attack sea birds as large as gannets. It is known to kill small gulls by drowning them. The great skua is especially common as a nesting bird on the *sandur* to the south of Vatnajökull. Skuas are migrant birds and spend the winter months along the more southerly shores of the North Atlantic.

Below: *Hexagonal blocks of basalt at Klaustur, once thought to be the floor of an old church.*

surface covering some 80m² (280ft²). This was always thought to be the floor of an old church, which was reasonable considering the ecclesiastical background of the area. It is now known, however, that this is an entirely natural feature – the smoothed upper surface of a series of basalt columns. Kirkjubæjarklaustur today has a small airstrip and acts as a service centre for the surrounding farming community, as well as making a good base from which to explore the area.

VÍK Í MÝRDAL ★

At the eastern end of the *sandur* is Vík, the southernmost town of mainland Iceland and also, reputedly, the rainiest. Once a fishing port, the town abandoned this activity during the 19th century as it lacked a harbour. It is now a service and transport centre. An attractive town of some 400 inhabitants, Vík has the Mýrdalsjökull as a backdrop, with the steep-sided, flat-topped headland of Reynisfjall to the west. To the east stretches a beach of black volcanic sand, pounded by huge North Atlantic waves. This was the only non-tropical beach to be listed by the US magazine *Islands* as one of the Top Ten in the world. However, this is definitely not a beach for sitting on, not only because of the weather, but because of the colony of aggressive Arctic terns who resent human interference at breeding time.

Below: *The small regional centre of Vík. Its black sand beach, pounded by the Atlantic waves, has a breeding colony of rather aggressive Arctic terns.*

Left: *The distinctive sea stacks off the coast of Vík have breeding colonies of sea birds such as fulmars and guillemots.*

In Vík itself there are few sites to visit, except perhaps the delightful church occupying a dominating clifftop position. Boat trips, in an amphibious vehicle, run to the sea-bird cliffs in summer, but calm seas are essential for the cruises to operate.

Along the Coast ★★★

Just offshore from Vík are the photogenic black sea stacks of **Reynisdrangar**. Both the stacks and the headland are filled with breeding sea birds during the summer months, including razorbills, fulmars, guillemots and a large colony of puffins. On the far side of Reynisfjall is another headland called **Dyrhólaey**. It is 120m (390ft) high and incorporates a natural arch, through which small boats can pass during calm weather. Nearby is the large shallow lagoon of **Dyrhólaós**, another good bird-watching site. Away to the northwest is the hill of Pétursey, about 275m (900ft) high, which was an island before it became surrounded by glacial deposits.

MÝRDALSJÖKULL ★★★

Mýrdalsjökull is one of Iceland's major icecaps. It is the fourth largest in size, covering some 700km² (270 sq miles) and reaching 1480m (4855ft) in height. Like the larger Vatnajökull to the east, it receives high precipitation, up to 8000mm (315in) annually, so that the accumulation of ice has been significant, reaching a

---

THE REYNISDRANGAR 'NEEDLES'

Sea stacks are erosion features formed by wave action. The distinctive Reynisdrangar 'Needles' near Vík are some of Iceland's best examples of stacks. The highest of the stacks rises over 66m (216ft) above sea level. Legend has it that they were formed one night when two trolls were trying to drag a three-masted ship ashore. When daylight broke it was revealed that the ship had turned to stone.

Above: *View south from the Mýrdalsjökull icecap to the coastal lowlands.*

depth of over 1000m (3281ft). Like Vatnajökull, it also has a subglacial volcano, **Katla**, which has erupted 16 times since Iceland was settled. Each *jökulhlaup* has deposited great quantities of sand and gravel, so building up the **Mýrdalssandur**, which covers some 70km² (27 sq miles). The Katla *jökulhlaups*, when in full flow, are estimated to contain a volume of water between five and seven times that of the Amazon River.

In early 2010 another Icelandic volcano, **Eyjafjallajökull**, became world news. Its eruption caused a cloud of ash to rise to over 20,000ft, while blasts carried finer material up into the North Atlantic jet stream. For several days the airlines of northern Europe were grounded, causing misery to thousands of stranded passengers. Ironically, the volcano revived Iceland's tourist industry and it is estimated that over 100,000 people came to see the spectacular eruptions. At the time of writing, Eyjafjallajökull, although still erupting, has quietened down. But there is a bigger concern. This volcano has erupted three times since the Vikings settled here in the 9th century. On each occasion it has been followed within a year by the eruption of Katla – a much more dangerous volcano capable of causing flooding.

To the north of Mýrdalsjökull and immediately east of Hekla lies the **Landmannalaugar** area, famed for the variable colours in the rhyolite rocks.

The Skógar Area ★★

The small settlement of **Skógar**, nestling beneath the Mýrdalsjökull icecap, makes a good centre from which to explore the area. Just east of the village is the short glacial **Jökulsá River**, which is often called the Fúlilækur, or 'foul river'. The stench is caused by large quantities of

---

sulphur which the river washes down from Katla. The main attraction in Skógar itself is the **Folk Museum**, which is located in a complex of turf farmhouses that have been reassembled on the site. The museum has over 6000 artefacts reflecting life in southern Iceland over the centuries. It is open from 09:00–18:00 during the summer months. Skógar's other attraction is one of Iceland's highest waterfalls, **Skógafoss**, where, just west of the village, the river Skóga drops 60m (197ft) into a narrow gorge. Further west is another waterfall worth visiting. This is **Seljalandsfoss**. It is possible to take the path behind the falls, although a change in wind direction can make this a drenching experience.

The West of the Region ★★★
There are two modern settlements located in the west of southern Iceland. **Hella** has developed in recent years as a market town, but has little to interest the tourist. **Hvolsvöllur**, to the east, is another market town which has a good view of snow-capped Hekla to the north. The Hvolsvöllur area has numerous associations with the *Njáls Saga* and guided tours to the main sites can be arranged from the town.

THE INTERIOR
Although one of the most seductive parts of the country, the interior of Iceland has a very limited access. It is only open to traffic from late June to the end of August, and even during this period four-wheel-drive vehicles are essential. Even during the summer months, bad weather can descend very rapidly and roads can become impassable. The interior is, nevertheless, a part of

FOLLOWING THE NJÁLS SAGA

The most popular and blood-thirsty of the Sagas is certainly the *Njáls Saga*, the setting for which was the land to the north of **Hvolsvöllur**. The story includes characters such as Hallgeður Longlegs, Gissur the White, and various members of the Njál family. The Saga features murder, arson, betrayal, love, and a continuous family feud – indeed, an ancient version of a modern-day soap opera! Archaeological digs in the 20th century suggest that much of the story may be true. Visitors can go to the **Saga Centre** in Hvolsvöllur, and guided tours are available to the sites mentioned in the *Njáls Saga*; tel: 487 8138.

Below: *A distant view of the volcano Hekla. It has erupted frequently over historic time.*

CROSSING RIVERS IN THE INTERIOR

One of the main hazards when driving across the interior of Iceland is the number of rivers which have to be crossed. Even with high-clearance four-wheel-drive vehicles, this exercise is fraught with danger. One of the main problems is the variable climate and its effect on river volume. Some of the river flows are dominated by rainfall, which has an immediate effect. Other rivers are fed by melting snows, which means that they may very well be at their peak volume on a sunny day. The best advice to drivers is to travel in convoy, and check on the river and weather conditions carefully before attempting a crossing. For information on conditions, telephone Public Administration on 563 1500.

Right: A super jeep with enlarged wheels crosses a river in spate in central Iceland.

Iceland which all visitors should experience if at all possible. It has been described as one of Europe's last wilderness areas, and travellers should be aware that there are few services available – no accommodation, no petrol stations, no restaurants and, in places, not even a road!

Kjölur Route

Most of the routes start in the southwest and end up in the north near Akureyri, Sauðarkrókur or Mývatn. The **Kjölur Route** runs northeast from the Gullfoss area and passes over the Central Highland desert, the track rising to over 700m (2300ft) between the Langjökull and Hofsjökull icecaps. It also passes the Hveravellir geothermal area, with its fumeroles and hot springs, before dropping down to meet the northern arm of the Ring Road near Blönduós. Although it is the easiest of the routes through the interior, it was unpopular for many centuries as it was often the haunt of bandits.

Sprengisandur Route

The alternative **Sprengisandur Route** initially follows the valley of the Þjórsá River before crossing the pass at around 800m (2625ft) between the Hofsjökull and the smaller Tungnafellsjökull icecaps. It then follows the Skjálfandafljót valley northwards to join the Ring Road near Goðafoss. This is a more difficult and hostile route, but gives some superb views of the icecaps.

South Iceland at a Glance

June–September has the best weather, but rain can be expected all year, with deep snowfalls on the higher land. On weekends in July–August popular spots like Skaftafell can become uncomfortably crowded. The interior is rarely open for tourists before late June. Winter snows begin again by mid-September.

BSÍ buses on the Reykjavík–Höfn service use the southern arm of the Ring Road and stop at the main tourist 'honeypots'. There are no internal airports in the region, although there are a few private airstrips.

Service buses using the Ring Road are few and far between and visitors on a budget may find it more convenient to hitch lifts in summer when the roads are busy. A private car is most convenient. This is also true of travelling in the interior, where four-wheel-drive is essential.

There is nothing in the luxury classification in south Iceland, but plenty of mid-range choices although these fill up rapidly in the height of the season.

MID-RANGE

The **Edda Group** have summer hotels at Kirkjubæjarklaustur, Skógar and Hvolsvöllur, tel: 505 0910.

Hotel Hvolsvöllur, Hliðarvegur 7, 860 Hvolsvöllur, tel: 487 8050, fax: 487 8058, website: www.hotelhvolsvollur.is
Hotel Ásgarður, v/Hvolsvöll, 860 Hvolsvöllur, tel: 487 8367, fax: 487 8387, website: www.asgardurinn.is Viking-theme hotel on edge of town. Some cottages available.
Hotel Edda Vík í Mýrdal, v/Klettsvegur, 870 Vík, tel: 487 1480, fax: 487 1302, website: www.hoteledda.is Between cliff and beach.

BUDGET

Gistiheimilið Húsið, Fljóshlíð, 861 Hvolsvöllur, tel: 487 8448, fax: 487 8748. Small guest-house on outskirts of town. Horse riding can be arranged.

Farmhouse accommodation, for details and booking, tel: 562 3640. There are **Youth Hostels** at **Fljótsdalur**, near Hvolsvöllur, at **Reynisbrekka**, outside Vík, and at **Vagnsstaðir**, west of Höfn. Booking, tel: 553 8110.

CAMPING

Official camp sites in the area have excellent facilities. The more popular ones, such as in the Skaftafell National Park, can become very crowded on weekends in the summer.

Good restaurants are rather hard to find. The best bets are dining rooms of larger hotels, though they may be expensive. Snack bars at petrol stations are good value and offer a wholesome tourist menu.

Most excursions here involve the icecaps of Vatnajökull and Mýrdalsjökull. Many of these can be booked in Reykjavík with firms such as Reykjavík Excursions or BSÍ. Local firms run snowmobile and glacier buggy tours on the icecaps. For trips on Mýrdalsjökull, contact **Geysir Snjósleðaferðir**, tel: 568 8888. For trips on Vatnajökull, contact **Glacier Tours**, tel: 478 1000. For boat trips on Jökulsá Lagoon, **Wonder Boat Trips**, tel: 478 1065.

There are several **Tourist Information Centres** in the area. The largest centre is in the **Skaftafell National Park**, tel: 478 1627. Others are at **Skógar**, tel: 487 8843; **Kirkjubæjarklaustur**, tel: 487 4620; **Vík**, tel: 487 1395; **Hvolsvöllur**, tel: 487 8781; and **Hella**, tel: 487 5165.

VÍK	J	F	M	A	M	J	J	A	S	O	N	D
AVE. TEMP. °C	-0.4	0.2	0.7	3.2	6.5	9.4	11.2	10.4	7.5	4.5	1.1	-0.4
AVE. TEMP. °F	31.3	32.4	33.3	37.8	43.7	48.9	52.2	50.7	45.5	40.1	34	31.3
AVE. RAINFALL mm	145	130	130	115	118	131	121	159	141	185	137	133
AVE. RAINFALL in	5.71	5.12	5.12	4.53	4.65	5.16	4.77	6.26	5.55	7.29	5.39	5.24

8
The Westman Islands

The *Vestmannaeyjar*, or Westman Islands, are a group of 15 islands and rock skerries some 11km (7 miles) off the southern coast of Iceland. Only one, the largest, known as **Heimaey** (pronounced *hay may*), is inhabited. The islands are located on the Mid-Atlantic Ridge and are of recent geological origin. They were formed of volcanic material, spewed out of submarine volcanoes between 8000 and 3000BC. This process has continued into the 20th century with the formation of the new island of **Surtsey**, created by an eruption which lasted for four years, between 1963 and 1967. The eruption was seen on television screens around the world, and scientific studies of the volcano have continued to this day. Ten years later, an eruption occurred on Heimaey, which forced the evacuation of the entire population, fortunately without loss of life. After this new volcano, named **Eldfell**, had quietened down, the inhabitants returned to find that the island had grown in size by 15% and that the lava flow had improved the shelter around the harbour.

A Violent History

The history of the Westman Islands has been typified by violence and tragedy. The islands were first inhabited by a group of **Irish slaves** (these 'Westmen' may have given the islands their name) intent on escape after murdering their master, Hjörleifur Hróðmarsson, the foster brother of Ingólfur Arnarson, in turn recognized as the first genuine Icelandic settler. When Ingólfur heard the

Opposite: *The sea cliffs of Heimaey, famous for their nesting puffins.*

CLIMATE

The Westman Islands' maritime position has the effect of moderating the climate, making it milder than that of Reykjavík in winter, but cooler in summer. **Rainfall** is high, with an annual total of 1713mm (67.5in). Average temperatures in **January** stay above freezing, and any snowfall is light. The average **July** temperature is 9.6°C (49°F), which is lower than that of the mainland. Fog and low cloud are common.

Below: *The town of Heimaey has frequently been threatened by volcanic activity. The last lava flow in 1973 destroyed some of the houses but actually improved the harbour.*

news, he quickly tracked down the slaves and killed them. The very first permanent settler in the Westman Islands, probably around 900, is believed to have been **Herjólfur Barðursson**, who was looking for a peaceful escape from the feuding on the mainland. The first church was built around 1000, and shortly afterwards the islands were purchased by the **Bishops of Skálholt**. Later British traders took over the islands as their headquarters in the North Atlantic until they were driven out by the Danes in the mid-16th century.

In 1627 the Westman Islands were attacked by a group of **North African pirates**, who murdered over 40 people and took away around 250 hostages, most of whom were sold as slaves in the markets of Morocco. By this time the Bishops of Skálholt had turned the islands over to the King of Norway. The succeeding centuries saw further tragedies – disease, starvation, scurvy and dysentry. The **Laki eruptions** in 1783 and the subsequent 'haze fires' killed most of the livestock and poisoned the sea. The 20th century saw a change in fortunes, with the development of the fishing industry, but a further setback came in 1973 with the **eruption of Eldfell**. After the evacuation of Heimaey, many of the inhabitants, who returned to find their houses destroyed by lava, decided to emigrate to other countries.

Left: *View of Heimaey harbour. The port accounts for 15% of Iceland's fish exporting business.*

Today, the Westman Islands are thriving. Prosperity is based almost entirely on the **fishing** industry and the majority of the 5300 residents are involved in fishing or tourism. The first freezing plant was installed in 1908 and shortly afterwards the islands were connected with the mainland by submarine electricity and telephone cables and a freshwater pipeline. The Westman Islands have a fishing fleet of over 100 vessels, which account for around 15% of Iceland's total exports. The main fish caught are sole, cod, halibut and haddock. There are also salmon farms which are located in the outer harbour. Some of the fish is exported fresh, but the majority is processed on Heimaey.

HEIMAEY ★★

The only inhabited island in *Vestmannaeyjar* is **Heimaey** (the 'home island'). The other islands are too steep-sided for harbours, although some are used for summer sheep pastures. The town of Heimaey, with a population of just over 4000, is attractively located around the **harbour** and stretches southward to cover about a third of the island. To the north of the town are some sheer cliffs, while to the south the lava flow from the 1973 eruption has contrived to make a sheltered entrance to the harbour. Look out for the **mural** on the side of one of the buildings near the harbour. It was painted by local schoolchildren and depicts the town on the morning of the 1973 eruption. Forming the southeastern background to the town are the two low volcanic peaks of **Helgafell** and the more recent **Eldfell**.

PJÓDHÁTÍÐ

The main social event of the Westman Islands' calendar is their annual **National Day** held over the first weekend in August. It began in 1874, when bad weather prevented the islanders from reaching the mainland to celebrate Iceland's National Day. They therefore decided to hold their own festival a month later, and this has now become an annual tradition. The festivities take place in a large valley called **Herjólfsdalur**, which becomes a huge camp site for the occasion. It is the location for singing, dancing, much drinking and a large bonfire. Some mainland critics disapprove, suggesting that the festival has become a mere showpiece for supporters of Vestmannæyjar independence. Nevertheless, it is hugely enjoyed by both islanders and those who come over from the mainland to join in the celebrations.

Visitors arrive at Heimaey by air or ferry, and there is enough to see here to make a two- or three-day stay worthwhile. Despite the existence of coaches and taxis, most of the island can be covered **on foot**.

Museums ★★★

Heimaey's **Natural History Museum**, at Heiðarvegur 12, was established in 1964. It has the usual selection of geological specimens and stuffed birds, but the highlight is the aquarium, which has a wonderful collection of Icelandic fish, both common and rare, plus a live video link to a puffin colony. Open from 11:00–17:00, May to September; tel: 481 1997.

The **Folk Museum** is located above the library. This museum combines an art gallery with a collection of stamps, currency and historic household artefacts. Open 10:00–17:00 daily during the summer; tel: 488 2040.

The **Volcano Show** is a film show which takes place in the Félagsheimilið theatre/community centre, with performances during the summer at 15:00, 17:00 and 21:00, each lasting 55 minutes. Two films are shown: one

Above: *An aerial view of Heimaey harbour.*
Opposite: *Eldfell rises to 205m (673ft) and can be climbed from Heimaey town.*

SURTSEY

In November 1963 a new volcano rose from the sea bed about 18km (11 miles) south-west of Heimaey. This was named **Surtsey** after the legendary Norse giant **Surtur**. The eruptions lasted for four years, and at their peak sent up a column of steam and ash over 10,000m (33,000ft) into the sky. When the activity calmed down, Surtsey had reached a height of 150m (492ft) and covered an area of 3km² (1.2 sq miles). Thereafter Surtsey became a natural laboratory for scientists, who have observed its gradual colonization by insects, birds, plants, and mammals such as seals. Surtsey is still off limits to visitors, but it is possible to fly over the dormant volcano in a chartered light aircraft.

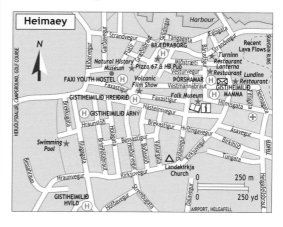

records the 1973 eruptions and the rescue operations, and the other tells the story of a fisherman whose boat capsized 5km (3 miles) offshore. He spent six hours in the icy waters before coming ashore over sharp lava rocks and reaching safety. A London medical expert later concluded that the fisherman had the body fat of a seal!

Other Points of Interest ★★★

Heimaey's modern white **church** is worth a look. Opposite the entrance is a memorial to lost fishermen. An older stone church, the **Landakirkja**, dates from 1788. It has an unusual interior arrangement, in that the pulpit is placed immediately behind the altar. The Landakirkja is open daily from 13:00–14:00 in July and August. The most recent **lava flows** are readily accessible and give good views over the harbour and also towards the mainland, where the Vatnajökull and Mýrdalsjökull icecaps can be seen on a clear day. **Eldfell**, which rises to 205m (673ft), can quite easily be climbed on the pathways, some with artificial steps, leading up to the crater rim. There are still plenty of hot cinders and fumeroles, so stout footwear is recommended. Be prepared, too, for the stench of sulphur. The slightly higher **Helgafell** can also be climbed. This was formed about 5000 years ago and rises to a height of 226m (742ft). Take the path from the end of the football pitch.

HEIMAEY'S LATEST VOLCANIC EPISODE

In January 1973 a serious volcanic eruption occurred on the eastern side of the island of Heimaey. The fishing fleet were able to evacuate the entire population of 5300 people. A massive amount of lava and ash threatened the town, demolishing houses and causing fires. The greatest danger was that the lava flow, which was 165m (540ft) high, would block the harbour entrance. Without the harbour, the evacuation of Heimaey would have been permanent. The flow was eventually stopped by spraying it with millions of gallons of sea water. The island had increased in size by 15% and over half the town had been destroyed. The good news was that the lava flow actually protected the harbour entrance, while the high underground temperatures provided the island with hot water and heating.

PUFFINS

The puffin (*Fratercula arctica*), with its upright stance and parrot-like beak on a disproportionately large head, is everyone's favourite sea bird. Both the birds and their eggs have always been eaten in Iceland, and puffin meat is still a traditional dish on the Westman Islands' National Day. The birds are caught in nets on the end of long poles, and in the past a good puffin-catcher has been known to capture over 1000 birds in a single day. Today, few puffins are caught. Baby puffins are usually deserted by their parents and left to find their own way to the sea. Many become disorientated by the lights of Heimaey and can be seen wandering around the town. At this time they are collected up by the children of Heimaey and released into the sea.

Below: *Too cute to eat? Puffin is still a delicacy in the Westman Islands.*

Boat Trips From Heimaey ★★★

There are a number of boat trips from Heimaey. The tours usually pass the salmon farms, the pen where Keiko the killer whale resided for a number of years (*see panel, page 12*), and the sea-bird cliffs. On calm days, the boats go right in amongst the caves and stacks along the coast. Sea-fishing and whale-watching trips are also available.

Sport ★★★

The Westman Islands have what is arguably Iceland's best 18-hole **golf course**, located in Herjólfsdalur. It is the country's most southerly golf course, and the mild climate that generally prevails in this part of the country means that it is playable for much of the year. There is also a superb **indoor swimming pool**, complete with sauna, jacuzzi, solarium and gym.

BIRD-WATCHING ON THE WESTMAN ISLANDS

The Westman Islands form one of the prime sea-bird haunts in Northern Europe. Several spectacular cliffs (particularly on northern Heimaey) and rich food in the sea have led to quite amazing numbers of nesting sea birds. The islands support Iceland's only breeding colonies of manx shearwater, Leach's petrel and storm petrel. However, as these birds are largely nocturnal in their habits, observation is difficult. There are vast numbers of **gannets**, particularly on the smaller outer islands. Other species include five types of auk, fulmars and gulls. By far the most common sea bird, however, is the **puffin**, with literally hundreds of thousands of nesting pairs. Though the puffin was once part of the staple diet of the Westman Islanders, human predation never seemed to affect the numbers of this endearing bird.

The Westman Islands at a Glance

BEST TIMES TO VISIT

Snowfall is low in winter, but rain and mist occur year-round. July and August are warmest. National Day (in August) is a good time to visit.

GETTING THERE

A **car ferry** from Þorlákshöfn (with bus connection to Reykjavík) to Heimaey runs daily, with extra crossings in summer and at weekends. The trip takes two hours on rough seas; tel: 481 2800, 481 3915 or 552 2300. By the time this edition is published the new, and much shorter, ferry route to **Bakki** may have opened. Air Iceland runs daily **flights** to Heimaey from Reykjavík Domestic Airport. It takes 30 minutes in good weather, but cancellations do occur due to fog. There is also an air link with Akureyri.

GETTING AROUND

Most of Heimaey can easily be seen on foot as it covers only 13.4km² (5.2 sq miles). For local **taxis**, tel: 481 2038. **Car hire** is also available, but very expensive, tel: 481 2038.

WHERE TO STAY

MID-RANGE
Hotel Þórshamar, Vestmannabraut 28, tel: 481 2900, fax: 481 1696, website: hotelvest mannaeyjar.is Heimaey's best hotel. Can arrange horse riding, sea fishing and bike hire.
Hotel Bræðraborg, Herjólfs gata 4, tel: 481 1515, fax: 481 2007. The Gistiheimilið

Heimir in the same building offers a cheaper alternative.

BUDGET
Gistiheimilið Árný, Illugagata 7, 900 Vestmannaeyjar, tel and fax: 481 2082. Near pool. Cooking facilities available.
Gistiheimilið Hvíld, Höfðavegi 16, 900 Vestmannaeyjar, tel: 481 1230. Good value.
Gistiheimilið Mamma, Vestmannabraut 25, 900 Vestmannaeyjar, tel: 481 2900, fax: 481 1696. Comfortable guesthouse near the harbour.
Gistiheimilið Hreiðrið, Faxastígur 33, 900 Vestmannaeyjar, tel: 481 1045, fax: 4811414. Good wheelchair access. Best budget option.
Faxi Youth Hostel, Faxastígur 38, 900 Vestmannaeyjar, tel: 481 2915, fax: 481 1497. Open Jun–Sep. Book in advance.

CAMPING
The **Heimaey camp site** at Herjólfsdalur, tel: 481 2922, has good facilities.

WHERE TO EAT

Heimaey has a wide variety of eating places to suit all pockets. Hotel restaurants are generally the best, though also the most expensive. The **Hertoginn** in the Hotel Þórshamar is particularly recommended.

Lundinn, Kirkuvegur 21, tel: 481 1426. Has a good range of Westman Island specialities, including puffin and fish dishes. Live music on certain days.
Lanterna, Bárustígur 11, tel: 481 3393. Yugoslav-run. Good local food and Balkan dishes. For cheap pizzas, try **Pizza 67**, Heiðarvegur 5, tel: 481 1567, and **HB Pub**, tel: 481 1515, which has live music.

TOURS AND EXCURSIONS

Páll Helgason Travel Service (PH Tours) run daily **coach tours** of Heimaey. Booking is through Hotel Bræðraborg. PH Tours also organizes **boat trips** around the coastline, visiting stacks, sea caves and bird cliffs. Other boat trips are run by Hjálmar Guðnasson, tel: 481 1195, and Ólafur Tyr Guðjónsson, tel: 481 2333. Margo Renner, tel: 481 2269, organizes **hiking trips** to bird cliffs and volcanic locations.

USEFUL CONTACTS

The **Tourist Information Centre** is at Vestmannabraut 38, tel: 481 1271, fax: 481 2792, www.visitwestmanislands.com Open 09:00–12:00 and 13:00–16:00, Mon–Fri; 13:00–16:00 on weekends. Small tourist information office at the Hotel Bræðraborg, tel: 481 2922.

HEIMAEY	J	F	M	A	M	J	J	A	S	O	N	D
AVE. TEMP. °C	1.3	2.0	1.7	3.4	5.6	8.0	9.8	9.6	7.4	5.0	2.4	1.4
AVE. TEMP. °F	34.3	35.6	35.1	38.1	42.1	46.4	49.6	49.3	45.3	41.0	36.3	34.5
AVE. RAINFALL mm	158	139	141	117	105	102	95	140	131	162	154	143
AVE. RAINFALL in	6.23	5.48	5.55	4.61	4.14	4.02	3.74	5.52	5.16	6.38	6.07	5.63

Travel Tips

Tourist Information

The **Icelandic Tourist Board** has offices in Copenhagen, Denmark; Paris, France; Neu Isenberg and Frankfurt, Germany; Tokyo, Japan; Zürich, Switzerland; London, UK and New York, USA. For information in UK contact Icelandair Holidays, 172 Tottenham Court Road London WIP OLY, tel: 020 7874 1000, website: www.icetourist.is The main office in Iceland is the **Tourist Information Centre**, Aðalstræti 2, Reykjavík, tel: 590 1550, fax: 591 1551. Information is also available at Reykjavík's City Hall in Vonarstræti. Regional offices in Akranes, Akureyri, Egilsstaðir, Húsavík, Ísafjörður, and Sauðárkrókur provide brochures and pamphlets, have information about tour operators and assist in booking accommodation and flights.

Entry Requirements

A valid passport is required for all visitors, except those from Nordic countries, who only need an identity card. Visas are needed for visitors from certain countries, which do not include Canada, USA, the EU, Australia and many others. If in doubt, ask at an Icelandic embassy or consulate before departure. An entry stamp in a passport is valid for 3 months.

Customs

Visitors over the age of 20 may bring in free of duty one litre of spirits/wine and 200 cigarettes. The duty-free shop at Keflavík Airport is open to arriving passengers and in view of the high cost of living in Iceland it is advisable to make use of this. There are restrictions on most meat and dairy products, but visitors may bring in up to 10kg of other foods. Icelandic VAT is high. Much of this can be refunded on leaving if goods are bought at tax-free shops.

Health Requirements

Iceland has no specific health problems and inoculations are unnecessary. All health services are publicly provided and free for citizens of Nordic and EU countries (bring EU Health Card). Dental services are privately provided and costs are on par with Europe and the USA.

Getting There

By Air: The main airline serving Iceland is the national carrier **Icelandair** (tel: 505 0100, www.icelandair.com), with services from Amsterdam, Baltimore, Barcelona, Bergen, Boston, Chicago, Copenhagen, Detroit, Faroe Islands, Frankfurt, Glasgow, Gothenburg, London, Luxembourg, Milan, New York, Orlando, Oslo, Paris, Salzburg, Stockholm and Washington DC. Icelandair offers passengers travelling between Europe and USA a stopover deal for up to 72 hours. **SAS** flies from Copenhagen, Oslo and Stockholm, while the budget airline **Iceland Express**, the 'no-frills' carrier, flies to Keflavik from London Stansted and Copenhagen. All incoming international flights land at **Keflavík** Airport (tel: 425 0330), 50km (31 miles) from Reykjavík. Regular non-stop Fly Bus coaches run from the airport to the capital, taking 45 minutes. The city terminal is at the Hotel Loftleiðir.
By Sea: The Faroes shipping company **Smyril Line** (tel: 472 1111) runs a car ferry service to Iceland throughout the year.

The weekly trip links Iceland with the Shetland and Faroe Islands, Bergen (Norway) and Esbjerg (Denmark). The *MS Norröna* accommodates some 1000 passengers and 250 cars. The ferry arrives in Seyðis-fjörður, which is over 700km (435 miles) from Reykjavík along the northern or southern routes of the Ring Road.

What to Pack

The unpredictable weather means that visitors should be prepared for anything. Wind and rain can be incessant, so water- and windproof jacket and trousers are essential. Sweater, scarf, hat and gloves are also advisable. A pair of hiking boots are necessary, even on a coach tour, as most of the sites involve a walk, often over rough ground. Bring a swimsuit for the geo-thermally heated swimming pools. Formal clothes are necessary in quality hotels and restaurants. The light provides marvellous conditions for photography. Binoculars are essential for observing wildlife.

Money Matters

Icelandic currency is the **króna** (Ikr), divided into 100 aurar. Notes come in denominations of 5000 Ikr, 2000 Ikr, 1000 Ikr and 500 Ikr, and coins in 100 Ikr, 50 Ikr, 10 Ikr, 5 Ikr and Ikr. Currency may be bought abroad (sometimes with diffi-culty), but the local exchange rate is better. If Iceland's application to join the EU is successful, the króna will be replaced by the euro in 2011. Three **banks** in Iceland –

Búnðarbanki Íslands, Íslands-banki and Landsbankí Íslands – usually open 09:15–16:00, Mon–Fri; opening hours may be erratic in rural areas. There are exchange facilities at Keflavík Airport from 06:30–18:30. **Travellers cheques** may be cashed at most hotels. **ATM**s are common in Reyjavík and other towns and are increas-ingly found in rural areas. **Credit cards** can be used to obtain cash from banks and are widely accepted in hotels, shops and restaurants, but not always at petrol service stations. **VAT** on most purchases is currently at 24.5%.

Accommodation

Prices are high, particularly in **hotels**. Reykjavík and Akureyri have international-standard hotels offering *en-suite* bath-rooms, restaurants, shops and often indoor pools. Tourist-class hotels throughout the country offer fewer facilities, but most have a restaurant and rooms with a private shower and toilet. A unique Icelandic feature is the **summer hotel**. These open for June and August but for the rest of the year they are boarding schools and colleges. Facilities vary: some offer only **sleeping-bag accom-modation**, while others also have restaurants and pools. Most common budget accom-modation is the **guesthouse**. Located throughout the coun-try, they usually offer bed and breakfast. A list of hotels and guesthouses can be obtained from tourist information centres. Advance booking is advisable during peak season.

Farmhouse accommodation is widely offered by Icelandic farmers, usually on a bed and breakfast or sleeping bag arrangement. Some farms provide self-catering cottages, others have horses and boats for rent. A list of farms offering accommodation is found in the booklet *Icelandic Farm Holidays* from information centres. **Youth hostels** are economical and there are around 30 in the country. Most close in the winter. They usually offer sleeping-bag accommodation and cooking facilities, though some provide family rooms and meals. Pre-booking is essential in July and August. Contact the Icelandic Youth Hostels Association, tel: 553 8110, fax: 567 9201. Despite the weather, **camping** is very popular. There are over

PUBLIC HOLIDAYS

New Year's Day • 1 January
Easter • Maundy Thursday, Good Friday, Easter Sunday, Easter Monday
First Day of Summer • Third Tuesday in April
Labour Day • 1 May
Ascension Day • May/June
Seamen's Day • Early June
Independence Day • 17 June
August Public Holiday • First Weekend in August
Rettir • September (sheep and horse round-ups in rural areas)
Christmas Eve • 24 December
Christmas Day • 25 December
Boxing Day • 26 December
New Year's Eve • 31 December

100 sites, often in national parks or scenic areas. Facilities vary – some are quite primitive, others have toilets, showers, snack bars, kitchens and pools. Note that facilities may not be on the site but in the nearest settlement. When camping in non-designated areas, obtain the landowner's permission. Because of possible wind and rain, tents should be durable. A booklet, *Camping in Iceland*, (obtainable from all tourist information centres) has a list of officially designated sites. Hikers in remote areas can make use of **mountain huts**, which usually have only basic facilities. They are owned by the Touring Club of Iceland, tel: 568 2533, who charge a small fee for their use. Accommodation is limited to 3 nights; pre-booking is essential.

Good Reading

Peterson, Mountford and Hollom (1993) *Birds of Britain and Europe* (Collins).
Love, Askell (1983) *The Flora of Iceland* (Almenna Bokafelagid).
Wolesey, Pat (1979) *A Field Key to the Flowering Plants of Iceland* (The Thule Press).
Carwardine, Mark (1986) *Iceland: Nature's Meeting Place* (Iceland Review).
Perkins, John (1983) *Iceland: A Geological Field Guidebook* (Cardiff University).
Magnusson, Magnus (1990) *Iceland Saga* (The Bodley Head).
Sale, Richard (2000) *The Xenophobe's Guide to Icelanders* (Oval Books).

Eating Out

Food is a major expense. With a service charge, plus alcohol, the bill may be double that which tourists would pay at home. There are plenty of **restaurants** in Reykjavík and to a lesser extent in Akureyri, but elsewhere they are mainly confined to hotels. Reykjavík has a range of ethnic restaurants, including Japanese, Indian, Thai, Italian and Chinese. Cheaper are the American fast-food chains, pizza restaurants and hot dogs stalls. In rural areas, cafés attached to service stations offer cheap, filling food, usually with a daily 'special'. In summer, look for the sign 'Tourist Menu' – this is usually soup, a main course and coffee for a set price. **Alcohol** is very expensive and can only be bought by those over 20, from State Monopoly Shops which have limited opening hours. The traditional Icelandic tipple is *brennivin*, a schnapps made from potatoes and flavoured with caraway. The main brand is Svarti Dauði, which means 'Black Death'!

Transport

Iceland has no railways, so travel is mainly by road and air. **Air**: Difficult surface conditions, particularly in winter, mean that flights are a common way to get around. Most routes are operated by Icelandair's subsidiary Air Iceland. Various bargain air passes are available, including Holiday Air Rover, offering round routing from Reykjavík via Akureyri, Egilsstaðir, Höfn, Ísafjörður and back to Reykjavík. The main centre for domestic flights is the Reykjavík Domestic Airport. **Road**: Iceland has a good network of roads, including Road No. 1, the so-called Ring Road, completed in 1974. About 80% of the Ring Road is metalled, the rest gravel. During dry periods, the gravel roads can be dusty, and flying stones can damage cars. Tracks through the interior are usually open only in July and August and involve fording rivers, so four-wheel-drive vehicles are essential. Petrol is expensive, though diesel is relatively cheap. Driving is on the right and seat belts are obligatory. Headlights must remain on. Speed limits are 50km/h (30 mph) in urban areas, 80km/h (50 mph) outside towns. Look out for sheep in rural areas. Drunk driving regulations are strictly enforced and the legal limit is low. Drivers bringing their own cars need a driving licence, registration document and green card. The Icelandic motoring organization (FÍB) will be allied to home organizations. Filling stations in Reykjavík are open until 23:30; earlier in other parts. **Car Hire**: Most international car-hire companies, like Avis, Hertz and Budget are based in Reykjavík. Car hire is expensive, mainly due to the 24% VAT. If you plan to go off the metalled roads, a 4WD vehicle is recommended. Minimum age for car hire is 21 for saloon cars and 25 for an off-road vehicle. There is a high demand for car hire in summer and pre-booking is advisable.

Buses: A network of long-distance bus routes covering all the inhabited areas is co-ordinated BSÍ, based at the main bus terminal in Reykjavík (tel: 562 1011, www.bsi.is). Discount passes, like the Full Circle Pass, allow a complete circuit of the Ring Road in either direction with as many stops as required. Included in the price are 10% discounts on accommodation and ferries. The Omnibus Pass allows unlimited travel on any bus route for a week and discounts on accommodation.

Taxis: Available in the main settlements, taxis are usually driver-owned but the fares are uniform and you pay what is on the meter. Fares are comparable to those in the USA and most European countries. You can also hire taxis for a flat rate to visit places of interest.

Ferries: Iceland has three car ferries – Reykjavík to Akranes, Þorlákshöfn to Heimaey, and a ferry linking Stykkishólmur, Flatey and Brjáslækur. There are several passenger ferries. Most are run by **Eimskip**, tel: 481 2800, www.eimskip.com

Maps: The Globetrotter Travel Map of Iceland is excellent. Free maps are available in tourist offices and hotels. The Ferdakort map (1:500,000) is good, but expensive. Maps are available at Landmælingar Íslands shop, Laugavegur 178, PO Box 5060, 125 Reykjavík.

Business Hours

Offices usually open 09:00–17:00, Mon–Fri. Shops stay open later, but may close on Sat in summer. Most supermarkets are open daily; also weekends and holidays. Banks open 09:15–16:00, Mon–Fri. Petrol stations open daily 07:00–23:30.

Tipping

Service is included in prices for hotels, restaurants and taxis. Tipping is not customary.

Time Difference

Iceland is on Greenwich Mean Time (GMT) throughout the year. In summer it is one hour behind British Summer Time.

Communications

All Icelandic towns have **post offices** and telephone offices –

ROAD SIGNS

Iceland's roads are generally well signposted and distances clearly marked in kilometres. Road signs are the same as those used throughout the EU. The danger signal (an **exclamation mark!**) should always be heeded. Even the Ring Road has gravel stretches, so slow down when the 'loose stones' sign appears. When a tarmac surface ends it is marked by the sign *Malbik Endar*. Icelandic roads, including the Ring Road, have many single-lane bridges marked by *Einbreid Brú*. Blind summits, shown by *Blindhæd*, should be approached with caution – never stop on the top or sides of a blind summit.

look for the sign *Póstur og Sími* – usually open Monday–Friday, 08:30–17:00. Stamps are available in supermarkets and hotels. Post boxes are red and often found near hotels. Allow 3–5 days for a letter to reach Europe or North America. The telephone system is very efficient. **Telephone booths** are usually in hotels, restaurants and service stations. Subscribers in the telephone directory are listed by their first names. There are no regional codes; the international code for Iceland is 354. If making international calls from Iceland, dial 00 first then the international code for the country concerned. For the UK dial 44. For Canada and USA, it is 1. Iceland has the highest per capita mobile phone network in the world. GSM is used in

CONVERSION CHART		
FROM	**TO**	**MULTIPLY BY**
Millimetres	Inches	0.0394
Metres	Yards	1.0936
Metres	Feet	3.281
Kilometres	Miles	0.6214
Square kilometres	Square miles	0.386
Hectares	Acres	2.471
Litres	Pints	1.760
Kilograms	Pounds	2.205
Tonnes	Tons	0.984
To convert Celsius to Fahrenheit: x 9 ÷ 5 + 32		

the more populated areas and most visitors will be able to use their cell phones, except in more rural areas, when an NMT phone may have to be hired. Prepaid local SIM cards can be hired locally.

Internet
Icelanders have enthusiastically adopted information technology. There are a number of Internet cafés in Reykjavík. It is estimated that there are 145,000 internet users.

Websites
www.destination-iceland.com
Excellent for hiking information.
www.south.is
Travel in south Iceland.
www.travelnet.is
History, geography, culture, accommodations, restaurants, and travel options.
www.iceland.is
Official government website.
www.icetourist.is
Iceland Tourist Board website.
www.visiticeland.com
The most comprehensive site for tourists visiting Iceland.

Electricity
Voltage is 220, 50 HZ AC, with two round pin prongs. Visitors may need adapters.

Weights and Measures
Iceland uses the metric system.

Health Precautions
Tap water often smells sulphurous, but is potable all over the country. Food is prepared under stringent health regulations. Visitors in winter should guard against **hypothermia**,

while those travelling over snow and ice during summer should use a block to prevent sun and wind burn.

Health Services
The public health service is excellent. There are over 40 hospitals providing 3600 beds. Staff are well trained and are familiar with English. Visitors should have travel insurance to cover unexpected health problems, particularly if planning risky outdoor activities.

Personal Safety
Iceland has one of the lowest crime rates in the world. If it does occur it is usually petty and alcohol-related. Visitors will seldom feel threatened, but should take the usual precautions with money, passports and valuables. The **emergency** telephone number for police and other services is **112**.

Etiquette
Icelanders are very friendly people who welcome all visitors . They are proud of their country and its lack of pollution. Litter is almost nonexistent so please respect this tradition.

Language
Icelandic is a Germanic language and most closely associated with Faroese and Norwegian. It has changed little – Icelanders are still able to read the **Sagas**, written 800 years ago. The alphabet has 34 letters, including a number of extra vowels and consonants. The grammar is extremely complicated. Icelanders try to

USEFUL WORDS AND PHRASES

Yes, No • *Já, Nei*
Hello • *Góðen dag*
Goodbye • *Bless*
Thank you • *Takk fyrir*
How are you? • *Hvad sergirdu gott?*
Toilet • *Snyrting*
Ladies, Gents • *Konur, Karlar*
How much is it? • *Hvad kostar petta?*
Airport • *Flúgvöllur*
Ferry • *Ferja*
My name is • *Ég heiti*
Where are you from? • *Hvaðan ert pú?*
Cheers! • *Skál!*
I don't understand • *Ég skil ekki*
Guesthouse • *Gistheimili*
Youth hostel • *Farfuglaheimili*
Open • *Opið*
Closed • *Lokað*
Beer • *Bjór*
Bread • *Brauð*
Coffee • *Kaffi*
Milk • *Mjólk*
Tea • *Te*
Water • *Vatn*
Days of the week:
Sunnudagur, Mánudagur, Priðjudagur, Miðvikudagur, Fimmtudagur, Fostudagur, Laugardagur
Some numbers:
0 • *null*   1 • *einn*
2 • *tveir*   3 • *prír*
4 • *fjórir*   5 • *fimm*
6 • *sex*   7 • *sjö*
8 • *átta*   9 • *níu*
10 • *tíu*
100 • *hundrad*
1000 • *thúsund*

protect their language from outside influence and develop their own words. Fortunately for visitors, Icelanders are excellent linguists.

INDEX

Note: Numbers in **bold** indicate photographs

NewYork

New York – The City That Never Sleeps

Lower Broadway bustle

If you are traveling to New York for the first time: expect anything to happen, except boredom. The only emotion that the place does not arouse is indifference.

'What is barely hinted at in other American cities is condensed and enlarged in New York,' said the writer Saul Bellow. True enough. Since its purchase by the Dutch in 1626, through its growth as a maritime hub, fueled by cheap immigrant labor, to its contemporary position as, arguably, the cultural and retail center of the world, New York has become a city that can't be ignored.

Culturally, New York has more than 150 museums, including the third largest in the world (the Metropolitan Museum of Art), around 400 art galleries, and more than 240 theaters. Broadway and the Metropolitan Opera are famous the world over.

The entertainment possibilities in 'the city that never sleeps' are immense: there's a choice of over 60 clubs, offering everything from jazz to blues, and hundreds of places to dance each night of the week. Hungry? There are more than 17,000 different places to eat. Amid all the bustle, there are quiet places too: the city has over 26,000 acres (10,500 hectares) of parks, the most notable and famous of which is Central Park.

5

A night on the town

Crime may have decreased in recent years, but New York is still famed for its frenetic pace of life. The streets are still filled with potholes, the sewage system is in disrepair, and the subway trains have a habit of getting stuck in tunnels. Added to this there's the social misery: the homeless are just as much a part of the city as its soaring skyscrapers and oversized limousines.

But New York can't be explained just in terms of its extremes. It's the New Yorkers themselves who make this city so exciting. There is a good reason why such well-known publicity-shy figures as Greta Garbo and Jacqueline Onassis, once chose New York as their home. It's the same reason that might inspire any number of people to pack their bags and head here some day. New York is the place where ordinary people can, if they are willing to be lucky, become stars, by performing in Washington Square Park, or by making it big in industry, and the place where real stars can walk down the street unnoticed. Or so we are lead to believe: New York is the city of myths, and making them is a part of it. True, New Yorkers do have a reputation for being hurried, even rude, but under their frequent brusqueness is a great sense of humor. Just remember that normality is said to bore them, while spontaneity delights them.

New York is a fast-paced town whose residents are possessed of a restless energy. Few people seem to have time

for anything not on their mental schedule; even asking for directions in the street is best done with an awareness of this, ideally while moving at the same pace and in the same direction as the informant.

New Yorkers have persuaded themselves that living at breakneck speed, under constant pressure, is stimulating. This is what gives them their edge and makes Manhattan the center of the universe (which all New Yorkers believe implicitly). It also helps to explain why few people, if they can help it, choose to live out their declining years in the city.

Location and Size

On the same latitude as Naples, Italy, ie roughly 41° north and 74° west, the entire city covers a surface area of 301 sq miles (780 sq km). Of its five boroughs, only the Bronx

lies on the mainland; Manhattan and Staten Island are islands, while Brooklyn and Queens form the westernmost point of Long Island. Manhattan, the smallest borough, has a surface area of just over 22 sq miles (57 sq km), but is the most densely populated part of the city. It is 13.4 miles (21.5 km) long and between 0.8 miles (1.3 km) and 2.3 miles (3.7 km) wide.

New York lies at the mouth of the Hudson River. The East River, which borders Manhattan to the east, is not actually a river at all, but a narrow strip of water connecting Long Island Sound and Upper New York Bay.

Manhattan is laid out primarily in a rectangular system of numbered streets and avenues. An exception is the island's oldest section, from Greenwich Village south to Battery Park, an area that can be confusing without the assistance of a map.

Climate

New York is generally blessed with plenty of sunshine during all seasons of the year. High pressure areas predominate, and spells of bad weather tend to remain just that – spells. Beware, however, of the summer months of July and August: the city gets unpleasantly hot and humid, and it's hard to summon the enthusiasm to go sightseeing in temperatures of 86–102°F (30–39°C). Although New York lies on the coast, the beaches that are accessible by public transportation tend to be crowded, especially on hot summer weekends. The nicest beaches are half a day's trip away from Manhattan on Long Island.

Winter in New York is cold, with temperatures in January and February regularly dropping as low as 10°F

No shortage of sunshine

(–12°C). An icy wind blows round the blocks. Snowfalls can often be heavy enough to bring traffic to a standstill, and photographs of people cross-country skiing down Fifth Avenue are not the montages they might appear.

On the other hand, temperatures in May, June, September, and October are very pleasant, making these ideal months in which to discover the city.

Population

According to the US Census Bureau, New York City has a population of 7.4 million. Of that figure, approximately 1.5 million live in Manhattan, 2.3 million in Brooklyn, 2 million in Queens, 1.2 million in the Bronx, and 413,000 in Staten Island. Of these, approximately 43 percent are of European descent, 25.2 percent are African-American or African-Caribbean, 24.4 percent are Hispanic, and 6.7 percent are Asian. But New Yorkers are more than faceless numbers – they represent every race, creed, and color in the world; they're the personification of 'the cultural melting pot', for which former mayor David Dinkins coined the apt, if optimistic, phrase 'gorgeous mosaic'. To walk on the sidewalks of New York is to hear English, Russian, Chinese, Japanese, Hindi, French, Italian, Spanish – in short, every language you can imagine.

Facing the world head on

7

Crime

No place on earth offers so many different cultures gathered in one spot; what's surprising is that, with the city's reputation for crime, crime statistics here are actually lower than in other large American cities. What usually catches the eye of the world, however, are lurid headlines about murders, rapes, and muggings, often involving innocent or unaware out-of-towners. Obviously, it pays to be careful, use your common sense and follow a few basic safety tips *(see page 100)*.

Most crime is drugs-related

Politics and administration

The city government has two major components: the mayor and the City Council. The mayor, who is elected for a four-year term, works in partnership with the Council, which acts as New York's main legislative branch. As the city's official law-making body, the Council monitors the operation and performance of the various city agencies. Among other tasks, it holds responsibility for analyzing and approving the city's budget. The 51 members of the Council represent all five boroughs and are also elected on a four-year basis.

Economy

A city of superlatives that match its soaring skyscrapers, at the start of the 21st century New York is the most

The New York Stock Exchange

World Financial Center

powerful financial center on earth. The New York Stock Exchange on Wall Street is the largest in the world, the New York Mercantile Exchange in lower Manhattan's World Financial Center is the world's largest Physical Commodity Futures Exchange, and the Nasdaq stock market recently unveiled the world's biggest video-screen sign in Times Square – a flashy if apt reflection of the growing new-media sector, which has earned parts of New York the catchy sobriquet 'Silicon Alley.'

Although just over 5 percent of the workforce is actually employed by investment houses and brokerage firms, the economy is more or less ruled by the vagaries of the stock market. At the same time, New York's influential banking community has expanded into the international arena, and this emphasis on a global economy has left the city more vulnerable to outside forces than in the past, when a diverse base of small manufacturers provided a safety net of autonomous strength and flexibility.

The local garment industry, for instance, for many years a mainstay of New York's economy, has lost around a quarter of its jobs since 1991 although it still produces close to $5 billion dollars' worth of apparel for national consumers. In another sign of the times, a number of new-media companies – businesses that develop and sell interactive software and on-line computer services – have moved into the loft buildings of the garment industry center along Seventh Avenue in midtown, as well as in areas as far-flung as Chinatown and the Flatiron and Financial districts further downtown. This trend, in turn, has helped to heighten an ongoing Manhattan real-estate boom, which had already forced some manufacturing concerns to relocate to more affordable areas in Queens, Brooklyn, Staten Island, the Bronx, and across the Hudson River in New Jersey.

As unskilled immigrants continue to arrive, there's also a widening gap between the rich and poor, with the middle class squeezed uncomfortably in-between.

The city is a major trading center. The combined Port Authority of New York and New Jersey still oversees a large percentage of the country's import-export trade by air and sea – and in addition to financial service sectors such as legal, insurance and accounting firms, important businesses include advertising, public relations, and the traditional media industries of newspaper, magazine and book publishing. The headquarters of the nation's major advertising agencies and publishing houses are located here, as are the leading television and radio networks. The local movie business is thriving, with over 200 feature films shot in the city during 1997 alone.

Outdoor activities

The retail, food, hotel, and other consumer-service areas continue to thrive as well, fueled by the city's status as the premier US destination for travelers from overseas: New York attracts up to 34 million visitors each year, one-fifth of them from other countries.

Media

New Yorkers are bombarded by information. People are driven by their addiction to knowing what's going on; in some circles it's not who you know so much as what you know. The *New York Times* is the paper of choice for most well-informed readers. Two tabloids compete for the rest of the audience: the *New York Post*, famed for its garish headlines and downmarket appeal, and the *Daily News*.

The *Village Voice*, most valuable for its comprehensive listings and classified advertisements, and its main competitor, the *New York Press*, are two of the best of the many free weeklies to be found around town.

The three major American television networks – ABC, CBS, and NBC – broadcast many programs from their Manhattan-based studios. Free tickets are occasionally available for specific shows, but unfortunately not for the quality programs broadcast by the Public Broadcast System (PBS), which is also based in New York. There are three other local stations, about a dozen UHF stations, and at least four cable companies offer a wide variety viewing, from 24-hour news to 24-hour vintage movies.

Life, liberty, and the pursuit of silliness

Newspapers, magazines, theater, art galleries, museums, and, at the flick of a dial, over 100 radio and television stations; add to this powerful corporations, award-winning modern artists, gorgeous skyscrapers, and the best music around drifting out of any number of dark, neighborhood clubs. Is it any wonder, then, that most people – locals and visitors alike – consider New York City the most vibrant place on earth?

Historical Highlights

1000 Algonquin Indian tribes use Manhattan for summer hunting and fishing.

1524 Italian maritime explorer Giovanni da Verrazano, under the patronage of Francis I of France, sights Manhattan but doesn't land.

1609 The Englishman Henry Hudson becomes the first white man to step on to the island known to the Algonquin as Mannahatta.

1624 The Dutch West India Company establishes a settlement on the southern tip of Mannahatta at the current site of Battery Park.

1626 The provincial director general of the New Amsterdam settlement, Peter Minuit, purchases Manhattan from the local Indians for 60 guilders' worth of trinkets – the equivalent of $24.

1643 Conflict with local Algonquin tribes leaves about 80 Indians dead at the Panovia Massacre.

1647 Peter Stuyvesant becomes director general. He soon suppresses all political opposition.

1653 Stuyvesant builds a fence along Wall Street to protect New Amsterdam from British incursion.

1664 In the first year of the sea war between England and Holland, Stuyvesant is forced to surrender the town to the British without a fight. New Amsterdam is renamed New York, after King Charles II's brother, James, Duke of York.

1673 The Dutch recapture New York and rename it New Orange, again without a shot being fired.

1674 New York is returned to the British as a result of the Anglo/Dutch Treaty of Westminster.

1689 James Leisler, a merchant, stages a revolt against British rule and is hanged for treason.

1690 With a population of 3,900, New York is the third-largest town in North America.

1712 Black slaves set fire to a home on Maiden Lane, hoping to incite an insurrection. Nine whites are killed. Six of the slaves commit suicide; 21 others are hanged.

1735 Newspaper publisher Peter Zenger is tried for slandering the British crown. He is acquitted, establishing the precedent for freedom of the press.

1765 In accordance with the Stamp Act, unfair taxes are levied aginst the colonists.

1770 A series of skirmishes between the Sons of Liberty and British soldiers culminate in the Battle of Golden Hill.

1776 The Revolutionary War begins and the colonies declare their independence from Great Britain. George Washington, in command of the colonial troops, loses the Battle of Long Island. British troops occupy New York until 1783.

1785 New York becomes capital of the newly founded United States of America, but only retains this status until 1790.

1789 George Wahington is inaugurated at the site of the Federal Hall, Wall Street.

1790 A first official census reveals that New York now has a population of 33,000.

1792 The stock exchange is founded beneath a buttonwood tree on Wall Street.

1811 An important decision is made affecting the city's future appearance: all streets are to be laid out in the form of a grid.

1825 The economic importance of New York increases sharply as a result of the construction of the Erie Canal, connecting the Hudson River with the Great Lakes.

1830 Irish and German immigrants begin arriving in great numbers.

1835 The part of Manhattan between South Broad and Wall Street is ravaged by the 'Great Fire.'

1848–9 Many political refugees arrive in New York after the failure of the German Revolution.

1857 William Marcy 'Boss' Tweed, elected to the County Board of Supervisors, launches a career of notorious corruption.

1858 Calvert Vaux and Frederick Law Olmsted submit plans for the city's Central Park.

1861 The American Civil War is declared.

1863 Draft Riots rage in the city for three days. Some 1,500 people are killed.

1865 Immigration continues unabated. Italians, East European Jews, and Chinese arrive in unprecedented numbers until well into the 1920s.

1871 'Boss' Tweed is arrested and later dies in jail.

1877 The Museum of Natural History opens.

1880 The Metropolitan Museum of Art opens.

1883 Brooklyn Bridge officially opens. The first performance is held at the Metropolitan Opera.

1886 The unveiling of the Statue of Liberty, a gift from France, takes place on Liberty Island.

1892 Ellis Island in New York Harbor becomes the point of entry for immigrants to the US.

1898 New York's five boroughs are united under one municipal government.

1902 The Flatiron Building is completed.

1911 The Triangle Fire alerts public to the appalling work and living conditions of immigrants.

1913 Construction of the world's tallest skyscraper: the Woolworth Building. It is only superseded in 1930 by the Chrysler Building.

1929 The Wall Street Crash, and the start of the Great Depression in the US and worldwide.

1931 The Empire State Building opens.

1933–45 Many Europeans take refuge in New York from ethnic and political persecution at the hands of the German Nazi regime.

1939 Ten years after its foundation by Abby Aldrich Rockefeller, the Museum of Modern Art moves into its new home on 53rd Street.

1941 The United States enter World War II.

1943 Serious racial unrest occurs in Harlem, a large African-American community since 1910.

1946 The United Nations begins meeting in New York. The permanent buildings on East 42nd–48th streets are completed six years later.

1959 The Guggenheim Museum opens its doors for the first time. Work begins on Lincoln Center

1965 A 16-hour-long power failure brings the city to a standstill.

1970 Economic decline sets in as firms start leaving the city in ever-increasing numbers. This decline continues until around 1976.

1973 The World Trade Center opens.

1975 The chronic financial situation in the city reaches its peak: bankruptcy is only avoided via a bridging loan from the federal government.

1977 A second major power outage, this time 27 hours' long. Looting and vandalism occurs.

1982 The IBM Building opens, followed, in 1983, by the AT&T Building. This affirms the resurgence of corporate development.

1983 The vast glass Trump Tower is completed.

1986 Battery Park City opens.

1987 'Black Monday' takes place on Wall Street. Shares suffer a sudden 30 percent drop in value.

1990 David Dinkins becomes the city's first ever African-American mayor.

1993 A bomb explodes below World Trade Center. Many are injured.

1993 Rudolph Giuliani becomes mayor of New York, and is re-elected in 1997. His 'get tough on crime' stance transforms the Big Apple into one of the safest cities in the US.

1998 Greater New York celebrates its centenary.

2000 Record crowds flock to the city's revitalized Times Square on New Year's Eve to see in the Millennium.

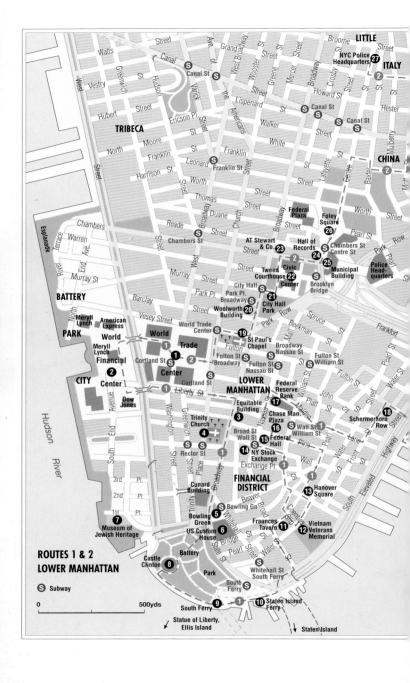

LITTLE

NYC Police
Headquarters **27** ITALY Ⓢ**2**

Broome Street

Watts Street
Canal Street
West Broadway
Grand Street
Wooster
Greene
Mercer
Broadway
Crosby
Howard St

Ericson Pl
Varick
Hudson
Greenwich
St
Vestry
Hubert Street
Canal St Ⓢ
Ⓢ Canal St

Lispenard
Walker Street
White Street
Ⓢ Canal St
Ⓢ Canal St
Hester
Mulberry

TRIBECA

Moore St
Franklin
North
Franklin St Ⓢ
Leonard St Franklin Street
Harrison St
Worth St
Thomas Street
Reade Street
St
Lafayette
Centre
Baxter
Mott

CHINA
Ⓢ**2**

Esplanade
River Terrace
Chambers

Duane Street
Church
Broadway

Federal
Plaza
Foley
Square
Worth Street
Street
Pearl
St
Park Row

Warren
West End Ave.
North End Ave.
Murray St
Chambers St Ⓢ
Reade
Murray Street
Street
Chambers St
Street
AT Stewart
& Co. **23**
Hall of
Records
Chambers St
24 Centre St
25 Municipal
Building
26
Police
Head-
quarters

BATTERY

Barclay
Park Pl
Vesey Street
Park Pl.
Broadway
City Hall
Tweed
Courthouse **22**
Civic
Center
Brooklyn
Bridge
Spruce
Frankfort

PARK

Meryll
Lynch
American
Express
World
Meryll
Lynch
Financial
World
Trade
Center
21
City Hall
Park
Woolworth
Building **20**
Park Row
Beekman

CITY

Ⓢ**2**
Center
Cortland St Ⓢ
World Trade
Center Ⓢ**19**
St Paul's
Chapel
Broadway
Nassau St
Fulton St
Fulton St Ⓢ
William St

Avenue
Dow
Jones
Ⓢ**1**
Ⓢ**2**
Cortland St Ⓢ
Liberty St
Fulton
Broadway
Fulton St Ⓢ
Nassau St
Ⓢ Fulton St Ⓢ William St
Fulton St

Hudson River
Washington
Greenwich Street
Equitable
Building **3**
**LOWER
MANHATTAN**
Federal
Reserve
Bank **17**
John
Platt
Water

South End Avenue
Trinity
Church
Chase Man
Plaza **16**
Ⓢ Wall St
William St
Maiden
Front
Schermerhorn
Row **18**

4
Broad St
Wall St **15**
Federal
Hall
Pine
Lane
Ⓢ Rector St
14 NY Stock
Exchange
Exchange Pl.
Wall
South Elevated Highway

3rd Pl.
2nd Pl.
1st Pl.
Cunard
Building
Ⓢ**1**
**FINANCIAL
DISTRICT**
Ⓢ**1**
13 Hanover
Square

7
Museum of
Jewish Heritage
5 Bowling Gn Ⓢ
Bowling
Green
US Custom
House **6**
Beaver
Fraunces
Tavern **11**
12 Vietnam
Veterans
Memorial
Coenties
Broad
Whitehall
Pearl Street
Water St
State St
Bridge

**ROUTES 1 & 2
LOWER MANHATTAN**

Ⓢ Subway

0   500yds

Castle
Clinton **8**
Battery
Park
Whitehall St
South Ferry
Whitehall St Ⓢ
South Ferry

South Ferry Ⓢ

South Ferry **9**
Ⓢ**1**
10 Staten Island
Ferry

Statue of Liberty,
Ellis Island
Staten Island

Delancey Street

Broome

Street

Grand Street

LOWER EAST SIDE

Chrystie Street

Forsyth Street

Eldridge Street

Allen Street

Orchard Street

Essex Street

Norfolk St

Hester Street

Canal Street

Elizabeth St

Bowery

Bayard St

TOWN

Pike

Henry Street

Madison Street

E. Broadway

Street

Market St

St James Pl.

Henry

Catherine

Madison St.

Monroe Street

Suard St.

Cherry St

Street Highway

South Elevated

Wagner

St

River

Brooklyn Bridge

East

South Street Seaport

Furman Street

Brooklyn Queens Expwy.

Columbia Heights

15

Route 1

Preceding pages: sky-high view from the Empire State Building

World Trade Center – Battery Park City – Statue of Liberty and Ellis Island – Financial District – South Street Seaport

Lower Manhattan is the original New York, where winding streets once led to bustling docks and clipper ships. Today these narrow byways, with names such as Pine Street, Pearl Street, and Wall Street, are lined by towering temples of finance. If you want to see the sights from the inside as well as the outside, it's best to plan two to three days for Route 1; otherwise the whole route can also be done on foot within a day. *See map, pages 14/15.*

A plaza measuring 24,000sq yds (20,000sq m), the largest enclosed shopping area in New York, with some 208 elevators, 50,000 workers, around 200,000 visitors daily, and two 1,377-ft (420-m) high towers – even for this city of superlatives, it's utterly gigantic. The ★★ **World Trade Center ❶** is no longer the world's tallest building, though it was for a few months in 1973, until Chicago set new standards with its Sears Tower (1,453ft/443m). Today both are outranked by Kuala Lumpur's Petronas Towers.

The most famous restaurant in the Trade Center is at the top of Tower 1 (North Tower): **Windows on the World**, where the prices are nearly as high as the establishment itself. The view of New York is stunning from here, though there's also a far cheaper way of enjoying it: an elevator takes just 58 seconds to get to the enclosed observation deck of the **Top of the World** on the 107th floor of Tower 2 (South Tower). Those with heads for heights could even try the rooftop promenade on the 110th floor (only open on clear, calm days). However fast the ride up is, though, be prepared for long delays in summer because of the crowds. Although the attractions up top include a simulated helicopter ride, on gloomy days you might want to check whether it's worth making an ascent at all: a display in the foyer provides information on visibility. By the way, a tip if you are a theater lover: a TKTS office is located on the mezzanine level of Tower 2 *(see page 83)*.

The construction of the twin towers was a magnificent technical achievement. Because of the sheer height involved, the building had to be assembled from the inside out: cranes installed in the lift-shafts hoisted tons of steel, and gradually built the outer walls. The building's aesthetic value remains controversial, however, and critics accused design architect Minoru Yamasaki of creating too bare and massive a structure.

The complex known as ★**Battery Park City**, overlooking the Hudson River, owes its existence to the World

The World Trade Center

The observation deck is on the 107th floor

The Esplanade in Battery Park City

Trade Center – it was built on top of the landfill that remained after its construction. The new land became state property and construction work was carried out according to a harmonious urban plan.

The commercial center of the complex is the ★ **World Financial Center** , which is reached from the World Trade Center via a glass bridge (North Bridge). The four stocky towers containing offices have a remarkably cozy air to them in contrast to the Twin Towers of the World Trade Center, and design of the squares and shopping arcades is most attractive. The atmosphere here is pleasant, with music playing, and people strolling and dining; marble and brass fittings add a note of majesty, and palm trees in the Winter Garden, a public space with a vaulted glass ceiling, lend a tropical air. Creating space accessible to everyone was one of the main objectives of the city planners; 30 percent of the area covered by Battery Park City fulfills this stipulation. The Esplanade along the river's edge is one of the most popular features here; it leads north to eight-acre Rockefeller Park and south toward Battery Park itself, past landscaped gardens and views of the Statue of Liberty to the dramatic **Museum of Jewish Heritage – A Living Memorial to the Holocaust** (18 First Place, tel: 212-978 1800, closed Saturday).

South Bridge, the southern connection between the World Financial and World Trade centers, leads to Liberty Street. Beyond it is Broadway, which leads south to the **U.S. Realty Building** (115 Broadway), the **Trinity Building** (111 Broadway), both elegant skyscrapers dating from 1906, and the **Equitable Building**  opposite. This huge structure caused such a stir when built in 1915 that new zoning ordinances, designed to prevent city streets from becoming sunless canyons and leading to the introduction of stepped skyscrapers, were introduced a year later.

World Financial Center – a pleasant atmosphere

17

The Equitable Building

The diminutive Trinity Church

Trinity tomb

Some like it hot: Bowling Green

Once upon a time, church towers rather than huge office blocks dominated the landscape. Today, nestling between the many temples of wealth around it, the red-sandstone **Trinity Church 4** (Monday to Friday 9–11.45am, Saturday 10am–3.45pm, Sunday 11am– 3.45pm) is a relic of that era. The first church on this site was built in 1697 but burned down in 1776, the year of the Declaration of Independence, during which the British began their siege of New York. A second structure, built in 1790, was torn down in 1839 and replaced with the current newly scrubbed neo-Gothic example. The church interior is simple and unpretentious; the bronze doors were added in the 20th century. The churchyard dates from 1681, and contains the pyramid-shaped tomb of Alexander Hamilton, first secretary of the US Treasury.

Trinity Church marks the first stage of a journey back in time. Further south, where Broadway crosses Exchange Place, is the presumed site of the camp of the Dutch explorer Captain Adriaen Block and his crew, who arrived here in 1614, six years before the Pilgrims landed on Plymouth Rock. They didn't intend to stay, but their ship burned, forcing them to remain on Manhattan Island for the winter while they built a new seagoing vessel – appropriately named *Restless*.

The next Europeans to arrive were eager to stay. Dutch colonists settled on the island of *Mannahatta* – as the Indians called it – in 1624, and in 1626 Peter Minuit, director general of the Dutch Province of New Netherland, 'purchased' Manhattan from the Indians for 60 guilders ($24) worth of trinkets. This transaction is said to have taken place in the fenced pocket park now known as **Bowling Green 5**. In the early days of the city, Bowling Green was a market-place and also used for troop exercises; later, during the struggle for independence from Britain, it devel-

Bowling Green: bull statue

oped into a center of resistance. Tensions were so high in the 1770s that a statue of the English king, George III, erected on the green in 1770, had to be protected just one year later from the angry crowds by a fence. In 1776, after the adoption of the Declaration of Independence, the statue and parts of the fence fell victim to popular sentiment.

To the north of Bowling Green is the **Cunard Building** (25 Broadway), with its fine lobby. It was built in 1921 to house the headquarters of the Cunard shipping line and now includes a post office and the **New York City Police Museum**. The Standard Oil Building (28 Broadway) houses the **Museum of American Financial History**.

The southern side of the green is dominated by the **US Custom House ❻**, a fine Beaux-Arts building designed by the architect Cass Gilbert and completed in 1907. The sculptures representing Asia, America, Europe and Africa are by Daniel Chester French. Twelve statues along the sixth-floor cornice symbolize historical trading centers: Greece, Rome, Phoenicia, Genoa, Venice, Spain, Holland, Portugal, Denmark, Germany, England, and France. (Anti-German sentiment in 1917 caused the statue for Germany to be renamed 'Belgium'.) Today the building is home to the **George Gustav Heye Center of the National Museum of the American Indian** (open daily, admission free), housing a selection of Native American artwork and crafts with religious or social significance. Exhibits range from a symbolic circle of beaded moccasins to interactive 'discovery boxes' with mini-histories of tribal artifacts.

US Custom House

19

A fortress stood on the site of the Custom House for 150 years. It was built by the Dutch, but they could not muster enough men to defend it and in 1664 the town and its fortifications fell to the British without a fight. Fort James, or Fort George as it was later called, was used by the British until the adoption of the Declaration of Independence, when it was finally pulled down. A Government house was built on its site and a president was supposed to move into it – New York was the country's capital from 1785 to 1790. In 1811, when England and France were at war, fortified defenses seemed necessary once more: England was threatening the young US nation, hoping to deter it from trading with the French.

Just to the south (across State Street) is Battery Park, where another fortress was built: originally called the West Battery, today it's known as **Castle Clinton ❽** (after an early New York City mayor, not the president). In 1824, the original fort – which then stood a few meters offshore – was converted to a place of entertainment known as Castle Garden. In the first half of the 19th century concerts and festivals of all kinds were held here, but from 1885 Castle Garden was used as an immigrant processing center. However, in 1896 the popular New York Aquarium (now

War Memorial in Battery Park

All aboard for Liberty Island

Ms Liberty mementos

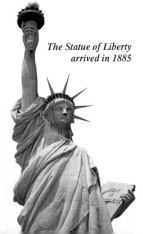

The Statue of Liberty arrived in 1885

located in Brooklyn) moved in. The old walls of the Castle were saved from demolition in the 1940s, and in 1950 the semi-circular fortress became a national monument.

Walk through Battery Park to **South Ferry ⓿**, where the ferries to both Ellis Island and **Liberty Island** dock. Tickets for both ferries are sold inside Castle Clinton, and the ferry to the latter runs daily between 8.30am and 4.30pm in summer (departures every 20 minutes) and between 9am and 3.45pm in winter (departures every 45 minutes). The ★★★ **Statue of Liberty** is even more popular since the celebration of its centenary in 1986. The ferry trip lasts 20 minutes, but there's waiting around once you get to the island: for the elevator inside that takes you half way up, and then for the flight of 168 steps leading to the crown (daily 9am–5.30pm, 5.15pm in winter; only passengers on the first boat or two are allowed admission to the very top).

The statue is 46m/151ft high, but its pedestal is nearly the same height; indeed, the history of the pedestal is perhaps even more interesting than that of the statue. *Liberty Enlightening the World* – was donated to America by the French as an expression of their admiration for the American Revolution, which they termed 'the completion of the French Revolution across the Atlantic.' The original proposal was made by the historian Edouard de Laboulaye; the sculptor responsible was Frédéric-Auguste Bartholdi; and Gustave Eiffel constructed the scaffolding inside.

Ms Liberty crossed the Atlantic in 200 packing cases, and arrived in New York Harbor in 1885. But there was a problem: the French had made it a condition that the New Yorkers build a suitable pedestal for their generous present. The fact that this was almost as expensive as the statue dampened the enthusiasm of many wealthy New Yorkers, who saw no point in paying indirectly for a present that had been forced on them.

Which explains why $100,000 for the pedestal were still missing when the crates containing the famous lady arrived in New York Harbor – until a man named Joseph Pulitzer saved the day. A prominent publisher (for whom the Pulitzer Prize is named), he organized a campaign for donations in his newspaper *The World*, promising that all benefactors would be mentioned by name. It was a clever move: within six months he had not only collected the required sum, but also significantly increased the circulation of his newspaper.

Liberty Enlightening the World was unveiled with much pomp on October 28, 1886. Then something strange happened. It may have had something to do with the site chosen for the statue – so exposed right out in the harbor, so high above the ocean and the masts of the ships – or perhaps the pose, with the arm outstretched as if in greeting. Whatever the reason, within just a few years the statue's original significance was forgotten and what the French saw as a symbol of Franco-American brotherhood was soon regarded as the incarnation of American freedom. *Liberty Enlightening the World* became the 'Mother of Exiles,' greeting all the immigrants with the words carved into a plaque at the entrance to her pedestal:

> 'Give me your tired, your poor,
> Your huddled masses yearning to breathe free,
> The wretched refuse of your teeming shore.
> Send these, the homeless, the tempest-tost to me,
> I lift my lamp beside the golden door!'

Over 16 million immigrants traveled through that open door between 1892 and 1954; the **Statue of Liberty Museum**, situated on the first floor of the pedestal, is dedicated to them.

The route taken by 12 million of the new arrivals first led them to ★★ **Ellis Island**, a small dot in the harbor where immigrants were asked embarrassing questions and searched. The 'tempest-tost' dreaded this humiliating inspection, for the reality of immigration was very different from the poetic promise. Laws, which were changed according to the current political situation and the number of immigrants arriving, barred the sick, the weak, the politically undesirable, the penniless, and even unmarried women from entering the land of the free. Those who failed the test were detained on the island and sent back on the next available ship – a cruel end to all those dreams of a bright new future.

Two thousand immigrants a day was no rarity in the record years of 1907 and 1914. And when one imagines what conditions must have been like in the Great Hall of the main building, the image of 'huddled masses yearning to breathe free' takes on new connotations. Restoration work was completed on the island's buildings in 1990, and the exhibits are as wrenching as they are fascinating.

Apart from the ferries to Liberty and Ellis islands, visitors should consider taking the **Staten Island Ferry** , which docks at the Whitehall Ferry Terminal at the eastern end of Battery Park. On its way to the borough of Staten Island *(see also page 75)* it crosses New York Harbor, providing superb ★★ **views** of the Statue of Liberty and the Manhattan skyline (there's a short wait at the other end before you reboard for the trip back to Manhattan).

From the ferry follow State Street north past the Shrine of Elizabeth Ann Seton (7 State Street), the first American-born saint, to **New York Unearthed** (17 State Street), a branch of the South Street Seaport Museum that special-

Ellis Island and the Great Hall

Manhattan from the ferry

Interior of Fraunces Tavern

Coenties Slip

Hanover Square statue

izes in urban archaeology. From here take Pearl Street to the intersection of Broad Street, and **Fraunces Tavern** ⓫, named after Samuel Fraunces who ran it from 1762. In 1776, Fraunces became George Washington's steward, and on December 4, 1783 the general returned here to bid farewell to his troops.

The present structure dates from 1907 and is an approximation of the original tavern, which was built in 1719. The museum on the upper storeys contains historical documents and period furniture, as well as items such as a lock of Washington's hair, a fragment of one of his teeth, and a shoe that belonged to his wife Martha. The ground floor restaurant is still a restaurant, frequented these days by bankers and stockbrokers working in the Financial District.

Before entering the world of Mammon, take a short detour east to the harbor and to **Coenties Slip**. A *slip* was an old docking bay for merchant ships, and several street-names still contain the word. Much of the southern tip of Manhattan was formerly water: the area east of Pearl Street is all reclaimed land. The ★ **Vietnam Veterans Memorial** ⓬, a 14-ft high monument erected by the city in 1985, now stands here at the foot of a brick amphitheater. Its simple wall of green glass is etched with excerpts from soldiers' letters – the senselessness of war and the desperation of those forced to take part has rarely been more eloquently conveyed.

The route now follows Water Street northwards and then bears left to attractive little **Hanover Square** ⓭, which derives its name from the time of the monarchy (George I was from the House of Hanover). While some wonder why its name wasn't changed under the young Republic, Hanover Square was a fine address, and in the course of the 18th century developed into the center of New York business. However, due to the Great Fire of 1835, which broke out on the corner of Hanover Square and Pearl Street and destroyed most of the area flanked by South, Broad and Wall Street, not a single original structure survives: over 600 buildings burned down during those three terrible winter days; the extreme cold made it almost impossible to extinguish the flames because the water froze in the hoses.

The finest buildings in Hanover Square are **India House**, which dates from the period of reconstruction, and **Delmonico's**, a long-time restaurant at 56 Beaver Street, dating from 1827. Built in Italianiate style between 1851 and 1854, India House originally served as a bank building and today houses a private club. But anyone can drop into the restaurant here, as well as **Harry's** on the ground floor. The latter is something of an institution in Wall Street banking and stockbroking circles: long before their minions have arrived at the office in the morning, Wall Street tycoons are already making decisions over 'power break-fasts' – and if you can get a table here or at nearby **Delmonico's** (56 Beaver Street) it's a good way of soaking up the legendary Wall Street atmosphere.

★ **Wall Street** is best observed at its most hectic time of day: shortly before 9am on weekdays. Limousines with tinted glass and smart young brokers talking on cell phones are everywhere. Thousands of them pour out of subways and vanish through the revolving doors of banks and office buildings – and then suddenly everything is quite still, and Wall Street seems almost deserted.

The street dates back to the early days of the city and is named after an earthen wall built to protect the Dutch settlement. When the English arrived in 1664 the wall was as effective a defense as the unmanned fort near Bowling Green. The conquerors pulled the wall down quite quickly after that, and the city spread northwards; a slave market was installed at the center of today's Financial District, and it later became a grain market.

The seeds of Wall Street's future fame were sown in 1792. Newly formed New York State was in severe financial difficulties as a result of the struggle for independence, and decided to issue bonds. To discuss conditions of trade, 24 brokers met beneath a buttonwood tree on Wall Street and founded the New York Stock Exchange. That same year they moved into the rooms of the Tontine Coffee House on the corner of Wall Street and Water Street, before building the Stock Exchange on today's site at 20 Broad Street. Wall Street remains a traditional locale for deal-clinching, though, and the sign-language used by today's brokers is supposed to date back to the time when partners in adjoining buildings had to be informed about buying and selling from the sidewalk below.

Wall Street wealth
The morning rush is over

23

A break from the floor

By the end of the 19th century, the industrial revolution had changed the face of the world, and some people had grown inordinately rich as a result of the American Civil War. Small businesses were *passé* and huge corporations began to form, most with a need for more money than they actually had at their disposal. The banks soon found the necessary capital and trade in securities reached record levels. Wall Street prospered. But on October 29, 1929, the day that came to be known as 'Black Friday', the bubble burst. The stock market dramatically collapsed, ushering in a global slump. Stories of bankrupt shareholders committing suicide by jumping out of skyscrapers went round the world.

Reports about corruption, artificially inflated share prices, and other semi-legal activities continue to provide Hollywood with much exciting material. Methods have changed on Wall Street in recent decades, though, and competition is tougher than ever: the real estate firms have become corporations now, and brokers' commissions can be freely negotiated.

Walking along Wall Street in the direction of Trinity Church, take a look inside the 19th-century lobby of the **Regent Wall Street** hotel at No 55. At No 23 is the **Morgan Guaranty Trust Company Building**. At the beginning of the 20th century, JP Morgan was the wealthiest and most influential banker in the world. The building was completed in 1914, and an anarchist's bomb went off outside it in 1920 – traces of the blast can still be seen on the walls.

Viewed from the outside, the ★ **New York Stock Exchange** ⑭ looks very much like a temple, with its huge pillars and elaborate frieze on the portico. It was built in 1903 and enlarged in 1923. Although there are plans afoot to move the Exchange to larger quarters, the entrance to

Stock Exchange messengers

Stock Exchange – the main floor

the Visitor Center is still at 20 Broad Street (Monday to Friday 9.15am–4pm); guards direct visitors to elevators that take them up to a gallery overlooking the main floor. Here, a number of interactive machines and displays attempt to shed some light on the feverish activities of the folks downstairs.

Opposite the New York Stock Exchange is **Federal Hall** ⓯ (Monday to Friday 9am–5pm), a magnificent neoclassical building on the corner of Wall Street and Nassau Street. The site was previously occupied by New York's old city hall, built around 1701 and the scene of a trial that became a milestone in the history of press freedom. In 1735, John Peter Zenger, publisher of the *New York Weekly Journal*, was arrested for libel after allowing the publication of several articles in his paper accusing British colonial governor William Cosby of corruption. To the delight of the general public, the colonial jury acquitted Zenger on the grounds that his charges were based on fact – a key consideration in libel cases since that time.

Another announcement – made on this site 41 years later – was just as unwelcome to the colonial government:

'We hold these truths to be self-evident, that all men are created equal, that they are endowed by their Creator with certain unalienable Rights, that among these are Life, Liberty and the pursuit of Happiness. That to secure these rights, Governments are instituted among Men, deriving their just powers from the consent of the governed. That whenever any Form of Government becomes destructive of these ends, it is the Right of the People to alter or to abolish it…'

Powerful words, which were translated into action 13 years before the French Revolution. They occur at the beginning of the Declaration of Independence that was approved and signed in Philadelphia on July 4, 1776 by the Second Continental Congress. The only colony that did not sign was New York, but this didn't prevent the rebels from reading out the document outside the old city hall 14 days later.

There was still a long way to go between declaring independence to creating a fully functioning state: a common constitution was finally agreed in 1787. In 1789, the first president was appointed: George Washington, whose statue stands outside Federal Hall. It was in his honor that the old city hall was renovated and had its name changed: for just over a year it served as the Capitol.

After New York had ceased to be the nation's capital, the old city hall fell into disrepair and was pulled down. Today's structure dates from 1842 and was originally the City Custom House. The museum inside is open weekdays, and serves as a reminder of the momentous events that took place here in the past.

The temple-like exterior

Federal Hall

Chase Manhattan Plaza

South Street Seaport

The historic ships – the big attraction at piers 15 and 16

On the other side of Federal Hall is Pine Street. Follow this, keeping to the right, and soon **Chase Manhattan Plaza** 16 comes into view, with its notable *Four Trees* sculpture by Jean Dubuffet. Cross the broad, windy square and then follow Nassau Street northwards. Liberty Street on the left (on the corner of Liberty Place) contains a marvelous Beaux Arts building dating from 1901, which housed the Chamber of Commerce of the State of New York until 1980.

The building that takes up the entire block between Maiden Lane, Nassau and Liberty is the **Federal Reserve Bank** 17. Its resemblance to the Palazzo Strozzi in Florence is intentional. Designed by architects York & Sawyer, it was completed in 1924, and its fortress-like appearance has a purpose: the building's underground vaults are rumoured to contain more gold than Fort Knox. The building's entrance lobby on Liberty Street is suitably impressive. (Tours are available on weekdays.)

Passing Louise Nevelson Plaza – named after the New York artist whose abstract sculptures it contains – the route now goes eastwards along Maiden Lane as far as Front Street. Keep left along it as far as Fulton Street and the ★ **South Street Seaport**. This area of the city is quite a mixture: it's a museum (with exhibitions on New York's maritime history, old ships, workshops, etc), a shopping center (with boutiques, gift shops, and galleries in the old houses, the Fulton Market Building, and the Pier 17 Pavilion), a starting-point for round harbor trips, a fine place to eat and a center of entertainment. A variety of open-air events are held here year-round.

New York owes its rise to prominence as a world capital to this port. It was here that overseas trade first began, and where the large sailing ships from all over the world used to dock. However, the arrival of the steamship in

the mid-19th century ushered in a period of steady decline, for there was more room for piers along the Hudson River. The area on the East Side thus fell into disrepair.

It was eventually awoken from its long sleep by a revitalization program, which was begun in 1967. An alliance was formed with commercial interests to underwrite restoration of the old harbor buildings and a growing collection of antique sailing vessels.

The area around South Street was always busy: the streets were bustling with seamen and traders; the brownstone houses along John, Fulton, Beekman, and Peck streets contained bars, brothels, and cheap boarding houses; markets were held in the squares; and chandlers, sailmakers, ropemakers and other craftsmen who relied on the harbor for their livelihood all had shops in the narrow houses here. Turning the place into a silent museum would not have done justice to the harbor atmosphere that existed in the 19th century.

The historic district of South Street Seaport is made up of 12 blocks of early 19th-century buildings and three piers. **Schermerhorn Row** , situated on the south side of Fulton Street, consists of a series of commercial buildings in the Georgian-Federal and Greek Revival style. The Museum Visitors Center, where maps and tickets for the museum and boat tours (as well as tours of the nearby Fulton Fish Market) can be obtained, is located at 12 Fulton Street. There is also a ticket office at Pier 16. The main attractions in this museum are the historic ships at Piers 15 and 16, which include the classic square-rigger *Wavertree* (1885), the four-masted *Peking* (1911) and the lightship *Ambrose* (1906).

Schermerhorn Row

The harbor trips organized by Circle Line Seaport cruises (tel: 212-630 8888) take an hour or so to go round the southern tip of Manhattan, with views of the Statue of Liberty, Ellis Island, the World Trade Center, and Battery Park.

From Pier 17, which is peppered with popular shops and restaurants, you can obtain an excellent view of the ★★ **Brooklyn Bridge.** This masterpiece of 19th-century bridge-building was designed by John Roebling. After his death during the first year of construction (he contracted tetanus after his foot was crushed by a docking ferry) his son Washington took over. Rising too fast from an underwater chamber, Washington suffered an attack of the bends and was wheelchair-bound from then on. Nevertheless, he and his wife oversaw the project to its conclusion, and the bridge was finally opened in May 1883. The best way to experience it is on foot; the entrance to the pedestrian walkway is located at the ends of Frankfort Street and Park Row, both of which are just a few blocks further north.

The Brooklyn Bridge

Route 2

World Trade Center – St Paul's Chapel – City Hall Park – Foley Square – Chinatown – Little Italy – Lower East Side

The area south of East Houston Street, on the Lower East Side, is another part of the city that deserves a full day to explore – if not longer. *See map, pages 14/15.*

The starting-point of this route is the ★★ **World Trade Center** again. There are two good reasons for this: first, it's the ideal subway stop and second, its two gigantic towers provide a fine contrast to **St Paul's Chapel ⑲**, on the corner of Broadway and Fulton Street. This is where the Old World meets the New: St Paul's is quintessentially European. Its architect, Thomas McBean, was probably a pupil of James Gibbs, who built St-Martin-in-the-Fields in London. The chapel was completed in 1766, and is authentic Georgian apart from the steeple, which was added 30 years later. It has two claims to fame: it is both the oldest church as well as the oldest civic building in Manhattan. George Washington worshipped here – his roped-off private pew in the north aisle is marked with a 'G.' The little churchyard in the back is an oasis of peace.

Vesey Street passes to the north of the square outside the church, and two buildings on it merit closer inspection: the **Garrison Building** (No 20), built in 1906, with its interesting triple facade, and the **New York County Lawyers' Association Building** (No 14), erected by Cass Gilbert in 1930. It is one of his less complex structures when compared with the US Custom House on Bowling Green *(see page 18)* and the **Woolworth Building ⑳**. This flamboyant 'Cathedral of Commerce,' which made Gilbert world famous, is a block further north on Broadway, between Barclay Street and Park Place, and in its day was considered by many to be the finest commercial building in the world. Frank Winfield Woolworth, the farm worker turned shop assistant and then retail entrepreneur, had this neo-Gothic temple built in honor of himself, his stores and his success story. By the time he died in 1919, his company controlled over 1,000 stores from its New York headquarters. The entrance hall with its mosaic ceiling contains statues of Gilbert and Woolworth, the former holding a model of the building, the latter counting coins.

With its 60 stories, the Woolworth Building had the additional distinction of being the tallest in the world (not counting the Eiffel Tower) for 18 years, from its construction in 1912 to 1930. Its 790ft (241m) were then superseded by the 1,043ft (318m) of the Chrysler Building *(see page 54)*, which was then dwarfed by the Empire

St Paul's Chapel

FW Woolworth counting coins and the exterior of his building

State Building (1,250ft/381m, *see page 45*) just one year later. At this stage it was clear how the focal point of the business world had shifted within the city, from downtown to midtown.

City Hall Park

29

In the 18th century, when only the southern tip of Manhattan island was inhabited, the area between Broadway, Park Row and Chambers Street, known today as **City Hall Park** , was a common. 'Commons' and 'greens' were an English export, and are still found at the center of most New England villages. The open area of lawn was used as grazing land or for military exercises and meetings. Public buildings such as prisons and almshouses were also situated here, as were the gallows.

When New York began to expand northwards in the early 19th century, and its inhabitants needed a new town hall – the third in just 170 years – they chose the common as a construction site. The architects' competition for the new **City Hall** was won by Joseph F Mangin and John McComb, a Frenchman and a Scotsman, and each added elements from their respective homelands: the building is a mixture of French Renaissance and English Georgian. It was opened in 1812, with a fine marble facade to the south and ordinary-looking brownstone (for reasons of economy) to the north. This magnificent building was threatened with closure and demolition on several occasions during its history. In 1956 the decision was finally made to thoroughly restore it and thus preserve one of the finest historic structures in the US. The original marble facade was refaced with Alabama sandstone.

City Hall was opened in 1812

Behind it stands the former New York County Courthouse , dubbed the **Tweed Courthouse** on its completion in 1878 after the scandalous revelation that 'Boss' Tweed, the fraudster and Democratic party boss who died that same year, had lined his own pockets with around $9 million of its final cost.

Hall of Records: facade detail

Fire station at the junction of Centre and White streets

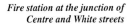

Between Chambers and Reade streets, the former **AT Stewart & Co. dry-goods store ㉓** at 260 Broadway was the city's largest emporium when it opened in 1846. In 1884, it was converted to offices, and in 1919, the old *New York Sun* moved in (the bronze clock dates from the paper's heyday). Home to various agencies, it now houses the headquarters of the city's Building Department.

The building with the twin towers, next door, was built for a bank in 1908. Today it is civic property, as is the **Hall of Records ㉔**, which was completed in 1911 and is one of the finest Beaux Arts buildings in New York. The facade, dominated by eight Corinthian columns, and several sculpture groups and statues, hides a rather sober interior: the building also contains the Surrogate's Court.

At the eastern end of Chambers Street is the **Municipal Building ㉕**, which dates from 1914. Despite the massive size of this structure, the team of architects who designed it – McKim, Mead, and White – managed to fashion an impressive contrast to City Hall.

Chambers Street disappears under the Municipal Building and ends up beyond it in Police Plaza – named after Police Headquarters, which is situated to the east of it. Park Row, formerly known as 'Newspaper Row,' connects here from the south: between 1840 and around 1900 this street contained the headquarters of every major paper in the city. Northwards up Centre Street is **Foley Square ㉖**. The row of administrative and judicial buildings belonging to the Civic Center continues here, with the two modern structures making up the **Jacob K Javits Federal Building** (1967 and 1976), the **New York County Courthouse** (1926), and the **US Courthouse** (1936). Other buildings along Centre Street include the New York City Department of Health and the nondescript Civil Courthouse – in short, government and administration buildings everywhere you look. From the lower end of Foley Square, it's worth making a detour to the corner of Duane and Elk Streets, where the **African Burial Ground** memorial commemorates Colonial-era slaves, whose graves were discovered during excavation of an adjacent Federal office building.

Centre Street continues north to White Street, where a right loop takes you to Baxter Street. From here, turn down Bayard Street and you're in another world. The telephone booths have pagoda roofs, the shop signs are all written in Chinese, and shopkeepers can be seen carrying crates and boxes full of exotic vegetables and spices. Red ducks dangle from shop windows, and a few steps further on shops sell satin shoes, jade, kimonos, kites, and cricket cages. This is New York's famous ★★ **Chinatown**. It has been estimated that this section of the city is home to about 150,000 people, and the population is increas-

ing all the time, with most residents coming from Taiwan and Hong Kong. Chinatown has now spread well beyond its original borders of Bowery, Baxter, Canal, and Worth streets and gradually made inroads into neighboring Little Italy and the Lower East Side.

Life in Chinatown is a rule unto itself. The overladen fruit-and-vegetable stalls, the broken English. The towers of the World Trade Center in the distance are the only reminders that that this is actually still New York and not Taipei or Hong Kong. A good way to learn more about this vibrant neighborhood is to stop by the **Museum of Chinese in the Americas**, at the corner of Bayard and Mulberry streets (70 Mulberry Street, 2nd floor, open Tuesday to Saturday), which has exhibits on local history and art.

Assuming there isn't a festival on – Chinese New Year, for instance, held in February – New Yorkers generally visit Chinatown to eat. There are hundreds of small, unpretentious restaurants here, all serving up magnificent delicacies. More often than not they are cramped, noisy and a bit shabby, and tables can't usually be reserved: sometimes lines form outside the most popular establishments on Saturdays and Sunday mornings, when the New Yorkers make their weekend pilgrimages here for a delicious *dim-sum* brunch. (*Dim-sum* is a collection of tasty steamed delicacies wheeled through the restaurant on a trolley; diners take as much as they like, and pay according to the number and type of plates they choose.) Some of the most popular spots include: **Nice Restaurant** (35 East Broadway), **Hee Seung Fung** (46 Bowery), and **New Silver Palace** (52 Bowery). As far as the other restaurants are concerned, each New Yorker has his or her favorite, and it's best to try them out yourself.

For coffee or dessert take a short walk across Canal Street back to Europe: ★ **Little Italy** has a fine selection of typical Italian food and espresso – but can be rather

A winning hand
The bustle of Chinatown

Mulberry Street in Little Italy

Welcoming staff

Pizza and pasta delights

on the expensive side. A slice of cake in Little Italy can often cost as much as a full meal in Chinatown. **Mulberry Street** is lined with restaurants, cafes, delicatessens and small houses with zigzag fire escapes, which give the neighborhood a certain European flair.

In mid-September, when Mulberry Street is decked out in honor of the Feast of San Gennaro, Little Italy turns into a huge block party, with food stalls, processions, and thousands of people. Along with the equally boisterous Feast of St Anthony in June, it's a New York experience not to be missed.

The former **NYC Police Headquarters** **27**, a 1909 French Renaissance-style palace, which takes up the entire block between Grand, Centre, and Broome streets, has been converted into million-dollar apartments, a reminder that as Chinatown spreads north and east, the well-heeled populace of SoHo keeps marching south. Beyond **Old St Patrick's Cathedral**, on the corner of Mott and Prince Street, a blossoming of new shops and restaurants – especially along Elizabeth Street – has transformed a once-traditional Italian neighborhood into a trendy acronym known as **NoLita** – for 'North of Little Italy.'

A few blocks further east is the **Bowery**, one of New York's most notorious byways – if Fifth Avenue is synonymous with wealth and success then the Bowery has been associated for decades with social deprivation and alcoholism. The street was famous for vagrants, bars, and cheap boarding houses – and as recently as the 1950s there were four or five down-and-out bars per block. Today, it's still pretty seedy, with a few notable cultural exceptions – including **CBGB** (315 Bowery), the club where punk started in the US. Other local landmarks include the tiny, family-run **Amato Opera House**, at the corner of 2nd Street, and the **Bouwerie Lane Theater**, a surviving relic of the era when this was a thriving theater center.

The Bouwerie Lane Theatre

Before it went into decline at the end of the 19th century in fact, the Bowery was a very fine street. The Dutch governor Peter Stuyvesant used it as an approach road for his country estate of *Bouwerij*, and anyone headed northwards toward Boston would gallop along it. In the second half of the 19th century the street developed a slight notoriety as an entertainment district, with German beer halls, theaters, and music halls.

Starting in the mid-19th century, successive waves of immigrants came to the New World, and many of them lived in the **Lower East Side** between the Bowery and the East River. Unlike the Irish, who were driven by famine, the German immigrants who settled in what became known as 'Little Germany' were mostly middle class and had emigrated for predominately political reasons, with thousands forced into exile by the failure of the German Revolution of 1848. From 1880, however, the community began moving northward to the former village of Yorkville (on today's Upper East Side), At the same time, spurred by the pogroms that followed the assassination of Tsar Alexander II in 1881, there was a massive new influx of immigrants, as Russian and Eastern European Jews began arriving in unprecedented numbers.

33

It was the latter, more than any other group, that shaped the character of neighborhood that stretched below East Houston Street to Delancey Street. Of more than 2 million Jewish immigrants who eventually came to the US, in fact, over 500,000 settled here. Grand Street, between Broadway and Essex Street, was the main shopping street in the city at that time, and textile wholesalers and suppliers had their warehouses along Canal Street. The area filled with garment trade sweatshops, kosher restaurants, and synagogues, and by 1900 the Lower East Side had become the most densely populated urban area in the world.

This was the new world ghetto, where the 'needle trade' was the cornerstone of the economy. Tenement rooms were often cluttered with piles of half-sewn clothes on the floor. Payment was made on a piecework basis. The working conditions were appalling and the wages pitiful. Those who didn't enter the needle trade often worked as peddlers or pushcart vendors, selling produce or cheap clothing in the markets on Hester Street and Orchard Street.

As the people of the Lower East Side painfully ground out a living, the area's substandard living conditions spawned various immigrant and labor rights movements. Emma Goldman preached her gentle anarchism here, socialist newspapers, such as the *Jewish Daily Forward*, flourished, and settlement houses that offered immigrants assistance with health and education were formed.

Today, the landmark building at 173 East Broadway where the *Daily Forward* was published has been converted to exclusive apartments (although the faces of Karl Marx and Friedrich Engels still peer from a frieze over the entrance). Other signs of change can be seen in stores with Jewish names but Chinese or Hispanic owners, and in the Bohemian bars, clubs, and boutiques along Ludlow and even Orchard Street. But the neighborhood retains the flavor of its early immigrant roots in classic Jewish restaurants such as **Katz's Delicatessen** (205 East Houston St) and **Ratner's** (138 Delancey Street), as well as at **Schapiro's** (126 Rivington St), a kosher winery that offers tastings on Sundays, and **Guss's** (35 Essex St), where fresh pickles are still sold out of a barrel.

★ **Orchard Street**, meanwhile, still gives an impression of what it must have been like to live here in those early days: tiny cramped shops heaped with clothes; amazing discounts that become even more attractive after a bit of haggling. (Note that many shop-owners are Orthodox and close their businesses on Friday afternoon and all day Saturday).

You can also experience the neighborhood the way it used to be by dropping into the **Lower East Side Tenement Museum** (90 Orchard Street, tel: 431 0233, closed Monday), which is centered around an almost perfectly 'preserved' 1863 tenement building. Cramped apartments from different eras of immigration have been recreated in all their bleakness, and there's a gallery with changing exhibits as well as hour-long walking tours sometimes led by guides in period costumes.

Orchard Street sign

Lower East Side Tenement Museum

Orchard Street Sunday Market

Route 3

TriBeCa – SoHo – Greenwich Village – East Village – Gramercy Park – Madison Square Park

It is best to allow two days for this route.

One of the most common criticisms of New Yorkers is that they never have any time for anything. They don't walk anywhere, they run. And they have no time to speak in complete words, let alone complete sentences: thus

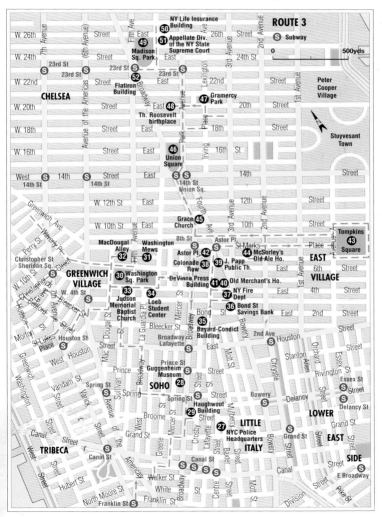

*TriBeCa: many warehouses
are now galleries*

SoHo: center for the avant-garde

Bloomingdale's becomes *Bloomie's,* Long Island becomes *the Island*, the area south of Houston Street is *SoHo*, and the triangular area below Canal Street is known familiarly as *TriBeCa*.

TriBeCa begins below Canal Street's western end and can be reached most easily via subway (get off at Franklin Street). In terms of geography, social make-up and origins, TriBeCa is an extension of **SoHo**. In the late 1960s, artists moved into the old houses and warehouses; it was they who saved the area south of Houston (pronounced HOW-ston rather than HEWston) from falling into decay. Gallery owners, painters and musicians suddenly realized that the spacious halls here were ideal for their purposes. Artists' studios could be set up with ease, and the rents were lower than those in Greenwich Village, the classic New York arty area. The first gallery was opened in SoHo in 1968, a second one followed a year later, and in 1971 four major gallery owners from uptown moved into the neighborhood. Restaurants followed, and real estate agents weren't far behind. Young artists who hadn't already made it had to move on. Then they discovered TriBeCa – and the whole procedure began again.

In the late 1990s the cycle turned yet again, with several important galleries moving from SoHo to Chelsea and artists forced to seek cheaper rents across the river in Brooklyn. TriBeCa, meanwhile, has become famous for the culinary arts and boasts some of the city's most expensive restaurants, including **Montrachet** (239 West Broadway) and **Chanterelle** (2 Hudson Street). In another sign of the times, the **Clocktower Gallery** (108 Leonard Street), a landmark artist's space at the top of the former New York Life Insurance Building, is rarely open to the public although the nearby **Knitting Factory** (74 Leonard Street) remains one of New York's best venues for avant-garde music.

SoHo's reputation as a mecca of the city's artistic culture has been tempered by its transformation into a shopping mecca, with stylish new boutiques, restaurants, and hotels adding to the dizzying array of things to see and do. There is still plenty of art to admire, though, with a branch of the **Guggenheim Museum ㉘** at 575 Broadway, along with the **New Museum of Contemporary Art** (583 Broadway) and the **Museum for African Art** (593 Broadway), as well as much noteworthy architecture. Between West Houston and Canal, West Broadway, and Crosby Street lies the ★ **SoHo Cast Iron District**. A favored material for 19th-century bridge and railway station construction, since large areas could be covered by prefabricated parts, cast iron was soon used for factories and warehouses. The material had another advantage: it was virtually fireproof, something much valued by New Yorkers due to the major conflagrations of 1835 and 1845.

Portrait painter

During the first half of the 19th century the area south of Houston Street was a busy business and residential quarter, particularly popular with New York's middle classes. There were theaters and places of entertainment; elegant hotels and large stores such as Lord & Taylor and Tiffany's lined lower Broadway, which around 1850 gradually started to supplant the Bowery as the city's most important entertainment district.

After the Civil War (1861–5) the neighborhood's character changed. The shops moved northwards, many people left, and industry moved in instead. Because it was much quicker to construct buildings with cast iron than with, say, stone, factories, warehouses, and workshops all sprang up virtually overnight. The aesthetic results of cast iron can be admired on the **Haughwout Building** ㉙, erected in 1857 on the corner of Broadway and Broome Street, and considered by many to be the finest example of American cast-iron architecture. The architect, John P Gaynor, gave it a Venetian-style exterior complete with Palladian arches; the building also contained the city's first-ever steam-powered passenger elevator.

The cast-iron construction boom vanished as quickly as it came: the development of steel skeleton construction *circa* 1890 meant that skyscrapers could now be built, and cast iron became a thing of the past. In the previous 30 years, however, New York had set a world record for the largest number of buildings with cast-iron facades. In the 1970s, many of these structures would have disappeared for good were it not for those New Yorkers who successfully protested against plans to raze of much of the area to make way for a highway.

Those who don't mind crowds, and like to be where the action is, should definitely visit SoHo on a Saturday, when the galleries are open and the streets are packed with locals and visitors. They all meet up in restaurants and cafes,

Controversial sculpture

Washington Square Park

A desirable address: the north side of the square

after indulging in some serious shopping, and dine out late. The area doesn't start to get busy until 10am or so, but activities continue very late into the night.

Another paradise for night-owls is ★★ **Greenwich Village**, easily reached from SoHo via Sullivan Street, which comes out into **Washington Square Park** ⏚. On sunny days and balmy summer evenings it seems as if all the colorful life of the Village is concentrated here: folk-singers strum guitars; students rollerskate and skateboard; esoteric street performers do their stuff. This little park was a center of the hippie movement in the late 1960s: the first ever 'smoke-in' took place here.

During its history, Washington Square has been used for almost every conceivable activity. Originally a potter's field, where the poor and unknown were buried, it later became a field of honor, a place of execution and a parade-ground. The first houses were built during the 1820s, and Washington Square soon became a desirable address. Several of these fine houses can still be seen along the north side of the square, where Fifth Avenue begins, and there is also an interesting view down **Washington Mews** ⏛, a small cobbled street of row houses where the wealthy used to keep their horses stabled, and which are now highly sought-after residences.

A counterpart to the mews, accessible from Washington Square West, is **MacDougal Alley** ⏜. Here too, former stables have been turned into attractive residential buildings. The 85ft (26m) high **memorial arch** dominating the square was originally planned as a temporary addition: the first version was made of wood, and stood here between 1889 and 1892 in commemoration of the centenary of the election of George Washington as the first president of the US. After the celebration no-one wanted to part with it, so Stanford White was commissioned to build a white marble version of the arch.

The southern side of the square is dominated by the **Judson Memorial Baptist Church and Tower** ⏝. Both the church and its tower were also designed by Stanford White in Italian Renaissance style, and completed in 1892 by White's firm of McKim, Mead, and White. Today the tower is used by New York University (NYU), the main building of which is situated on the southeastern corner of Washington Square Park.

Further east, the **Loeb Student Center** ⏞ on the corner of La Guardia Place is also part of NYU. It was built in 1948 on the site of Marie Branchard's boarding house, an institution known as the 'house of genius' because of her illustrious guests, including writers Eugene O'Neill, Theodore Dreiser and Stephen Crane. The studio of painter John Sloan, a member of the group known as The Eight *(see page 52)*, was situated a few houses further on.

A village of genius

In fact it's one big 'village of genius'. Since the Art Nouveau period, Greenwich Village has been the home of the artistic avant-garde. The radical paper *Masses*, whose contributors included Maxim Gorki, Bertrand Russell, and John Reed, had its offices here. In 1914, Gertrude Vanderbilt Whitney opened a gallery and provided a platform for contemporary artists, much of whose work was highly controversial. In 1916, members of the Playwrights' Theater settled on MacDougal Street and very soon achieved fame – Eugene O'Neill among them.

39

After World War II the Bohemian image of 'the Village' persisted. In the 1950s, the beatnik movement flowered (Jack Kerouac and Allen Ginsberg); in the 1960s and early '70s the area was home to hippies and anti-Vietnam war activists (Abbie Hoffman and Jerry Rubin). Christopher Street, on the other side of Sixth Avenue, became the center of the New York gay community. And suddenly the Village was chic – and expensive. The artists and activists moved out, the smart boutiques moved in. This is most evident on **Bleecker** and **MacDougal Streets**, with their rows of restaurants, cafés – some of which are very attractive – gift shops and souvenir stores.

Gay Pride on Christopher Street

Beyond Sixth Avenue, the Village is less commercialized. A stroll through Waverly Place, Grove Street, Bedford Street, or St Luke's Place – to name but a few of the loveliest byways – is a good introduction to the truly village-like character of this part of the city. It's almost like being in Europe: low houses, almost all of them 19th-century, with rooftiles, pretty portals, leafy front gardens and plenty of trees. Unlike SoHo, where the streets are laid out more or less in grid-form, the streets in this part of the Village take the same twisty routes that they followed in the 18th century, when the bucolic village of Greenwich – as it was then known – was a popular summer refuge for colonial New Yorkers.

Funky McDougal Street

Shops for all tastes

Neo-Romanesque building at 376–383 Lafayette Street

Skidmore House: early 19th-century architecture

To discover the East Village, go back to Washington Square. From here, Washington Place leads to a stretch of Broadway (just north of the museums mentioned on *page 36*) that's part of 'NoHo', a rather undefined area **north** of **Houston**.

Once just a dingy pause before SoHo, today this part of Broadway is crammed with stores selling everything from crazy toys and souvenirs to jeans and housewares. **Tower Records** has a huge selection of music at 692 Broadway. A few blocks further north, at the corner of 12th Street, the **Strand Bookstore** is one of the last survivors of what was once known as 'Booksellers' Row,' offering 'eight miles' of used books.

Those interested in architecture and history should go via Bleecker Street to Lafayette Street: At No 65 Bleecker Street is the **Bayard-Condict Building** ❸ (1897–9), the only work of Louis H Sullivan in New York. Sullivan worked predominantly in Chicago. He was a major exponent of the Chicago School, whose members became famous for the construction of the earliest skyscrapers; he also taught Frank Lloyd Wright. The six angels adorning the facade are not quite in keeping with the remainder – Sullivan was apparently forced to add them against his better judgment.

The former **Bond Street Savings Bank** ❸ on the corner of Bond Street and the Bowery is worth a short detour south; it is a fine example of cast-iron architecture dating from 1874. Note too the former headquarters of the **New York Fire Department** ❸ at 44 Great Jones Street, built in the Beaux-Arts style in 1898; and also the imposing neo-Romanesque structure at **376–383 Lafayette Street** (corner of Great Jones Street); it was built in 1888 by architect Henry J Hardenbergh, famous for designing the Plaza Hotel and the Dakota Building *(see pages 58 and 69)*.

Great Jones Street formerly connected with **Lafayette Place**, the precursor of today's Lafayette Street, which looked very different during the first half of the 19th century from how it appears today. It was a tree-lined cul-de-sac, and home to wealthy residents such as Jacob Astor and Cornelius Vanderbilt. They lived in **Colonnade Row** ❸, which consisted of nine mansions and owes its name to their impressive colonnaded porticoes. Four of these buildings, which were erected in 1833, can still be admired today along the western side of Lafayette Street.

On the opposite side of the street is the **Joseph Papp Public Theater** ❸, originally the Astor Library, and named after the late founder of the New York Shakespeare Festival. Around the corner, the **Merchant's House Museum** ❹ (29 East 4th Street, open Thursday to Monday 1–5pm) is located in an 1832 Greek Revival-style townhouse that was home to same family for generations,

The Old Merchant's House is a museum

and remains eerily intact. At the junction of 4th Street and Lafayette, the **DeVinne Press Building** was erected in 1885, and is a reminder of a time when the area around Lafayette Street was the center of the city's print trade.

Astor Place 42 angles east from Broadway to Third Avenue and contains two other things definitely worth seeing: the first – above ground – is the **kiosk** at the subway entrance, a copy of the cast-iron original, and the second is the restored subway station itself. The ceramic tiles on the walls display beavers – a clue to how the Astor family became so wealthy. It all began when the 20-year-old John Jacob Astor emigrated from Germany to the US in 1783. His career was a rags-to-riches story, though the rags in his case involved working in a fur shop. He worked his way up the ladder so quickly that he managed to open his own store within three years. Soon he was the most important fur dealer in the US, and by the year 1800 had amassed a fortune of roughly $250,000, which he increased still further by investing in trade with Asia and in the New York property market. Branches of his firm sold furs across the entire continent. When he died in 1848 he was the richest man in America, and left behind a fortune of $20 million.

From here walk down St Mark's Place, one of the city's liveliest thoroughfares, crammed with clubs, restaurants, boutiques, and street peddlers. Geographically and historically, the **East Village** is part of the Lower East Side *(see page 33)*. The German names on some of the buildings are a reminder that this once used to be part of 'Little Germany' during the 19th century. It had its heyday at the beginning of the 1870s. **Tompkins Square** 43, further east, was the heart of the neighborhood. Avenue B, the commercial artery, was nicknamed 'German Broadway'. The basements contained workshops, the ground floors were shops, and goods were even sold outside on

41

Cast-iron kiosk at Astor Place

'Strength in unity' – remnant of Little Germany

the sidewalks. There were beer halls, oyster saloons, and grocery stores all along the avenue.

The area around Tompkins Square shared the fate of the Lower East Side. After the German community had moved away, other nationalities moved in: Russian Jews, Ukrainians, and, later, Puerto Ricans to name but a few. They all came to the New World seeking a better life, but found living conditions were squalid to say the least: whole families had to make do with one dark room without a lavatory. In the summer they suffered from the intense heat, and in winter they had to use coin-operated gas-heaters in order to keep warm.

The Lower East Side became increasingly impoverished as the 20th century progressed. In the decades that followed World War II no self-respecting person ventured further than First Avenue, which now formed a sort of demarcation line: the world of vice and the 'golden triangle' of the drug-dealers lay beyond it, in the ABC avenues and the streets around Tompkins Square. The fact that today you can poke around whimsical boutiques and eat soya bean salads and other hearty fare in local cafés is not just because the police stormed the center of the drug trade years ago. The area was most radically transformed by the young artists and musicians who found SoHo too expensive and moved here because rents were considerably cheaper than elsewhere.

Unfortunately the East Village is undergoing the same transformation as SoHo, TriBeCa, and the West Village: artists followed by galleries followed by restaurants followed by property dealers. Already, rents around the recently restored Tompkins Square Park go at prices quite unaffordable for young artists.

The clubs and performance spaces that made the East Village so popular still exist, though things really only get

Street talk

A true survivor

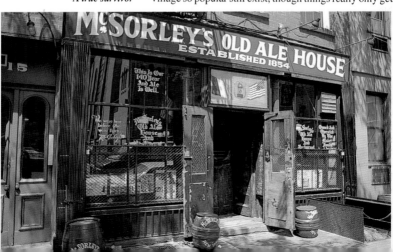

going after 10pm. During the daytime the best policy is simply to stroll through the streets, pausing at places like **McSorley's Old Ale House** back on the corner of 7th Street and Third Avenue, which dates from 1854 and successfully survived the decline of the area. A true drinking man's pub where women didn't break the sex barrier until 1970, it was one of Irish playwright Brendan Behan's favorite hangouts.

Between 8th and 9th Street on Broadway is where AT Stewart *(see page 30)* built his second department store in 1862; it took up an entire block and marked the start of Ladies' Mile, which extended as far as 23rd Street and owed its name to the fact that most of the customers patronizing the many department stores here were female. Carry on along Broadway, passing **Grace Church** , one of the city's loveliest ecclesiastical structures. Built in 1846, its exterior white marble, now a muted grey, was mined by convicts at infamous Sing Sing prison in upstate New York.

Grace Church

Continue as far as **Union Square** . A fashionable area in the mid-19th century, until recently this square had deteriorated and become a hangout for vagrants. Today it bustles with life, thanks partly to the **Greenmarket** that brings upstate farmers to the northern edge of the square four days a week. While there are similar markets elsewhere in the city, this is the pick of the bunch – and a great place to walk around on a Saturday morning. An outdoor café operates in warm weather, and there are several restaurants nearby, including the highly rated Union Square Café *(see page 87)*.

43

Fresh greens on Union Square

At the northeastern corner of Union Square, Park Avenue begins: follow it only briefly before turning right into 18th Street and then immediately left again into Irving Place. The block between Irving Place, Third Avenue, 18th Street, and Gramercy Park South is known as 'Block Beautiful.' Its architects were strongly influenced by Paris and London. This is also true of **Gramercy Park** , situated between 20th and 21st streets. It was established in the 1830s by a wealthy lawyer named Samuel Ruggles along the lines of a London square; the pretty brick houses surrounding it – some with fancy iron balconies – were and still are inhabited by wealthy intellectuals and successful artists. Unfortunately for visitors, like many of its European counterparts the well-maintained park itself is open only to local residents (who have keys to the wrought-iron gate).

Gramercy Park

Just around the corner on 20th Street, at No 28, is the house where US president **Theodore Roosevelt** was born (now a museum run by the National Park Service). Another landmark worth admiring is the National Arts Club (15 Gramercy Park South), built as a private home in 1884.

Since 1888, the magnificent building next to it has housed the **Players' Club**, a famous meeting-place for actors and theater people.

There's still a tradition of entertainment in this neighborhood, as evidenced a few streets further north by **Madison Square Park** ㊾, which lies between Fifth and Madison avenues, from 23rd to 26th Street. Just to the north is the site of the original Madison Square Garden. There are in fact two gardens – the first one was designed by the celebrated architect Stanford White in 1890; it was a palace, complete with theater, concert hall, roof-garden, restaurant, café, and the second-highest tower in the city at that time. Another version was built further north, but was torn down in 1924, more than 20 years before Madison Square Garden moved to its present locale *(see page 48)*.

Into the hands of justice

Today the first original site is home to the **New York Life Insurance Building** ㊿, the work of Cass Gilbert who also designed the Woolworth Building *(see page 28)*. Designed in a mixture of styles, it was completed between 1926 and 1928. The lobby is particularly worth seeing. Along the park's eastern edge is a building that looks like a Greek temple but is actually the **Appellate Division of the New York State Supreme Court** (51), and was built between 1896 and 1900. The statues adorning the building indicate its function: Justice can be seen, as can Moses, Solomon, Justinian, and Confucius.

Somewhat further south is a tower that looks best after dark. It is part of the complex of buildings belonging to the Metropolitan Life Insurance Company, and was modeled by the architect Napoleon le Brun after the Campanile of St Mark's in Venice. Built in 1893 (and added to in 1909, 1932 and 1964), it's never been as eyecatching as its neighbor to the south, the **Flatiron Building** (52). Originally called the Fuller Building, this triangular skyscraper really does resemble an iron when observed from the corner of Fifth Avenue and Broadway.

The Flatiron Building

What really caused a stir when it was erected in 1902 though was not the building's appearance so much as its extraordinary height: 250ft (76m). People on the ground were convinced it would collapse if stormy weather broke out, but thanks to the new 'steel skeleton' construction methods of the day, the Flatiron Building is still standing today. The new construction technique came from Chicago, as did the architect of the Flatiron, Daniel H Burnham. The erection of the Flatiron Building ushered in the skyscraper age, which radically changed the face of New York City over the next few decades.

Reflecting the area's trendy reputation in media circles, the neighborhood is colloquially known as 'SoFi,' which stands for 'South of Flatiron.'

Route 4

Empire State panorama

The Empire State Building – Garment District – Times Square – Rockefeller Center – Museum of Modern Art

This route through midtown Manhattan needs one or two days to complete. *See map, page 46/7.*

The route starts in a famous building on the corner of Fifth Avenue and 34th Street. The souvenir shop on the 86th floor sells giant plastic gorillas made in Taiwan: yes, it's King Kong, swatting at bi-planes from the top of the ★★★ **Empire State Building** ⑤. When the film *King Kong* was shot in 1933, this was the obvious building to choose for its grand finale: the Empire State Building was just two years old and considered to be the eighth wonder of the world. At 1,250ft (381m) it was the tallest building on earth, and was only outdone by the World Trade Center in 1973. No less wondrous was the speed at which the Empire State was constructed: the whole thing took about a year and a half. Its 6,500 windows need to be washed twice every month, and there are 73 elevators.

The lobby is superb: three stories high, faced with marble and decorated with bas-relief. There's more than enough time to admire it because the lines for the elevators tend to be very long indeed. The view from the top is worth the wait, however: the 86th floor has a glass-enclosed area and an outdoor promenade, while the observatory on the 102nd floor is completely enclosed (the viewing terraces are open till midnight; tickets are on sale until 11.25pm). Manhattan by night – or at dusk, when the lights start coming on – is particularly memorable.

The route now continues westwards along 34th Street as far as the **Garment District**. This area extends roughly

Going up

A stitch in time

from 30th Street to 40th Street, and from Sixth to Eighth Avenue. The garment trade, originally located on the Lower East Side *(see page 42)*, shifted north at the beginning of the 20th century. In the traditional immigrant sweatshops, mostly dingy, windowless cellars, tailors and seamstresses slaved long hours for miserable wages. The move northwards brought an improvement in work conditions, less because of the new location than because the first trade unions had recently been formed, and were growing increasingly powerful. Work conditions in the

Moving carpets

clothing industry were still an affront to human dignity, however, and it was only after 146 young women, mostly immigrants had lost their lives in a Greenwich Village fire at the Triangle Shirtwaist Company in 1911 that strikes and mass protests finally brought about an improvement.

While the Garment District still produces a great deal of the country's wearing apparel, many buildings here are being converted for use by mostly new-media companies. But the weekday atmosphere in the streets around Seventh Avenue – the main commercial artery through the Gar-

General Post Office

Macy's

ment District, and known locally as 'Fashion Avenue' – is still hectic. Trucks block the streets, and pushcarts and clothing rails laden with skirts, coats, and blouses clutter the sidewalks.

In the southern part of the Garment District, the previously uninspiring **Pennsylvania Station** 🞢, which replaced a grand, early 20th-century railway station in 1968, is currently being transformed. **Madison Square Garden**, world famous as a venue for sporting events and concerts (*see also page 44*), remains on the modern building's flat roof, but an ambitious renovation project encompassing the **General Post Office** 🞣, across Eighth Avenue at 33rd Street, provides a majestic new portal for visitors arriving by train. Like the Penn Station, the 1913 post office building was designed by McKim, Mead and White.

The area further west although the **Chelsea Piers** complex, which stretches south from 23rd Street along the Hudson River, features a multitude of fitness and sports activities – from a golf driving range to ice-skating and even horseback riding – plus a marina and restaurants.

Further north, there's the **Intrepid Sea-Air-Space Museum** situated at Pier 86 on West 46th Street, which is centered around the *USS Intrepid*, a converted World War II aircraft carrier. And the enormous **Jacob K Javits Convention** Center, which opened in 1986 and was designed by the firm of IM Pei & Partners, sprawls along Twelfth Avenue from 38th Street back down to 34th Street. The 165ft (50m) high Crystal Palace lobby is particularly impressive.

From here it's back to the junction of Broadway and Sixth Avenue, and into the world of consumption. Here, at Herald Square, stands **Macy's** 🞥, which claims to be the biggest department store in the world. It's worth a stroll across the ground floor just to take in the huge selection of goods.

Macy's was built on the site of a former opera house where, in a major mid-19th century scandal: Mrs William H Vanderbilt, whose husband's fortune was estimated at $94 million, was denied the use of a paid box at the opera, since the opera house was firmly in the hands of old-established New Yorkers who wanted to have nothing to do with *parvenus* such as the Astors and Vanderbilts. Her indignation did not last long, however: 65 millionaires joined forces, and built their own opera house on the corner of Broadway and 40th Street, with 122 boxes – more than enough for all the Astors, Morgans, Rockefellers and Vanderbilts. It was opened in 1883 and was named the Metropolitan Opera House. The celebrated building finally closed its doors in 1966 after a nostalgic farewell gala; the Metropolitan Opera was re-opened that same year at Lincoln Center (*see page 69*).

From Herald Square, follow Broadway northwards as far as 40th Street and **Broadway** 'proper,' the street famous throughout the world. The name Broadway today is synonymous with theaters, shows, musicals, entertainment, and the glitzy world of the Great White Way, as this section of Broadway between 40th and 53rd streets was referred to after electric light made its appearance for the first time. Its heyday was in the 1920s and '30s, when there were over 80 theaters on and around Broadway. The most famous section was 42nd Street – so famous in fact that theater owners whose properties were actually on 41st or 43rd Street had passageways constructed through entire blocks of buildings just to be able to boast a 'Forty-Second Street' address.

But in the late 1920s the cinema learned to talk, and Broadway theater began to decline. The Great Depression added to Broadway's woes, turning many of the theaters along 42nd Street into burlesque houses and then cinema palaces. As it fell into decay the street developed a very different kind of fame – as a red-light district, becoming synonymous with drugs and prostitution.

Times Square

Nearby ★ **Times Square** 🔢 is named after the famous *New York Times* newspaper, which moved into offices here in 1904. At the junction of Broadway and Seventh Avenue, this is the traditional center of the busy Theater District; it is also the site of the city's boisterous annual New Year's Eve celebration. In the immediate vicinity, more than 35 Broadway theaters attract audiences to over 30 new theatrical productions a year. Several vintage theaters in the area have recently been renovated and reopened; new hotels, restaurants, stores, and attractions are everywhere; and after a long period of decline, Times Square is again one of the city's most popular tourist destinations.

As in other parts of the city, however, you still need to be careful. Walk with purpose (even if you don't know where you're going), take care in the subway and keep your eye on any valuables. For a bird's-eye view, step into one of the glass elevators at the **Marriott Marquis Hotel** 🔢, which go up to a revolving restaurant. Or stop by the **Times Square Visitors Center** (1560 Broadway between 46th and 47th streets), across from the TKTS booth that sells tickets for current Broadway shows at half the regular price.

Diamond Row has 80 percent of the US diamond trade

The route now continues onwards to 47th Street, to the brief section between Sixth and Fifth avenues known as ★ **Diamond Row**. Eighty percent of the US diamond trade is transacted along the 270yds (250m) of street here – either inside the shops with their glittering displays, or out on the street: a few of the sellers carry their wares in their pockets in a piece of tissue paper that is traditionally folded. There are no contracts; deals are completed with a handshake. The Diamond Dealers Club supervises everything to ensure that no one breaks the strict code of honor. Anyone accused of double-dealing can expect to be banned from the international diamond trade altogether.

After a stroll along 47th Street, turn left into **Fifth Avenue**, historically one of the city's most famous shopping streets *(see page 58)*.

St Patrick's Cathedral

Shortly before ★ **St Patrick's Cathedral** – a neo-Gothic structure built between 1858 and 1874 on the corner of Fifth Avenue and 50th Street – a small pedestrian mall, known as the **Promenade**, appears on the left-hand side between 49th and 50th Street, and leads to ★★ **Rockefeller Center**. This huge compound of office towers is a 'city within the city,' and extends from Fifth to beyond Sixth Avenue and from 48th to north of 51st Street. It was designed to integrate several functions within a single complex: accommodation, work, shops, restaurants, and entertainment. The basic architectural concept behind the scheme can be formulated as follows: an attempt to create space in all its different dimensions. Depth: the complex is served by an underground network of walkways. Height: the buildings grow narrower the higher they get, so that light can penetrate, and the high and low buildings were designed to avoid conveying any sense of being 'cooped up.' There is an abundance of space on the horizontal plane too: squares, open areas, broad streets, and narrow passageways.

50

The centerpiece of the complex is the **Sunken Plaza** ⑥⓪, which serves as a skating rink in winter and an outdoor cafe in summer. Colorful flags flap quietly, and a golden *Prometheus* hovers in front of the waterfall. This work by Paul Manship is the most well known but not

Statue of Prometheus

the only artwork here in Rockefeller Center: there are over 100 paintings and sculptures here by more than 30 artists. Outside the **International Building** on Fifth Avenue, for instance, is Lee Lawrie's *Atlas*; another work by the same artist, *Wisdom*, can be seen above the entrance portal of the General Electric (formerly RCA) Building, at 30 Rockefeller Plaza. With its restrained art deco elegance, this is the most important structure in the complex; it's also home to the NBC **Experience** (entrance on 49th Street), which includes tours of the National Broadcasting System's studios (for details, call 212-664 3700.)

The International Building

The entire compound was financed by just one man: John D Rockefeller Jr. The Rockefeller name is of course synonymous with wealth, but the surprising thing about the Center is that is John D managed to come up with the $125 million needed for its construction at a time when America was going through the worst depression in its history. The first 14 buildings were constructed between 1931 and 1940. Thousands of people who would otherwise have remained unemployed found work here.

Rockefeller Center, Lower Plaza

The whole complex is extremely harmonious and self-contained, a fact that becomes clearer when one crosses over to Sixth Avenue and takes a look at what architects added to it during the 1960s: three similarly-shaped blocks, ugly, faceless, and gloomy looking. However, the entrance to one of the highlights of the Rockefeller Center, the art deco ★ **Radio City Music Hall** ❻, is right here on Sixth Avenue. This theater, too, was built during the Great Depression – it was opened in 1932 – which makes the sheer amount of pomp, luxury, and splendor inside all the more surprising. The six-story foyer contains a magnificent staircase, the seats are all upholstered in soft velvet, and the stage is as wide as a city block. The satin curtain weighs 3 tons and is raised and lowered by 13 motors. The sun, the moon, and the stars appear at the touch of a button; likewise lightning and storm effects.

Radio City Music Hall

The enormous 6,200-seat auditorium was always sold out, even during the worst years of the Depression, when the theater either presented the famous Rockettes revue group, or the very latest movies on the huge screen. It was only much later, with the arrival of television, that the owners began to have difficulty in filling the house. Rumors of demolition were rife, but local New Yorkers amassed a small fortune to save their last great entertainment center, and Radio City Music Hall underwent restoration. Today it is a landmark building, and hosts extravagant shows as well as popular-music concerts on a year-round basis. A guided tour is more than worthwhile (for times, tel: 212-247 4777.)

The ★★★ **Museum of Modern Art** ❻ (11 W 53rd Street) is well worth a visit, even for those who think

MoMA – mecca for modern art

Matisse at MoMA

Relax in the Sculpture Garden

they don't like modern art. Just as the Whitney Museum was the brainchild of Gertrude Vanderbilt Whitney (*see page 67*), so New York's MoMA was founded by one of the city's first ladies. Abby Rockefeller, the wife of John D Rockefeller Jr, was a passionate collector of modern art, and her collection included works by such artists as Georgia O'Keefe, Pablo Picasso, and Georges Braque, as well as painters from the group known as The Eight, who were exponents of the so-called Ashcan School.

The museum was opened in 1929, and ten years later the collection was shifted to its present home on 53rd Street. The building has undergone quite a few alterations since that time. In 1951, the acclaimed architect Philip Johnson added two wings; during the 1960s several neighboring buildings were acquired; and in 1983 the western part of the building was extended and provided with a 42-story apartment tower. The latter was highly controversial: architecture critic Ada L Huxtable spoke of a 'marriage of culture and commerce' – for in order to finance its extension work the museum had sold its air rights *(see page 55)* to a private corporation. This made it possible to construct a much higher tower than local regulations permitted and led, in Huxtable's view, to the destruction of '53rd Street's special New York character.' With its 'little old buildings, brownstones and municipal structures,' 53rd Street had been 'one of the most attractive and cosmopolitan side-streets in all Manhattan.' This unlikely marriage had obvious advantages, though: the museum's exhibition space was doubled, finally providing room for Cubists, Expressionists, Pop Artists, Dadaists, etc. But even that wasn't enough. Exhibition space is currently being doubled again, thanks to another major expansion that will absorb an adjacent hotel and provide an additional entrance on 54th Street. Due for completion by 2004, this latest renovation is designed by Yoshio Taniguchi.

MoMA is considered by many to be the most important museum of modern art in the world – modern art here defined as starting with the Impressionists in the 1880s: Van Gogh, Monet, Chagall, Matisse, Toulouse-Lautrec, De Chirico, Picasso, Miró, Pollock, and Warhol are just a few of the artists represented. There is also an architecture and design section, with works by Tiffany, Thonet, Marcel Breuer, and many others. Photography also has its own section, and MoMA is famous for its films. Foreign films, classics, works by young unknowns, plus all kinds of lectures and seminars – there's always something going on. In the midst of it all, an oasis of calm is provided by the Abby Aldrich Rockefeller Sculpture Garden, designed by Philip Johnson. Trees, benches, ponds, terraces, even summer evening concerts, are enhanced by the works of Miró, Picasso, Rodin, and Moore.

Route 5

United Nations Headquarters – Grand Central Terminal – Park Avenue – Fifth Avenue – Upper East Side – Harlem

One day is enough for a stroll from United Nations Headquarters (including a tour inside) as far as the Roosevelt Island Tramway. More time should be allowed for the Upper East Side and Harlem. *See map, page 46/7.*

The feeling one gets that each neighborhood in New York has its own special set of rules, often incomprehensible to outsiders, is nowhere more clear than in the small area bounded by the East River, First Avenue, 42nd and 48th Street: not even the US laws are valid here. Don't worry, though: this route starts in a very respectable area, far from any crime or squalor. The fact that the area occupied by ★ **United Nations Headquarters** has its own rules is a sign of exclusivity. The representatives from over 150 countries who work here enjoy a special kind of diplomatic immunity – often a source of irritation to the people of Manhattan because it means that UN employees can park their cars wherever they like.

United Nations Headquarters and sculpture

53

United Nations Headquarters consists of four buildings behind a long row of colorful flags – one for each member country. There are artistic contributions from each country here too: the buildings and gardens contain many different sculptures, tapestries, and paintings.

Before the UN arrived, the site was occupied by slaughterhouses, glue factories, breweries and light industry. Not only the smell and the noise but also the sight of the area must have been very unpleasant: the architects who designed and built the apartment complex known as **Tudor City** 🔞 on 42nd Street avoided putting any windows in its east facade, despite a good view of the river.

Tudor City

The turnaround came at the end of World War II. The United Nations Organization was founded in San Francisco in 1945, as the successor to the League of Nations. The problem of financing and finding it a suitable headquarters was solved by New York's John D Rockefeller Jr; he purchased an $8.5 million-site overlooking the East River and made a present of it to the UNO, while the US issued an interest-free credit of $67 million. The **Secretariat Building** 🔢, with its narrow tower, was completed in 1950. It was followed by the **Conference Building** 🔢, the lowest building in the complex, the **General Assembly Building** 🔢, which serves as an auditorium, and finally by the **Dag Hammarskjöld Library** 🔢.

The team of architects who worked on the buildings was also multinational: Le Corbusier (France), Oscar

Ford Foundation atrium

*A famous landmark:
the Chrysler Building and lobby*

Niemeyer (Brazil), and Sven Markelius (Sweden), among others. The complex as a whole is by no means an architectural masterpiece – Le Corbusier distanced himself from it in later life. Nevertheless, this center of international decision-making is still worth a visit (tickets from the lobby of the General Assembly Building; *see page 81*). In addition, the UN's giftshop contains some very fine crafts and souvenirs from all over the world.

From the main exit, walk a few steps southwards before turning right, i.e. west, on 42nd Street. The eastern end of the street is very different from the section further west around Times Square *(see page 49)*. With exceptions such as the new Trump World Tower, which overshadows the UN from its lofty perch at 47th Street, the area is a paradise for lovers of art deco. First, though, how about a quick dose of tranquillity: the 130ft (40m) high atrium of the **Ford Foundation Building** ➏➑ (321 E 42nd Street). This is no ordinary atrium, but a third of an acre of mature trees and shrubs. There's even a brook. Passers-by are welcome to step inside and relax.

Opposite the Ford Foundation Building, between Second and Third Avenue, is the old **Daily News Building** ➏➒ (220 E 42nd Street). Built in 1930, it has a fine entrance hall with a huge revolving globe. The newspaper moved to new digs in 1995, but the name and character of the high-rise immortalized in the film *Superman* (as headquarters for the fictional *Daily Planet*) has been retained.

Another art deco jewel can be found on the corner of 42nd Street and Lexington Avenue: the ★★ **Chrysler Building** ➐➎. Its unconventional tower, with stainless steel arches glinting in the sun and illuminated at night, is one of the most aesthetically satisfying sights in the New York skyline. The lobby is also fascinating, with its marble-and-chrome decor, enhanced by epic murals depicting transportation and human endeavour. Commissioned by automobile maker Walter P Chrysler, this 1,048ft (320m) high building was the tallest in New York on its completion in 1930, but was soon surpassed by the Empire State.

On the other side of Lexington Avenue is a more modern but far less stirring architectural effort: the **Grand Hyatt Hotel** ➐➊, which replaced the old Commodore Hotel in 1980 and was designed by Gruzen & Partner and Der Scott. The lobby seems typical of that decade's impersonal glitz. Reflected in the glass facade of the hotel are two other buildings with fine lobbys of their own: the **Chanin Building** ➐➋ and the **Bowery Savings Bank** ➐➌, both of them dating from the 1920s.

The **Whitney Museum of American Art at Philip Morris** ➐➍, on the corner of 42nd Street and Park Avenue, holds alternating exhibitions of contemporary art (admission to the gallery and sculpture court is free).

Now a short detour, to Fifth Avenue and the **New York Public Library's Center for the Humanities** **75**. This Beaux Arts building dates from 1911. Designed by Carrère & Hastings, it contains 9 million books, as well as a magnificent Reading Room and an ongoing series of exhibits. The steps outside the library are a popular oasis for resting shoppers, students and tourists; Bryant Park, which stretches behind the library to Sixth Avenue, is another pleasant spot, planted with shrubs and flowers, and the site of various special events.

Amazingly enough, one of the best places to eat around here is inside ★★ **Grand Central Terminal** **76**, but that shouldn't deter gourmets unduly. The **Oyster Bar** between the station's main and lower levels is considered by many to be the best seafood restaurant in the city, although there are plenty of other food outlets (along with shops) to explore here. You can even eat in two restaurants overlooking the main concourse, which with its pale blue ceiling depicting the celestial constellations is 115ft (35m) high, 125ft (38m) wide, and more than twice as long. Either offers a good perch from which to watch commuters dashing to meet their trains. Built in 1913, the Beaux Arts-style station has been a landmark building since the 1970s.

Towering above Grand Central is the **MetLife** (formerly PanAm) **Building** **77**, built in 1963 by Walter Gropius. It is an early example of something that has become a bit of a hobby with the city's property dealers: the buying and selling of 'air rights,' whereby the owner of a low-rise building promises not to use up the construction height available to him and sells the air rights to his neighbor. The latter is then allowed either to build over the lower building, or add the same number of feet to his building that were lacking in the lower one. It all turns out to be highly lucrative for the owners of smaller buildings, despite contributing little to the aesthetics of the city skyline.

Grand Central's Oyster Bar
New York's Public Library

MetLife towers above the station

The Waldorf-Astoria remains a top-class establishment

It's possible to walk straight through the station and up an escalator to the lobby of the MetLife Building to reach **Park Avenue**, one of New York's most exclusive thoroughfares. Some of the shops here only open their doors to customers by appointment, and those who live here can be said to have 'made it'. The avenue also boasts the famous **Waldorf=Astoria Hotel 78**. Though less exclusive now than several other hotels in the city, alongside the Plaza it remains one of the most famous old hotels in New York. The reception for the Apollo 11 astronauts (after the first moon landing) took place here; kings, queens, heads of state and the world's wealthiest stay here, as do famous politicians and artists. One side-effect of all this fame is that the lobby is often packed with tourists admiring the art deco work and soaking up the Waldorf atmosphere.

On the corner of Lexington Avenue and 51st Street, the original General Electric Building was built in 1931. The facade has several neo-Gothic features and the art deco lobby is worth a visit.

The stroll back to Park Avenue via 52nd Street also passes two buildings of historic importance. The **Seagram Building 79** was designed by Ludwig Mies van der Rohe in 1958, who caused a stir by being the first architect in Manhattan not to use all the construction space he had available: he left a plaza out in front. Others soon followed his example, and several other plazas for public use appeared. **Lever House 80** between 53rd and 54th Street was also a trendsetter: built in 1952 it was the city's first ever glass-curtained skyscraper.

Walk eastwards along 53rd Street as far as Lexington Avenue and the **Citicorp Center 81**, built in 1978. Apart from its aesthetic appeal – with its distinctive sloping roofline, it's considered the most attractive post-modern structure in New York – it also contains restaurants and shops, located within an interior 'landscape' of flowerbeds.

The Seagram Building

trees and fountains. The Citicorp Center is 915ft (279m) high, and rests on 130ft (40m) high pillars. Air rights had to be bought here, too. St Peter's Church owned them, surrendering them on condition that the church be incorporated into the new building.

The route now continues westwards via 54th Street, and then bears right onto Madison Avenue. Two controversial examples of post-modern architecture stand side-by-side between 55th and 57th Street. The **Sony Building** 🟡, designed for AT&T by Philip Johnson and completed in 1983, was both heralded and criticized as a post-modernist leap back to earlier styles. The building is inhospitable, though, and the general opinion seems to be 'nice material – shame about the design.' Next door to it, the former IBM **Building** 🟡, built in 1984, contains a 'gift to the community' in the form of a spacious ground-level atrium sculpture garden, a good place to relax with a cup of coffee.

It also includes a passageway to **Trump Tower** 🟡, one block over on Fifth Avenue, where the atrium's brass, polished-marble, five-story waterfall and corner terraces, reflect its owner's sense of showmanship. The shops here are pricey, to say the least; the rents for them and the luxury condominiums overhead astronomical. Most visitors, have to make do with a spot of window shopping.

Trump Tower shop

Donald Trump's success story is in many ways typical of New York. It began in the 1970s, when the city was threatened with bankruptcy and the large firms all seemed to be leaving. It was during this period that Trump bought real estate at knockdown prices – later on, of course, property prices rocketed. The city had Trump and similar speculators to at least partially thank for its new lease of life during the 1980s and late 1990s, but he and others like him were also largely responsible for increasing the gap between rich and poor. Formerly, millionaires often counterbalanced their wealth with philanthropy, and supported the city's social and cultural life. Trump's philosophy seems clear, however: New York is a city for the super-rich, with no room left for the poor.

Next door to Trump Tower is the famous **Tiffany & Co.**, the perfect old-money foil to Trump's flashy excesses, where jewelry, pearl-studded combs, diadems, and all that glitters can be bought for a great deal of money indeed. Despite its high-carat name, Tiffany's was on the verge of bankruptcy at the end of the 1970s and was purchased by the Avon cosmetics firm. But the combination turned out to be bad for business – those happy to fork out for Tiffany's wares were unhappy to be reminded of cheap Avon products (the store has regained its independence since then). Meanwhile, Donald Trump, who had just purchased a bankrupt department store next door, exploited this situation and offered $5 million for Tiffany's air rights.

Diamonds are forever

This allowed him to build 68 stories high one of the most expensive parts of Manhattan.

The section of ★★ **Fifth Avenue** just below Central Park is a very desirable address; further south, a series of discount electronic and import-export stores arrived just as proper department stores such as B Altman went bust. Now transformed into the Science, Industry and Business branch of the New York Public Library, this former emporium caused quite a scandal when it first opened on the corner of 34th Street in 1906: the neighbors were against the idea of a commercial building in their select residential area. In the 1880s, the corner of Fifth Avenue and 34th Street was a mecca for the city's high society. The elegant brownstone mansion belonging to Mrs Carolina Astor, for instance, contained a ballroom large enough to accommodate 400 guests, and those not accepted into 'The Four Hundred,' as it was called, could say goodbye to social life altogether. Family feuds finally forced Mrs Astor to move to the remote northern part of Fifth Avenue, but no sooner had she moved there than all the city's wealthy followed. Magnificent mansions sprang up and the southern part of Fifth Avenue became what it has always been since then: a shopping street.

Today, the most exclusive shops can be found from 49th to 59th streets between the flagship **Saks Fifth Avenue** department store and the celebrated FAO Schwarz toyshop. Many of the luxury stores have their own liveried doormen, and distinguished-looking ladies can often be observed alighting from long black limousines. All the big names are here: Cartier, Bergdorf Goodman, Van Cleef & Arpels, Harry Winston, and Tiffany & Co. However, lately Fifth Avenue has seemed less exclusive than in the past, with mass-merchandising emporiums such as the Warner Bros Studio Store and Niketown all springing up near 57th Street.

Still, the ★ **Plaza Hotel** ㉟ overlooking Central Park provides a glorious finale to this stretch of Fifth Avenue. Emperors, film stars, and presidents have all stayed in this legendary hotel, which was built in 1904 in the style of a French château. Despite its high room prices, even the Plaza offers occasional specials on room rates and is definitely worth visiting. A drink in the Oak Bar (a lavish wood-paneled salon with a gorgeous view of Central Park) or a meal in the Palm Court is definitely less of a strain on the pocket than booking a suite.

In front of the hotel, the Pulitzer Fountain commemorates the journalist and publisher of that name, while horse-drawn carriages stand on the corner of Central Park and **Grand Army Plaza**, waiting to whisk their passengers away from the noise and bustle (for a description of Central Park *see page 63*).

58

Brentano's for books

Fifth Avenue transportation

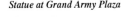
Statue at Grand Army Plaza

Your carriage awaits

The route now heads east along 59th Street, back to Lexington Avenue. Renowned Chicago architect Helmut Jahn, designed the pointed, blue-glass high-rise building  at 750 Lexington Avenue, which is particularly interesting when observed from 57th Street. On the corner of Lexington Avenue and 57th Street is another modern structure, designed by William Pedersen, which has received acclaim for the originality of its 'corner solution.'

Helmut Jahn building

Back into the world of consumerism: the department store of **Bloomingdale's** ❻ takes up the entire block between Lexington and Third Avenue, 59th and 60th Street. 'Bloomie's' is part of New York mythology, a perfectly organized, seven-story consumer paradise. Whatever you're looking for, this store has it all.

Located on the corner of Second Avenue and 60th Street is the **Roosevelt Island Tramway** ❻, a cable car that travels across the East River to Roosevelt Island, a middle-income housing complex with one main street, a church, and scenic walkways.

The border between two worlds – midtown and the **Upper East Side**, where the city's hectic pace suddenly gives way to shady side streets and elegant house – is marked by 59th Street. The new **Bridgemarket** complex in the cathedral-like vault beneath the Queensboro (i.e. 59th Street) Bridge at First Avenue includes a branch of the London-based **Conran Shop** home furnishings store. But the most famous shopping opportunities hereabouts lie along Madison Avenue, where **Barneys New York** at 61st Street marks a splendid northward sweep of stylish designer boutiques. From here, the Upper East Side continues as far as 96th Street. The traditionally Hispanic East Harlem begins north of 96th Street and leads into **Harlem** itself.

Named Nieuw Haarlem by the Dutch, Harlem became post-colonial New York City's first suburb: Alexander Hamilton, the country's first Secretary of the Treasury, had a home here, which today is a national park site. The railroad, and later the subway, led to an influx of European immigrants, but by 1910 or so, when African-Americans began moving into homes on 134th Street, white residents started to move out, and central Harlem, at least, soon became a primarily black neighborhood. As in certain other areas of the city, it's not necessarily a good idea for first-time tourists to wander around on their own; better to join with a tour that stops at such landmarks as the **Studio Museum in Harlem** (West 125th Street); the **Schomburg Center for Research in Black Culture** (Lenox Avenue and 135th Street); the famous **Apollo Theater**; and the beautifully preserved townhouses along 138th and 139th Streets, between Seventh and Eighth Avenues, which were designed by Stanford White and are commonly known as '**Striver's Row.**'

Streetwise shopping in Harlem

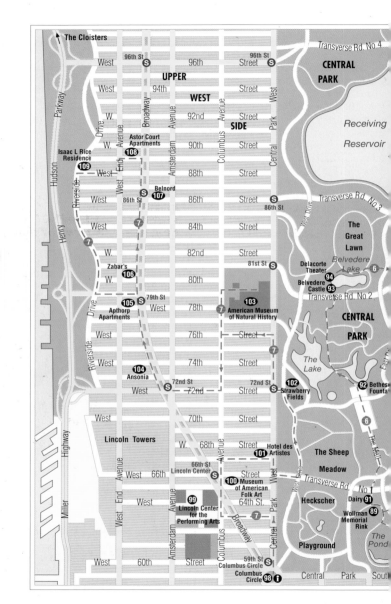

ROUTES 6 & 7
CENTRAL PARK

Ⓢ Subway

0   500yds

Fifth Avenue
East

96th St Ⓢ

East Avenue

Madison Avenue

East

Park Avenue

East

Lexington Avenue

Soloman R
Guggenheim
Museum ❾❺

East

Ⓢ 86th St

East

The
Metropolitan
Museum
of Art

East

East

East

East

East

Whitney Museum
of American Art ❾❻

East

Frick Collection ❾❼
East

East

68th St
Hunter
College Ⓢ

East

East

Fifth Avenue
Madison Avenue
Park Avenue
Lexington Avenue

❾❶
Zoo

East Avenue

East

63rd St Ⓢ
Lexington Ave

Lexington
Ave

Helmut Jahn
Building Ⓢ ❽❻

Ⓢ 5th Ave
L

Third Avenue

96th   Street

94th   Street

92nd   Street

90th

88th

86th

84th

82nd

80th

78th

76th

74th

72nd

70th

68th

66th

64th

62nd

60th St.

Second Avenue

Avenue

First Avenue

East Avenue

Street

Street

Street

Street

Street

Street

Street

Street

Street

Street

Street

Street

Street

Street

Street

Street

York Avenue

East End Avenue

Carl
Schulz
Park

Avenue

YORKVILLE

UPPER

EAST

SIDE

Street

Rockefeller

University

York Avenue

Franklin Roosevelt Drive

West Channel

Roosevelt
Island

Roosevelt Island Aerial Tramway

Queensboro Bridge

❽❼
❽❻ Bloomingdale's

❽❽ Roosevelt Island
Tramway

Route 6

Central Park – Metropolitan Museum of Art – Solomon R Guggenheim Museum – Whitney Museum of American Art – Frick Collection

A substantial Sunday brunch is the best preparation for a pleasant stroll through Central Park. Even if you stop every few yards to marvel at the weekend antics of New Yorkers, it won't take more than half a day to cover the route to the Metropolitan Museum of Art described here.

If the plans of those who designed Manhattan had been followed to the letter, today it would be nothing more than a concrete jungle. There wouldn't have been anywhere to jog, picnic, ice-skate, or sunbathe; in short, there *Bladerunners* wouldn't have been any ★★ **Central Park**. The members of the commission that decided Manhattan's architectural future in 1811 had only allowed enough room for four tiny squares of green; they wanted the rest of the island to be developed. If fate had placed New York on a small river such as the Thames or the Seine, they claimed, open spaces would certainly have had to be created to guarantee enough fresh air. However, since Manhattan was next to the sea, the situation was different. Also, land prices were so high that economic considerations had to be given priority.

New Yorkers soon experienced the consequences of this way of thinking. Between 1820 and 1840 the city's population swelled from 124,000 to 313,000, and Manhattan island's riverside spaces were suddenly covered with warehouses, dockyards, and other installations. Voices were soon raised in protest. William Cullen Bryant, the publisher of the *New York Evening Post* and also a poet, the internationally famous author Washington Irving,

painters, landscape architects, and many others all insisted that an area of land at the center of the island be kept free of development and turned into parkland. In 1856 the decision was finally made: the city purchased a 2½ mile (4km) long, narrow strip of land between Eighth and Fifth Avenue, 59th and 110th Street. The hefty $5.5 million price for the 840 acre (240ha) area was attributed to the fact that the local property speculators had had more than enough time to prepare for the deal.

Strolling along the paths today, listening to the birds and admiring the lakes, meadows, and trees, it's hard to imagine that the park is man-made and that in the mid-19th century this whole area was nothing but an evil-smelling swamp full of thin brushwood, boulders, and stones. The only proper buildings here were a blockhouse and the city arsenal; the other 'structures' – as far as they could be termed such – provided temporary and miserable accommodation for goat-herders and squatters. They were quickly driven out when the developers turned up. The swamps were drained, bridges, and roads were built, and wagonloads of earth were brought in so that thousands of trees and plants could grow. The workmen followed the plans of Frederick Law Olmsted and Calvert Vaux, the two architects who had won the Central Park design competition in 1857 and were now making their dream a reality.

Central Park sports

Landscape architects must possess certain visionary qualities, for how else can they predict how their work will evolve? It's doubtful, though, whether Olmsted and Vaux had the slightest idea of the range of activity that goes on in Central Park today: youths, stripped to the waist, dancing deliriously on roller-skates, film stars jogging along almost hidden by their bodyguards, tens of thousands of people covering the meadows for open-air concerts, and now and then the odd mugging or murder making the headlines.

Which brings us to the theme of safety in Central Park. Generally speaking, crime on average is lower in the park than elsewhere in the city. However, there are a couple of basic rules that should be followed:

1 Leave the park before dusk. Never come here at night, unless for one of the summer evening concerts.
2 Stick to the routes where people are, and avoid quiet, secluded corners.
3 Bring a friend (or two); there's always more safety in numbers.

The best day of the week to appreciate Central Park is on summer Sundays, when most of Manhattan is deserted and there are 1.5 million fewer people in the city than on the hectic weekdays. The commuters stay in the suburbs,

Bethesda Fountain

Belvedere Castle

and the Manhattanites have the island to themselves. New York suddenly becomes calmer, cozier, and more relaxed, and Fifth Avenue fills with pedestrians who, after a substantial brunch, are irresistibly drawn to the park to stroll, play, cycle, canoe, drink coffee, or just to see and be seen. Everyone seems to be part of the same big show: from well-to-do ladies from the Upper East Side walking their poodles to athletic teenagers showing off their skateboarding prowess.

The best route to take for a stroll is from the park entrance near Grand Army Plaza, 59th Street and the corner of Fifth Avenue, up to the Lake. This route passes the Pond, the western side of which is a bird sanctuary, and also the **Wollman Memorial Rink** 89, which offers either rollerskating or iceskating depending on the time of year. The newly renovated **Zoo** 90 is definitely worth visiting. Information about the park's other attractions can be obtained from the Visitor Center at the **Dairy** 91; this is the place to go for maps and directions to places such as **Strawberry Fields**, Yoko Ono's memorial to John Lennon, as well as special exhibits on the park's history and the excellent daily tours led by Urban Park Rangers. Continue along the mall – a long avenue lined with trees and busts of famous artists (Beethoven, Burns, Shakespeare, Scott, etc) where there's always something going on – as far as **Bethesda Fountain** 92 and the Lake. To the north of the Lake, at the highest point of Central Park, **Belvedere Castle** 93 exudes medieval romanticism; next door is the open-air **Delacorte Theater** 94, and not far away, the **Great Lawn** is traditionally where music lovers spread their blankets for evening concert performances.

It's only a few steps from here to one of New York's most famous cultural institutions, parts of which overflow into the park: the ★★★ **Metropolitan Museum of Art** (on Fifth Avenue between 80th and 84th Street). Calvert Vaux had a hand in its design and the original carriage entrance, dating from 1880, is still intact, though on view in the museum's sculpture court. More sections and wings have been added continually to cope with the massive amount of art here, and the present-day building – although stretching between 80th and 84th Streets – still holds less than half the museum's permanent collection of over 3 million objects. The two most recent architectural additions are the three-story American Wing (1980) and the Lila Acheson Wallace Wing (1987); the latter includes a roof-garden with a superb view of Central Park. In addition, the museum recently completed its new Greek and Roman galleries and has also created a number of new exhibit spaces, all of which are contained within the framework of the existing structure.

There's no way round it, unfortunately: in order to avoid spending several weeks inside the Metropolitan Museum one does have to concentrate on just a few rooms. There is an information desk in the museum's 'Great Hall' (just inside the main entrance). Here is a short summary of what can be found inside:

65

Ground Floor: *Costume Institute* (clothing from 17th to 20th centuries; alternating exhibitions); *Robert Lehman Collection* (private collection taking up two floors; 3,000 works of art donated to the museum by Robert Lehman, most of them European including works by Rembrandt, Goya, Van Gogh and Matisse); *Uris Center for Education* (classrooms, library and auditorium).

Main Floor: *Egyptian Art* (world-famous Egyptian art collection; highlight here is the Temple of Dendur); *Greek and Roman Art* (parts of the collection are among the museum's oldest exhibits; of particular interest is the bedroom of a villa from Boscoreale near Pompeii dating from AD79); *Medieval Art* (magnificently presented exhibits, 7th–16th century); *European Sculpture and Decorative Art* (various galleries containing reconstructions of rooms from European palaces and mansions); *Arms and Armor*; *Michael C Rockefeller Wing* (Precolumbian art, tribal art and cult artifacts from Africa, Oceania and the Americas); *American Wing* (four floors of gallery and study areas containing every possible manifestation of American art, including paintings, sculpture, decorative art, plus 25 period rooms); *Lila Acheson Wallace Wing* (three levels of exhibition space devoted to modern art and design, including large-scale sculpture displayed on the magnificent roof garden.)

The Chess Players

One of the Met's Monets

Second Floor: *Ninteenth-Century European Paintings and Sculpture* (a recent 21-gallery addition); *European Paintings* (including a number of Rembrandts); *Islamic Art; South and Southeast Asian Art; Japanese Art; Chinese Art; Korean Art; Ancient Near Eastern Art* (oldest exhibits here date from 6000BC); *Drawings, Prints, and Photographs* (artists represented include Leonardo da Vinci, Titian, Michelangelo, Turner, and Degas); *Musical Instruments* (including three Stradivari); *Greek and Roman Art* (including new galleries added in 2000); plus modern art and American Wing exhibits continued from the main floor.

This great treasure trove of art, along with a regular series of spectacular special exhibitions, has made the Metropolitan Museum of Art one of the world's most impressive centers of culture. And names such as the Robert Lehman Collection and the Lila Acheson Wallace Wing make it clear that, like many American cultural institutions, the Metropolitan has historically benefited from the largesse of wealthy patrons. Something which may also explain why such a large number of museums are found nearby: when Mrs Caroline Astor moved house to the Upper East Side *(see page 58)*, the northern part of Fifth Avenue became the most desirable place to live in the whole of the city. Whoever could afford it built villas facing Central Park, and many of the buildings have now become foundations and institutes, as well as museums. The **Cooper-Hewitt National Design Museum**, for instance is inside the former villa of millionaire Andrew Carnegie (Fifth Avenue/91st Street); Solomon R Guggenheim, meanwhile, had the architecturally bizarre Guggenheim Museum *(see below)* built on his land.

New York's so-called 'Museum Mile' actually extends more than a mile (from 82nd to 104th streets) and includes the **International Center of Photography** (94th Street) and the intriguing **Museum of the City of New York** (103rd Street). Because of the sheer number of cultural institutions in the vicinity, a certain amount of selectiveness is required. The following three, however, shouldn't be missed:

Outside and inside the Guggenheim

The ★★ **Solomon R Guggenheim Museum** ❺ (Fifth Avenue/89th Street) is worth visiting for its wonderful architecture alone: it was designed by Frank Lloyd Wright. From the outside it resembles an upturned snail-shell; inside, the spiral ramp affords continually new perspectives on the artworks displayed.

The museum was opened in 1959 somewhat later than planned – 16 years in fact – due to bureaucracy and protests from local residents. Guggenheim and Frank Lloyd Wright were both already dead by this time. When it was finally ready it was an architectural sensation, but still had far too little room for Guggenheim's mammoth collection – the copper magnate owned over 4,000 paintings, sculptures, and drawings. A new building – which rather dominates the original – was opened in 1992 to provide more exhibition space. Highlights include the largest collection of Kandinskys in the world, plus works by Picasso, Chagall, Mondrian, Marc, Miró, Renoir, Manet, and many others.

The ★ **Whitney Museum of American Art** ❾❻ has a midtown branch, too *(see page 54)*, but its main building is on the corner of Madison Avenue and 75th Street. The collection was the idea of Gertrude Vanderbilt Whitney, a wealthy sculptor who helped young artists to exhibit their work in Greenwich Village as early as the 1930s.

In contrast to the Museum of Modern Art, the Whitney Museum exclusively exhibits 20th-century American art. The latest paintings and sculptures are always presented each autumn. 'Classics' among the moderns include Lichtenstein, Pollock, Rauschenberg, and Shan. One real highlight here must not be missed: the 2,000 or so works by Edward Hopper.

Little Big Painting by Lichtenstein

The ★ **Frick Collection** ❾❼ (Fifth Avenue/70th Street), a collection of art treasures assembled by steel manufacturer Henry Clay Frick, is housed in his former palazzo, which was built in the French neoclassical style in 1913. Efforts have been made to keep the house more of a house and less of a museum; it's like being the guest of a man who can afford to surround himself with select works of art. The tiny roofed inner courtyard is particularly attractive. Goya, Titian, El Greco, Vermeer, and Renoir are just a few of the artists represented here.

67

Portrait by Titian
The Frick's Garden Court

The Dakota

Route 7

Upper West Side and The Cloisters

It's best to plan a full day for Route 7, not including a visit to The Cloisters in the north. *See map, pages 60/1.*

West of Central Park, something strange happens to Manhattan: the avenues that had to content themselves with being plain numbers as far as 59th Street are suddenly given names again. Eighth becomes Central Park West, Ninth turns into Columbus Avenue, Tenth becomes Amsterdam Avenue, and Eleventh turns into West End Avenue.

Why the name change? It's all to do with image. When the Upper West Side came into existence at the end of the 19th century, local property owners planned to create an elegant residential area for the wealthy. The negative image of Eighth, Ninth, Tenth, and Eleventh Avenue stood in their way. These weren't 'good addresses,' and didn't look good on visiting cards. So they were renamed, suddenly sounded more exclusive – and local property prices started to rise.

The first building to raise the tone of the area west of the park was the American Museum of Natural History, which was opened in 1877. Seven years after that, the first wealthy entrepreneur moved up to the west: Edward Clark. As heir to the Singer Sewing Machine Company fortune, Clark had more than enough money to build an apartment house resembling a castle next to the park, on a level with 72nd Street, and he even surrounded it with a moat. Clark created this elevated atmosphere on purpose, to set his future tenants at ease: New York's upper class of that time still found the idea of an apartment house extremely vulgar. As for the location of the 'castle': Fifth Avenue society turned up its nose at it. So far removed from city life, well, it was just as if one lived in the Dakota Territory out west, they joked – and suddenly the house had a nickname: the *Dakota*.

Despite all the reservations everyone may have had, the Upper West Side had its way. The construction of the 'Ninth Avenue El' (1878), one of New York's first and once prevalent raised railways, brought the Dakota closer to the rest of the city, and many apartment houses were built that provided accommodation for people who found downtown or the Lower East Side too cramped and who could still afford to escape. For them, moving to the Upper West Side symbolized the first rung on the ladder to social success. Even though some luxury apartment houses and addresses, like Central Park West or Riverside Drive, were reserved for the very wealthy, the atmosphere of the Upper West Side during the first phase of its settlement was solidly middle class.

In later decades, the Upper West Side developed into a favorite address for intellectuals. Actors, musicians and writers who have lived and continue to live here include Hannah Arendt, Anaïs Nin, Yehudi Menuhin, John Lennon, Scott Fitzgerald, Isaac Bashevis Singer, Billy Joel, Mick Jagger, Harry Belafonte, and Paul Simon, to name but a few.

A stroll round the Upper West Side begins on **Columbus Circle** 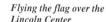, a busy traffic roundabout. At its center, Columbus stands on a column, and on its northern side is the **Trump International Tower and Hotel**, on the site of the old Gulf & Western Building.

Columbus Circle

Broadway is the shortest route from here to the ★ **Lincoln Center for the Performing Arts** 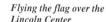, but a more scenic way to get to Lincoln Center is to stroll along Central Park and then turn down 63rd Street, which leads directly to it. This conglomeration is the heart of mainstream New York culture: the **Metropolitan Opera House**, the **New York State Theater**, which is shared by the **New York City Ballet** and the **New York City Opera**, **Avery Fisher Hall**, home of the New York Philharmonic, **Alice Tully Hall**, headquarters of the Lincoln Center Chamber Music Society, and the **Juilliard School**, where young hopefuls study and give concerts (often for free).

Flying the flag over the Lincoln Center

Twelve blocks had to be demolished to make way for this 'temple of the muses', and thousands of people rehoused. Five architects were commissioned for the various buildings: Max Abramovitz, Philip Johnson, Wallace K Harrison, Eero Saarinen and Pietro Bellusci. The condition was that they use the same construction material (pollution-resistant Italian travertine), but otherwise each architect was given creative freedom. The buildings' neoclassical exterior elevations give them a certain degree

Metropolitan Opera House

Café des Artistes

Outside the Museum of Natural History

of unity. Lincoln Center was built during the 1960s, and the last building to be completed was the Metropolitan Opera (1966).

Those not eager to see a performance here can still go on a guided tour *(see page 80)*. Don't miss the two large murals by Marc Chagall in the foyer of the 'Met.'

From Lincoln Center it's a short walk across to the **Museum of American Folk Art** ⓐ (near the corner of Columbus Avenue and 66th Street). This little museum contains various exhibitions devoted to particular themes that are often highly original (admission free).

Walk back up 67th Street in the direction of Central Park; at the junction with Central Park West is the **Hotel des Artistes** ⓐ, an establishment that has had several illustrious guests in its time, including Isadora Duncan and Noel Coward. On the ground floor is the famous **Café des Artistes** restaurant, with its European atmosphere and 'old world charm' that Americans love so much.

Enter Central Park now and turn north at the famous **Tavern on the Green**; soon you will arrive at West Drive and **Strawberry Fields** ⓐ. This peace garden with plants from 123 countries was created by Yoko Ono in memory of her husband, ex-Beatle John Lennon, who was shot dead in 1980, right outside the **Dakota**, where he lived (1 West 72nd Street). Over the years this famous building has remained the grandest residence on Central Park West, attracting tenants including Boris Karloff, Leonard Bernstein, and Lauren Bacall *(see pages 68–9)*.

A little further north on Central Park West is the ★★ **American Museum of Natural History** ⓐ. The bombastic facade of this 23-building complex (1872–1933) is reminiscent of a gloomy and forbidding Teutonic fortress. But the enormous exhibition space inside is devoted to an impressive series of exhibits on natural history, anthropology and ethnology. The museum is ideal for children: there are dinosaur and whale skeletons; the gem collection contains the largest cut sapphire in the world (the *Star of India*, 463 carats); the Hall of South American Peoples contains shrunken heads and blowpipes; and the **Naturemax Theater** shows films on a screen four stories high and 66ft (20m) wide.

Next door, the museum's dazzling **Rose Center for Earth and Space** opened in 2000 and includes the **Hayden Planetarium**, which features the world's most technologically advanced space show. The centerpiece is a four-story sphere that houses a super high-tech star projector. Shows are scheduled daily from 10.30am.

If you're visiting the museum on a Sunday, it's worth heading for the corner of 77th Street and Columbus afterwards: the weekly **Green/Flea market** here sells fresh vegetables, antiques, clothing, toys, comic books, etc.

A walk along 76th Street is a good idea anytime, though: the section between Columbus Avenue and Central Park West is one of the city's numerous historic districts. Those keener on the present than the past are advised to stroll down **Columbus Avenue**. This is a good place to observe the way in which the Upper West Side has changed in recent decades. After young urban professionals began flocking here in the 1980s, boutiques, street cafés, and bistros sprang up to accommodate them. Old apartments were bought and refurbished, prices went up, and what used to be a relatively affordable part of the city has become as expensive as everywhere else in New York.

Columbus chic

Gentrification is not only evident on Columbus: Amsterdam Avenue and Broadway have also been affected. This stretch of Broadway has some very fine old apartment houses along it, one such being the **Ansonia**  on the corner of 73rd Street. It was built in 1901, and its owners caused quite a stir: they had two swimming pools, real seals frolicking in the fountain in the foyer, and a live bear cruising around the roof-garden.

The Ansonia

Less ostentatious but more architecturally interesting are the **Apthorp Apartments** , which take up the entire block between Broadway, West End Avenue, 78th, and 79th streets. They were built for William Waldorf Astor between 1906 and 1908.

71

On the corner of 81st Street and Broadway is a sight of a very different kind: **Zabar's** . To the uninitiated, Zabar's probably looks like just another delicatessen, albeit one with an amazing amount of assorted wares: hundreds of different types of cheese, sausages, imported beers, Italian noodle machines, Chinese woks, French copper saucepans. For New Yorkers, though, Zabar's is a place of pilgrimage and the original gourmet paradise. This is where neighborhood residents and non-residents alike meet and exchange the latest news – just like a marketplace in medieval times.

Walk further up Broadway from Zabar's and soon some more fine apartment buildings will come into view: the **Belnord** , situated between 86th and 87th Street, Broadway, and Amsterdam Avenue, is typical of the Upper West Side, and like the Apthorp, is built around a central courtyard. Between 88th and 90th Street (on the corner with Broadway) stand the impressive **Astor Court Apartments** . From here the route continues via West End Avenue and 88th Street to **Riverside Drive**, the Upper West Side's most majestic boulevard. This street was once lined with magnificent detached villas, offering views across leafy Riverside Park that attracted New York's wealthier citizens by the end of the 19th century.

Riverside Park

One mansion still conveys a sense of that era: the **Isaac L Rice Residence** (corner of 89th Street), which was built in 1901. Rice, a well-to-do industrialist, named his home Villa Julia after his wife. Apart from another mansion on 107th Street this is the only detached residence remaining on Riverside Drive; the rest are huge terraced apartment buildings.

Up at 122nd Street and Riverside Drive is the imposing **General Grant National Memorial**, which contains the tomb of this famous Civil War general (who became the 18th president of the US) and his wife. Maintained by the National Park Service, the memorial is said to have been inspired by the Invalides, Napoleon's final resting place in Paris.

Those interested in art have a good reason to travel even further north at this point (bus M4). Fort Tryon Park, at West 192nd Street in Washington Heights, contains ★ **The Cloisters** *(see map, page 60)*. What is on offer here seems a world away from contemporary America and highly unexpected in New York – this is the world of the European Middle Ages.

Detail of The Cloisters

72

During the 1930s, John D Rockefeller Jr had sections of French and Spanish monasteries dismantled, shipped across the Atlantic and reassembled here in the New World – all at great expense. The result is not as bizarre as one would suppose: Romanesque cloisters, Gothic chapels, portals, and vaults – the entire architectural history of the Middle Ages stands here in one harmonious ensemble, surrounded by gardens on a hilltop overlooking the Hudson River.

The Cloisters contains the medieval art collection from the Metropolitan Museum of Art *(see pages 65–6)*, mostly comprising French, Spanish, and Flemish works: stained-glass windows, manuscripts, goldsmiths' work, and sculpture, as well as the much-prized Unicorn Tapestries, six handwoven tapestries from the 15th century.

The Cloisters

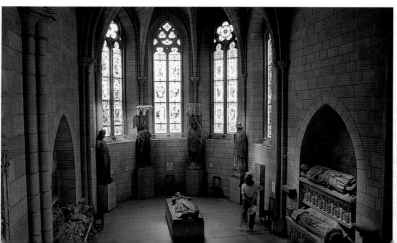

Excursions

Brooklyn – Queens – The Bronx – Staten Island

See map, page 6.

Although most people always say 'New York' when they actually mean 'Manhattan,' the city has four other boroughs. New York City's population of 7½ million is distributed across all five of them: Manhattan, Brooklyn, the Bronx, Queens, and Staten Island. Only around 1.5 million people actually live in Manhattan itself. Its population doubles on weekdays because of commuters from the other boroughs, and also from New Jersey and Connecticut. They arrive on buses, trains, and the subway, and their cars stand in traffic jams on the bridges and inside the tunnels. There's a term for them in Manhattan: the B&T ('bridge and tunnel') crowd, and it's not kindly meant. Those who dwell in Manhattan regard it as the spiritual as well as the geographical center of the city. Even residents from other boroughs refer to it as 'The City,' and the postal address for Manhattan is 'New York, NY,' while the other four boroughs have to be mentioned by their individual names.

But there are plenty of sights to see in the other boroughs; with all the attractions of Manhattan, though, the problem is actually finding the time. Manhattan's great competitor on the other side of the East River, **Brooklyn**, is rich with cultural highlights. The **Brooklyn Museum** *(see page 81)*, for instance, has a superb Egyptian collection. And few people know that Brooklyn, with its population of 2.3 million, would now be the fourth largest city in the US if it hadn't been swallowed up by New York in 1898.

You can actually reach Brooklyn on foot, across the famous ★★ **Brooklyn Bridge** *(see page 27)*, which was considered the eighth wonder of the world on its completion in 1883. The view of the Manhattan skyline it affords is breathtaking.

Bridge with a view

Those eager to see Manhattan from another dramatic perspective should take a stroll along the **Promenade** in Brooklyn Heights, one of Brooklyn's most attractive neighborhoods. Although the 19th-century brownstone mansions here have long been popular with artists and writers, today the rents are as high as in Manhattan.

Brooklyn's Promenade

Brooklyn's population has more African-Americans than that of Harlem, a substantial Orthodox Jewish community, and smaller enclaves of Italians, Arabs, and Chinese. There's a large contingent from the Caribbean, and some sections, such as Brighton Beach, are home to Russian and other East European immigrants. Famous

Brooklynites include Norman Mailer, Arthur Miller, Barbara Streisand, and Woody Allen.

Brooklyn lies on the westernmost tip of Long Island, so it's actually possible to go swimming here. Although these days not the most savory of prospects, **Coney Island Beach**, the 'poor man's Riviera,' is packed on hot summer days. **Coney Island** itself, formerly the site of one of the world's largest and most exciting amusement parks, was laid out in the 1880s and thrived until the 1960s. Today the area is a jumble of apartment blocks and empty lots, but you can still ride on the Cyclone, a roller coaster dating to 1927, and stare at the weird acts presented by **Sideshows by the Seashore** (Surf Avenue/ West 12th Street). You can still savor Nathan's Famous hotdogs and admire the sea lions at the **New York Aquarium** (Surf Avenue/8th Street).

Another popular Brooklyn destination is **Prospect Park**, which, like Central Park, was laid out by Frederick Law Olmsted and Calvert Vaux. To the northeast of the park is the lovely **Brooklyn Botanic Garden**; across the street is the **Brooklyn Museum**. Alongside its impressive Egyptian collection, the museum also has a vast collection of art from all over the world. In another part of the borough, the **Brooklyn Academy of Music** (30 Lafayette Avenue) is best known for its annual autumn 'Next Wave Festival,' which features international avant-garde theatrical and musical performances.

To the north of Brooklyn, and also technically on Long Island, is **Queens**, the largest of New York's boroughs. About 2 million people live here – all of them fast asleep, if Manhattan rumors are to be believed. Queens is considered the 'bedroom' of Manhattan, and is also referred

Coney Island delights

Brooklyn Botanic Garden

to as 'the borough of cemeteries.' Not that it's necessarily a quiet place: broad highways cut through endless, monotonous rows of terraced houses, and La Guardia and John F Kennedy airports keep the noise level high.

Every visitor who lands at JFK International Airport and takes a taxi to Manhattan goes through Queens. Tennis fans watching television coverage of the US Open at the National Tennis Center are actually looking at Queens, too, though they may not realize it. During the silent movie era, Queens was the equivalent of today's Hollywood – the center of the motion-picture industry – and movies and TV shows are still produced at the Kaufman-Astoria studios here. **The American Museum of the Moving Image** (35th Avenue/36th Street, Astoria) celebrates this early movie history. Also worth visiting is the **Queens Museum of Art**, in Flushing Meadows-Corona Park (site of the National Tennis Center), which features a detailed model of all five boroughs created for the 1964 World Fair.

Queens may be hard to define, but as far as **The Bronx** is concerned, many associate it with a rough, fairly tough, image. However, not all its population of 1.2 million live behind burned-out facades. Only the southern part of New York's only mainland borough corresponds with the notorious image – and even parts there are experiencing a rebirth; the northern part, with its leafy enclaves along the Hudson River, contains magnificent villas and stately mansions, testifying quite clearly to their owners' wealth. The main attraction of this borough is the **Bronx Zoo/Wildlife Conservation Park** (Bronx River Parkway/Fordham Road), the largest municipal zoo in the US. Right next to it is the **New York Botanical Garden**, originally laid out in 1891 and modeled after Kew Gardens in London.

With a population of just 413,000 and a surface area of 56sq miles (150sq km), **Staten Island** is by far the most thinly populated of New York's boroughs. It remains rather isolated from the other boroughs, and its relatively bucolic atmosphere can be a refreshing contrast to the bustle and noise of Manhattan. The **Staten Island Ferry**, which docks close to the Battery Maritime Building and connects the Island to Manhattan, has been in operation in one form or another since 1840. Until the construction in 1964 of the **Verrazano-Narrows Bridge**, it was the only connection between Staten Island and the other boroughs. The trip *(see also Route 1, page 21)* provides a fine view of the southern tip of Manhattan and its skyline.

One of Staten Island's most interesting sites is the reconstructed village known as **Historic Richmond Town** (441 Clarke Avenue, next to LaTourette Park), an open-air museum documenting life in Richmond – Staten Island's former name – between the 17th and 19th centuries.

A memento from the Museum of the Moving Image

75

Historic Richmond Town

Planning and Architecture

City planning in the European sense does not exist in New York. There were no religious or secular despots here eager to realize their visions, and no overall plan. The city's earliest landmarks were responses to the demands of the time, such as the defensive wall to the north, today's Wall Street, or the parade-ground, today's Washington Square. Basically, everyone built what they liked where they liked – or rather, what they could afford to build, and the city didn't interfere. Grand Central Terminal was built by the Vanderbilts, who owned the railway lines; the city's first opera house was financed by wealthy citizens. Even today's museums, theaters, and concert halls are dependent to a large degree on patronage.

Central Park was bought by prominent New Yorkers

The city fathers' first real attempt at city-planning took place in 1811, and it had far-reaching consequences: they covered the island of Manhattan with a grid of streets. In so doing, though, they neglected to add any areas of green; the section of the city now occupied by Central Park was only bought back at the behest of several prominent New Yorkers in 1856 – at an astronomical price.

77

The second time the city intervened was in 1916. By this time, 'steel skeleton' construction made it possible to build skyscrapers. The first one in New York was the Flatiron Building, erected in 1902 and relatively restrained with only 22 storeys. However, the Equitable Building, which appeared on Lower Broadway in 1916, was a monster on an 'H'-shaped ground plan, with 40 floors, and filling an entire block. The walls were perpendicular from top to bottom, without any tiering, and thus the whole neighborhood was plunged into shadow. There were so many complaints that the city found itself compelled to pass a zoning law – the first of its type in the US. It stipulated that the upper floors of a skyscraper should be tiered to allow light through to the streets below. This resulted in the so-called 'wedding-cake' style of building, examples of which include the Chrysler and Empire State Buildings.

The 1902 Flatiron Building

This zoning law was amended in 1961. The cause this time was a building the public liked rather than hated: the Seagram Building, a simple tower with a straight facade on Park Avenue, built by Mies van der Rohe and Philip Johnson in 1958. It followed the rules of the International Style, an extension of the Bauhaus concept. In a break with New York architectural tradition, the design team incorporated a plaza at the foot of the building, over a priceless section of Park Avenue real estate.

It is hard to imagine today how this rather dull plaza could have been such an important innovation, but from then on the law favored skyscrapers that created public space in this manner. The positive side to this was that

Rockefeller Center:
wonderfully harmonious

Trump Tower

peaceful foyers and lobbies were introduced, creating oases of tranquility in midtown or downtown: good examples include the lobby of the IBM Building on Madison Avenue, or the one at the Ford Foundation on 42nd Street. Museums providing free access to the public also qualified as public space under the amendment.

The negative effect of the change in the zoning law can be seen on 6th Avenue, where the western extension of Rockefeller Center consists of four uninviting-looking skyscrapers towering above draughty squares. Rockefeller Center itself, however, is wonderfully harmonious and self-contained: several blocks were designed and built according to a unifying concept, creating one of the world's largest business-and-entertainment complexes – a 'city within the city.' The man responsible for this scheme – realized in the middle of the Great Depression – was the multi-millionaire John D Rockefeller Jr.

Another example of successful city-planning can be seen at the southern tip of Manhattan: Battery Park City, built in the 1980s on landfill left over from the construction of the World Trade Center.

Postmodern architecture in Manhattan is concentrated in the northeastern section of midtown; one of the most notable buildings here is at 135 East 57th Street. Another example, an elliptical tower known locally as 'the Lipstick Building,' is at 885 Third Avenue. Standing next to the IBM Building on Madison, the AT&T Building, now occupied by Sony, represents a return to more classical ornamentation after the austerity of the International Style.

The 1990s ushered in a new sense of humility and self-criticism among architects and planners. The city learned from past mistakes: the planners responsible for the multibillion dollar renovation of Times Square, for example, have successfully struck a balance between work and leisure.

Whereas in the past New York was a little too 'trigger-happy' as far as the demolition of fine buildings was concerned, there is now a more thoughtful approach. After the old Penn Station was torn down in 1963, public outcry resulted in the Landmark Preservation Act of 1965. Ironically, the current redevelopment of Penn Station encompasses the adjacent General Post Office, which – like the original station – was designed by McKim, Mead and White. The recent multi-million dollar restoration of Grand Central Terminal and the ongoing development of the Hudson River Park, resulting in new public piers and walkways stretching from lower Manhattan up to 59th Street and beyond, are other hopeful signs.

The fact that city and state are working hand-in-hand on such projects, and not abandoning them to the force of private greed, is something new in New York's history, and shows how open the city is to fresh ideas.

Museums

New York has over 150 museums, most of which are privately run and receive little or no money from public funds. Most ask visitors for contributions towards their upkeep. Here is a list of some of the more famous cultural institutions (note: opening times often change seasonally):

Manhattan

American Museum of Natural History (Central Park West/79th Street). Natural history, ethnology, and anthropology. Sunday to Thursday 10am–5.45pm, Friday and Saturday 10am–8.45pm *(see page 70)*.

Natural History habitat

The Cloisters (Fort Tryon Park). Medieval art in reassembled sections of European monasteries. Tuesday to Sunday 9.30am–5.15pm, 4.45pm in winter *(see page 72)*.

Cloisters column

Cooper-Hewitt National Design Museum (Fifth Avenue/91st Street). Textiles, jewelry, furniture, graphics, ceramics, etc. Tuesday 10am–9pm, Wednesday to Saturday 10am–5pm, Sunday noon–5pm *(see page 66)*.

Ellis Island/Statue of Liberty Immigration Museum (Ellis Island). History of immigration to the US. Daily 9am–5.30pm, later in summer. Ferry (Circle Line) leaves hourly from Battery Park, half-hourly in summer *(see page 21)*.

79

El Museo del Barrio (Fifth Avenue/104th Street). Art and culture of Latin America and Puerto Rico. Wednesday to Sunday 11am–5pm.

Fraunces Tavern Museum (54 Pearl Street). Historic inn, with period furniture from 18th and 19th centuries, as well as some intriguing memorabilia of Washington. Monday to Friday 10am–4.45pm, *(see page 22)*.

Frick Collection (Fifth Avenue/70th Street). European masterpieces from the 14th–19th centuries. Tuesday to Saturday 10am–6pm, Sunday 1–6pm *(see page 67)*.

Renoir at the Frick
Chagall at the Guggenheim

Guggenheim Museum (Fifth Avenue/89th Street). Impressionist, modern, and contemporary art in Frank Lloyd Wright's architecturally acclaimed building. Sunday to Wednesday 9am–6pm, Friday and Saturday 9am–8pm *(see page 66)*. Also in SoHo (575 Broadway). Thursday to Monday 11am–6pm, *(see page 36)*.

International Center of Photography (Fifth Avenue/94th Street). Photographic exhibitions. Tuesday to Thursday 10am–5pm, Friday 10am–8pm, Saturday and Sunday noon–6pm.

Jewish Museum (Fifth Avenue/92nd Street). Historic manuscripts, art, and artifacts. Sunday, Monday, Wednesday, Thursday 11am–5.45pm, Tuesday 11am–8pm.

Lower East Side Tenement Museum (90 Orchard Street). Documents history of Lower East Side immigrants. Tuesday to Friday noon–5pm, Saturday and Sunday 11am–5pm *(see page 34)*.

Not to be missed:
the Met

Folk Art at its finest

Metropolitan Museum of Art (Fifth Avenue/82nd Street). One of the largest and wealthiest museums in the world, full of art from all over the globe. Not to be missed. Tuesday to Thursday and Sunday 9.30am–5.15pm, Friday and Saturday 9.30am–9pm *(see pages 65–6)*.

Museum of American Folk Art (Columbus Avenue/66th Street). Folk paintings, furniture, and decorative arts (moving to 53rd Street in 2001). Tuesday to Sunday 11.30am–7.30pm *(see page 70)*.

Museum of Jewish Heritage: A Living Memorial to the Holocaust (18 First Place/Battery Park City). Exhibits, photos and archival films that focus on 20th-century Jewish history. Sunday to Wednesday 9am–5pm, Thursday 9am–8pm, summer Fridays 9am–5pm; closed Saturdays, Thanksgiving and Jewish holidays *(see page 19)*.

Museum of Modern Art (11 West 53rd Street). Modern art from the turn of the 20th century. Saturday to Tuesday, and Thursday 10.30am–5.45pm, Friday 10.30am–8.15pm *(see page 51–2)*.

Museum of the City of New York (Fifth Avenue/103rd Street). The history of New York from colonization by the Dutch until the present. Wednesday to Saturday 10am–5pm, Sunday noon–5pm.

National Museum of the American Indian (1 Bowling Green). A celebration of the living cultures of the indigenous peoples of the Western Hemisphere. Admission free; open daily 10am–5pm.

Studio Museum in Harlem (144 West 125th Street). Noted African-American artists and others represented here. Wednesday, Thursday, Saturday, and Sunday noon–6pm, Friday noon–8pm.

Whitney Museum of American Art (Madison Avenue/75th Street). 20th-century art. Tuesday, Wednesday, Friday to Sunday 11am–6pm, Thursday 1–9pm *(see page 67)*.

Other Manhattan museums and attractions
Federal Hall National Memorial (26 Wall Street). Exhibits on George Washington and the new republic. Monday to Friday 9am–5pm *(see page 25)*.

Intrepid Sea-Air-Space-Museum (Pier 86 at 12th Avenue and 46th Street.) US Navy missiles and aircraft, on the *USS Intrepid* World War II aircraft carrier. Monday to Saturday 10am–5pm, Sunday 10am–6pm; later in summer.

Lincoln Center for the Performing Arts (Columbus Avenue/64th Street). Guided tours daily; to sign up, tel: (212) 875 5350 *(see page 69)*.

Morgan Library (29 East 36th Street). Paintings, sculpture, manuscripts, all collected by the banker John Pierpont Morgan and his son. Tuesday to Thursday 10.30am–5pm, Friday 10.30am–8pm, Saturday 10.30am–6pm, Sunday 2–6pm.

NBC Experience (Rockefeller Plaza/West 49th Street). Interactive TV exhibits plus tours of the NBC studios, including those of *The Today Show*. Monday to Saturday 8.30am–5.30pm, Sunday 9.30am–4.30pm *(see page 51)*.
Radio City Music Hall (Sixth Avenue/50th Street). Regular tours of this art deco palace; call (212) 247 4777 for details *(see page 51)*.
South Street Seaport Museum (Visitors Center, 12 Fulton St). 12-block museum-without-walls, with historic sailing vessels and exhibits, plus shopping and restaurants. Daily 10am–5pm *(see page 26–7)*.
United Nations (First Avenue, between 45th and 46th Street). Free tickets to General Assembly, plus tours. Daily 9.30am–4.45pm *(see page 53)*.

The Bronx
Bronx Zoo/Wildlife Conservation Park (Bronx River Parkway/Fordham Road). The country's largest urban zoo. Daily 10am–5pm *(see page 75)*.
New York Botanical Garden (Southern Boulevard and 200th Street). Landscaped gardens, classes, lectures, and events. Tuesday to Sunday 10am–6pm *(see page 75)*.

81

Brooklyn
Brooklyn Botanic Garden (100 Washington Avenue, at Prospect Park). Popular garden, with conservatory. Tuesday to Friday 8am–4.30pm, Saturday, Sunday and public holidays 10am–4.30pm, until 6pm in summer *(see page 74)*.
Brooklyn Children's Museum (145 Brooklyn Avenue). Interactive exhibits for the younger set. Monday, Wednesday to Friday noon–5pm, Saturday and Sunday 10am–5pm.
Brooklyn Museum of Art (200 Eastern Parkway, Prospect Park). Art from all epochs and continents; very good Egyptian collection. Wednesday to Friday 10am–5pm, Saturday and Sunday 11am–6pm *(see page 73)*.

Queens
American Museum of the Moving Image (35th Avenue/36th Street, Astoria). Historical documentation of the motion picture industry. Tuesday to Friday noon–5pm, Saturday and Sunday 11am–6pm *(see page 75)*.

Historic Richmond Town

Staten Island
Historic Richmond Town (441 Clarke Avenue). Authentic village, with costumed guides and buildings from the 17th to 19th centuries. Open year-round Wednesday to Sunday 1–5pm, longer in July and August *(see page 75)*.
Snug Harbor Cultural Center (1000 Richmond Terrace). An 83-acre combination park, historic site, botanical garden, and cultural center, plus the Newhouse Center for Contemporary Art offering changing exhibits.

Music and Theater

The number and variety of entertainment options available are enormous: open-air concerts in Central Park, jazz in Greenwich Village, cinemas, musicals, Broadway theaters, off-Broadway, off-off-Broadway, the Met, music and dance clubs. To keep pace with what's happening, consult the Friday edition of the *New York Times*, which contains a preview of the forthcoming weekend's events. Weekly publications containing culture sections include *New York Magazine*; *The New Yorker; Time Out New York*, the *Village Voice,* and *New York Press*, which have excellent guides to events where admission is cheap or free.

Music and dance

New York offers every kind of music and dance imaginable, from opera and classical music to jazz, pop, blues, country, reggae, classical ballet, modern-dance workshops, and master classes. Admission to many of the concerts is free: the summer concerts in Central Park, for instance, or the lunch-time concerts held in the Financial District and midtown, which liven up the day for office workers.

The two largest concert halls in the city are **Carnegie Hall** and **Avery Fisher Hall**; the latter forms part of the **Lincoln Center for the Performing Arts** *(see page 69)*, where the **Metropolitan Opera** is also located. Another fine opera company is the **New York City Opera**, which shares the use of the **New York State Theater** (also located in Lincoln Center) with the **New York City Ballet**.

Popular venues for contemporary music include **Madison Square Garden**, **Radio City Music Hall** *(see page 51)*, **Symphony Space**, **Town Hall**, the **Beacon Theater**, **Nassau Coliseum** on Long Island, and the **Apollo Theater** in Harlem *(see page 59)*.

There are numerous dance troupes in the city, such as the **Martha Graham Dance Company**, the **Alvin Ailey American Dance Group**, and the **Dance Theater of Harlem**. Dance venues include the **Brooklyn Academy of Music**, **City Center** on West 55th Street, **Dance Theater Workshop** on West 19th Street, and the **Joyce Theater** on Eighth Avenue and in SoHo on Mercer Street.

Annual events include the Brooklyn Academy of Music (BAM)'s Next Wave Festival from September to December, tel: (718) 636 4100, and the New York Philharmonic's season at Avery Fisher Hall, which begins in September, tel: (212) 875 5030. The New York City Opera performs at the New York State Theater from September to November and starts again in March, tel: (212) 870 5570; the same venue hosts the New York City Ballet performances of *The Nutcracker* from late November to early January.

The Blue Note is for jazz

Carnegie Hall

Theater

The main Broadway theaters are near Times Square. These stage all the large-scale musicals. The alternative to Broadway is off-Broadway, where performances scarcely differ in quality from the former category, albeit performed in smaller theaters. The vast majority of off-Broadway theaters, and indeed, the more experimental off-off-Broadway theaters, are downtown in the East Village area. Here you'll find the **Public Theater** complex – seven theaters in one building at 425 Lafayette Street, tel: (212) 260 2400 – where shows including *Hair* and *A Chorus Line* originated before being transferred to uptown venues. **Theater for the New City** at 155 First Ave, tel: (212) 254 1109 and **La Mama** at 74A East 4th Street, tel: (212) 475 7710; are two of the showplaces for work by experimental theater artists, while along West 42nd Street between Ninth and Tenth Avenues, the group of off-Broadway theaters known as Theater Row includes **Playwrights Horizons**, tel: (212) 279 4200. Useful numbers for tickets and/or information include NYC/On Stage, tel: (212) 768 1818; and The Broadway Line, tel: (212) 302 4111.

83

Since popular shows are often sold out months in advance, anyone keen to see a specific show should order the tickets via their travel agent before arriving in New York – or call Telecharge, tel: (212) 239 6200, which takes a small fee but handles ticket sales for over 30 Broadway and off-Broadway theaters.

There are several ways of getting hold of tickets in New York itself: if you are staying in a good hotel and don't mind tipping generously, the hotel concierge should be able to obtain tickets on your behalf. Otherwise go to the box offices, or to the **Convention & Visitors Bureau** *(see page 98),* where discount coupons may be available.

Half-price tickets on the day of performance can be obtained from TKTS, which has branches at Times Square and Tower 2 of the World Trade Center – the lines at the World Trade Center tend to be much shorter than those at Times Square. The general rule is first come, first served; you can't reserve. Cash or travelers' checks only.

Times Square, 47th Street/Broadway: tickets for matinee performances from 10am, for evening performances from 3pm.

Tower 2 World Trade Center, mezzanine level: Monday to Friday 11am–5pm, Saturday 11am–3.30pm. Limited tickets for matinee and Sunday performances are available on the day prior to and on the day of performance; evening-perfomance tickets are only available on the same day only.

The 'Backstage on Broadway' tour provides a behind-the-scenes glimpse of Broadway theater life *(see page 97).*

TKTS on sale here

Pandora's Box

Pandora's Box

Pandora's Box

wholesale

export

FREE
DIP IT YOURSELF
COLDERAM FINISHES

Food and Drink

In New York, you can eat Brazilian, Italian, French, Indian, Spanish, Korean, Cuban, Turkish, Russian, Jewish, Chinese, Tibetan, Vietnamese, and Mexican food, wonderful steaks, great hamburgers, the freshest of seafood, the most organic of health foods. It can be enjoyed in incredibly expensive restaurants or more cheaply in smaller, more humble establishments. The culinary possibilities are unlimited – the city has 17,000 restaurants, cafes, pubs, and snack bars.

A good guide through the gastronomic jungle is *Zagat*, an annually updated book that contains restaurant reviews and classifies eateries according to location and specialties served.

Tips on eating out:

It's always a sensible idea to reserve a table by phone in advance. Wherever this can't be done (eg Chinatown), expect long lines outside many establishments at weekends. Restaurants that happen to be 'in' can often be fully booked whole weeks in advance.

Cafe culture

Cakes to go

85

Even when a restaurant appears to be empty, don't go straight over to a table and take a seat. 'Wait to be seated' is the local custom. If you're a smoker, also note that smoking is permitted only in certain restaurants.

The service charge isn't usually included in the price, so a tip isn't just to show your appreciation to the waiter – it's a substantial part of his or her actual wages. This direct payment system has many positive effects: the waiters are almost all friendly, and service is usually very good indeed. Tips in restaurants should be no less than 15 percent of the total price of the meal (it's easy to work out this figure in New York: just double the 8¼ percent tax shown on the bill and round up or down). If you feel the service was unsatisfactory, reduce the percentage. It is customary to leave the gratuity lying on the table in cash after you have paid the bill.

Beware, though: some waiters who know they're serving tourists will add their tip to the final amount in advance, so check first to see whether service has already been included.

If the waiter brings the bill without being asked, it is a hint to vacate your table. New York is not like other more relaxed cities, where you can carry on sitting and talking over a drink. Restaurant owners keep a steady eye on their turnover, and their next customers are likely to be waiting for the table – business, after all, is business.

The helpings are almost always enormous. If you can't finish all the food on your plate, don't be embarrassed to ask for a 'doggy bag.'

Service with a smile

Lower East Side diner

Meal times

New York breakfasts can be huge, with fried eggs, bacon, sausages, pancakes covered with maple syrup, cornflakes, and, of course, toast and jam or marmalade. Lunches are somewhat less filling, usually for professional reasons. Businessmen in New York tend to grab a sandwich from the local 'deli' or eat a quick meal at a coffee shop or fast-food outlet.

The main meal of the day is dinner, typically preceded by a drink at the bar. Sunday brunch – a late breakfast that can often last until early afternoon – is a New York institution. A lot of establishments, including the large hotel restaurants, offer their own brunch specialties on Sundays. One good place to go for brunch is Chinatown, where tiny steamed delicacies known as *dim sum* can be consumed in vast quantities.

Drinks

Most but not all restaurants have liquor licenses. Several of the smaller, cheaper establishments advertise themselves as 'BYOB' – 'bring your own bottle' – meaning that you can buy your own wine or beer in the local supermarket and are then given a corkscrew and a glass by the restaurateur. Meals in these establishments work out a lot cheaper than in fully licensed restaurants, where alcohol is often very expensive. Most places serve French and Californian wines; some also offer selections from Australia and South America. Beer is either served in bottles or 'on tap' (i.e. draught).

Coffee is everywhere, thanks to Starbucks and similar coffee chains. Traditional afternoon tea is served at places such as the Lowell Hotel on the Upper East Side and Tea & Sympathy, 108 Greenwich Avenue, tel: (212) 989 9735 in Greenwich Village.

Men at work

Broome Street Bar detail

Restaurants

Below is a small selection of recommended restaurants:
Le Bernadin, 155 West 51st Street, tel: (212) 489 1515; though expensive, this is the best French seafood restaurant in the city.
Broome Street Bar, 363 West Broadway, tel: (212) 925 2086; one of the oldest bars in the neighborhood, in business long before SoHo became chic. Very good burgers.
B. Smith's, 320 West 46th Street, tel: (212) 315 1100; an excellent Theater District choice – chic but still not too expensive; specializes in the very best of Southern-style cooking.
Cucina Stagionale, 275 Bleecker Street, tel: (212) 924 2707; a very popular BYOB restaurant in Greenwich Village, serving excellent-value and delicious Italian food (no reservations).

Ferrara, 195 Grand Street, tel: (212) 226 6150; a Little Italy landmark and a good place to wander to after a meal in Chinatown. The cakes here are infamous.

Hard Rock Café, 221 West 57th Street, tel: (212) 459 9320; a mainly young clientele enjoys the high-decibel ambience here in the city's original theme restaurant.

Hatsuhana, 17 East 48th Street, (between Fifth Avenue and Madison Avenue); tel: (212) 335 3345; some of the best Japanese *sushi* and *sashimi* in the city.

Kiev, 117 Second Avenue, tel: (212) 674 4040; an unpretentious East Village establishment serving traditional Jewish and East European fare.

Lutece, 249 East 50th Street, tel: (212) 752 2225; one of the finest French restaurants in town.

Nice, 35 East Broadway (near Catherine Street), tel: (212) 406 9510; this Chinatown favorite is the place to go to sample some *dim-sum*.

O'Neals', 49 West 64th Street, tel: (212) 787 4663; friendly Upper West Side bar and restaurant offering reliable American food at reasonable prices. Also very convenient to Lincoln Center.

Odeon, 145 West Broadway, tel: (212) 233 0507; a hip TriBeCa mainstay that has reasonably priced food and stays open late.

The Oyster Bar, Grand Central Terminal, Vanderbilt Avenue/42nd Street, tel: (212) 490 6650; excellent seafood – some say the best in town.

Raoul's, 180 Prince Street, tel: (212) 966 3518; well-established SoHo bistro serving great French food.

Rosa Mexicano, 1063 First Avenue (58th Street), tel: (212) 753 7407; arguably the best Mexican food in New York. Great Margaritas too. Reserve in advance.

Spark's Steakhouse, 210 East 46th Street, tel: (212) 687 4855; excellent steaks and very fine wines too. Expensive.

Tavern on the Green, Central Park West/67th Street, tel: (212) 873 3200; wonderfully situated on Central Park. New American cuisine. The trees are hung with thousands of lights. Touristy and expensive, but good for a splurge.

Two Boots, 37 Avenue A (between 2nd and 3rd streets), tel: (212) 505 2276; funky East Village pizza place with a Cajun twist. Another branch in Grand Central Terminal.

Union Square Café, 21 East 16th Street, tel: (212) 243 4020; offers a *nouvelle cuisine* American menu with the emphasis on fresh, regional ingredients. Dishes are delicious and sensibly priced, considering its popularity. Reservations necessary.

Vong, 200 East 54th Street, tel: (212) 486 9592; stylish mid-town restaurant, serving exotic, French-flavoured Thai cuisine. Expensive, but worth it.

Zen Palate, 663 Ninth Avenue/46th Street, tel: (212) 582 6669; one of the best vegetarian restaurants in Manhattan.

Tavern on the Green

SoHo Kitchen and Bar

Wooden wares for sale

Shopping

Manhattan's busiest shopping streets – its avenues – are a consumer's paradise. The only mid-to-uptown areas still relatively peaceful and free of crowds are Central Park West, the section of Fifth Avenue next to Central Park, and Park Avenue. The smaller stores – newsagents, supermarkets, grocery stores, dry cleaners, etc – tend to be found all over neighborhoods such as the Upper West Side, Upper East Side, Harlem, Greenwich Village, Chelsea, etc. Most Manhattan residents have no car; they either buy necessities from the nearest store in their neighborhood, or they have the store deliver provisions to their apartments.

The most exclusive shops are on Madison Avenue, between 60th and 79th streets; on 57th Street between Lexington and Sixth Avenues; and in the 50s blocks of Fifth Avenue. Fifth Avenue also contains cheap stores peddling discount electronic goods, leather goods, Asian vases, and other imported articles.

Boutiques selling avant-garde fashions, original gifts and souvenirs, children's fashions, toys, and other essentials can be found along Columbus Avenue, and also Amsterdam Avenue between 66th and 84th streets. The city's jewelers are concentrated on 47th Street, in the section of it known as 'Diamond Row.'

The Village and SoHo have dozens of eccentric stores with unusual window displays; many of the city's galleries are here as well as in Chelsea.

Sundays are busy on Orchard Street, on the Lower East Side *(see page 34)*: this is a good place for discount clothing, shoes and leather goods. Further downtown, discount designer wear and goods are the specialty at Century 21 on Cortlandt Street near the World Trade Center.

For an eclectic mix of antiques, head over to the

Shop till you drop

weekend flea market on Sixth Avenue between 25th and 26th streets. Another flea market (one of several around the city) is held every Sunday on the Upper West Side, on the corner of Columbus Avenue and 77th Street.

Books

Most of the major publishers in the USA have their head-quarters in New York. The city has a plethora of large bookchains (Barnes & Noble, etc.), along with notable independent shops including:

Biography Bookshop, 400 Bleecker Street. Histories of the famous and infamous.

Books of Wonder, 16 West 18th Street. Good assortment of children's books.

Gotham Book Mart, 41 West 47th Street. A great place to browse.

Strand Bookstore, 828 Broadway/12th Street. One of the last survivors of what was once known as Booksellers' Row. Superb selection of used books.

Strand Bookstore

Department Stores

Barneys New York, Madison Avenue/61st Street.
Bloomingdale's, Lexington Avenue/59th Street.
Lord & Taylor, Fifth Avenue and 39th Street.
Macy's, Herald Square.
Saks Fifth Avenue, 611 Fifth Avenue.

Macy's

Electronics

Photographic goods and video recorders, CD players, etc are all very good value in New York. Try:

J&R Music and Computer Worlds, 15–31 Park Row (across from City Hall). Cameras, computers, stereos, etc.

Jeans

Canal Jean Co, 504 Broadway, between Broome and Spring Streets. Jeans, T-shirts, sweatshirts.

Museum Shops

The MOMA Design Store, 11 West 53rd Street. Designer furniture, household articles.

Metropolitan Museum of Art Gift Shop, in the museum on Fifth Avenue and also at Rockefeller Center (15 West 49th Street). Art books, posters, jewelry, reproductions.

MOMA store

Records, tapes, CDs

Tower Records, 692 Broadway/East 4th Street.
Virgin Megastore (1540 Broadway/45th Street).

Toys

FAO Schwarz, 767 Fifth Avenue. The Fifth Avenue flag-ship of America's most famous toyshop.

Decked out for the evening

Nightlife

Nightlife in New York tends to get under way at around 11pm, not before. Most of the city's nightclubs are very short lived. Bars and clubs that are 'in' one month can be 'out' the next. The only way to find out is to do your own research on the spot, and then hope to be admitted by the all-powerful doorman. The 'right' clothes may help.

Dance and music clubs

Bowery Ballroom, 6 Delancey Street
Well-known bands and great acoustics make this venue well worth a pilgrimage to the Lower East Side.

CBGB & OMFUG, 315 Bowery at Bleecker Street
The club where punk started in the US.

Hush, 7 West 19th Street
A stylish, intimate Flatiron District club with drinking, dining, and dancing all under one roof.

The Knitting Factory, 74 Leonard Street
An eclectic mecca for avant-garde sounds in the heart of TriBeCa, offering everything from jazz to rock and poetry.

The Pyramid Club, 101 Avenue A
Typical East Village hangout.

S.O.B.'s, 204 Varick Street
A SoHo bastion of Latin-American and world music.

The Pyramid Club

Club scene

The Supper Club, 240 West 47th Street
A classy mid-town establishment offering everything from dancing to big-band music to big-name rock acts.

Twilo, 503 West 27th Street
A sprawling Chelsea dance club with well-known DJs and a largely gay crowd. Usually stays open all night.

Vinyl, 157 Hudson Street
A dance club without alcohol but with quirky hours, for instance, Sunday 4pm–midnight. Extremely popular with youthful devotees of house and similar music.

Webster Hall, 125 East 11th Street
A large club in East Village with all-night dancing to everything from rock and reggae to house.

Wetlands, 161 Hudson Street, below Canal
Casual club in TriBeCa where regulars groove to the sounds of reggae, folk, jazz, and funk.

Jazz clubs
The following classic clubs are all in the West Village:

*Hot sounds for a
cool clientele*

Blue Note, 131 West 3rd Street
The very best of mainstream jazz and blues, from time-honored greats to more contemporary acts.

Sweet Basil, 88 Seventh Avenue South
Another venue for fine mainstream jazz.

Village Vanguard, 178 Seventh Avenue South
The club that helped to launch legendary talents including Miles Davis and John Coltrane.

Bars
Barmacy, 538 East 14th Street
Bar located in a former pharmacy.

Chumley's, 86 Bedford Street at Barrow
A 'speakeasy' from Prohibition days.

The Greatest Bar on Earth, 1 World Trade Center
The view from here is awesome, and the bar offers live music on some nights.

McSorley's Old Ale House, 15 East 7th Street
Old-fashioned tavern with sawdust floors.

Oak Bar in the Plaza Hotel, Fifth Avenue/59th Street
Cozy, elegant club atmosphere.

Getting There

By Plane

There are a number of ways to get to Manhattan (15 miles/
24km away) from **John F Kennedy International Airport** in Queens.

The cheapest method is to take the shuttle bus marked
'Subway' to the Howard Beach/JFK Airport subway
station, where the 'A' train connects directly with Manhattan for $1.50. However, if you're unfamiliar with the
subway system, take the more expensive **New York Airport Service** to midtown Manhattan (every 15–30 minutes until midnight). The fare is under $15; for more
information, tel: (718) 706 9678.

*Opposite: NY cabs
are legendary*

Gray Line Air Shuttle minibuses (daily, 7am–11pm)
stop at most hotels in Manhattan between 23rd and 63rd
Streets and cost about $14. For more information, tel: (212)
315 3006 or (1-800) 451 0455.

Carey Airport Express

The most comfortable way to Manhattan is by taxi. This
costs a flat rate of $30, plus bridge and tunnel tolls and
a 15 percent tip. Ride only in yellow (licensed) cabs.

The city's other international airport, **Newark International**, lies 16 miles (26km) east of Manhattan, in New
Jersey. There are bus connections from here (including
Olympia Trails Airport Express Bus, tel: (212) 964 6233
or (718) 622 7700 to Pennsylvania Station, to Grand Central
Terminal and to the World Trade Center (fares are $11
and above). The **Gray Line Air Shuttle** minibuses (between $14 and $19) pick up and drop off at several Manhattan hotels. The taxi fare from Newark is around $40;
in the other direction, it is the amount on the meter plus
$10. Bridge and tunnel tolls are extra, as is a 15 percent tip.

93

Domestic flights land at **La Guardia Airport**, only 8 miles
(13km) east of midtown Manhattan in Queens. **New York
Airport Service** buses (every 30 minutes, $10) connect
with midtown Manhattan; **Gray Line Air Shuttle**
minibuses (under $14) connect with several hotels in Manhattan; and taxis are metered and cost between $18 and $26,
with bridge and tunnel tolls (and 15 percent tip) extra.

By Train

Long distance Amtrak trains arrive at and depart from
Pennsylvania Station (Seventh Avenue/32nd Street), as
do commuter trains to and from Long Island. **Grand
Central** (Park Avenue/42nd Street) is generally for commuter trains only.

By Bus

All buses arrive at the **Port Authority Bus Terminal**
(Eighth Avenue/41st Street).

Getting Around

Orientation

Getting your bearings in Manhattan is remarkably easy. Apart from Lower Manhattan, where the thoroughfares twist and turn, and may even be named, all the straight thoroughfares running from west to east are called 'streets' and are numbered from south to north (1st, 2nd, 3rd, etc). In addresses, the addition of a 'West' (W) or an 'East' (E) after the address number show whether it lies to the west or east of Fifth Avenue.

The avenues run north-south, intersecting with the streets at right angles. They too are numbered, from (starting in the east) First to Twelfth Avenue. Some have their own names, eg York Avenue, Lexington Avenue, Park Avenue and Madison Avenue; and Sixth Avenue is officially called Avenue of the Americas. There's just one street that doesn't conform to this pattern: Broadway cuts across the island diagonally.

Don't rent a car. Parking spaces are almost non-existent, and you are soon likely to become a victim of gridlock.

Underground opportunities

The New York subway

The New York subway may have a bad reputation, but when one considers that 4 million people use it each day without problem, there seems to be no reason to avoid it completely. It is the fastest way of getting around, and the city couldn't function without it.

As far as your personal safety on the subway is concerned, a few basic rules should be followed:

- Always stick with the crowd whenever you get on or off a train. Avoid remote entrances or exits.
- Have the exact amount of money for the trip ready; keep your wallet or purse hidden.
- Don't get into carriages that are empty or unilluminated.
- Remember to keep a firm grip on your bags.

A subway token costs $1.50 and is bought at the official booth in the station. A single fare allows you to travel as far as you like. The MetroCard – a stored-value plastic card available in denominations from $3 to $120 – allows unlimited transfers throughout the system, including buses. Note that express trains leave out certain stations, local trains make all stops on a particular line.

Traveling at peak times (7.30–9am and 4.30–7pm) is not recommended, unless you happen to be fond of crowds. Free subway maps are sometimes available from the token booths or by calling (718) 694 4903. Finally, make sure you know the direction you're traveling in, i.e. *downtown* (southwards), *uptown* (northwards).

MTA New York City Subway

Buses

Buses are safer and generally more pleasant than the subway, and they connect most of Manhattan's east-west streets (the subway is north-south oriented).

A bus trip costs either $1.50 or one token. Have the exact amount ready – drivers provide no change. If you want to switch buses, ask the driver for a free transfer ticket. You can also use the MetroCard *(see page 94)*.

Manhattan bus maps are (sometimes) available from token booths at subways, or at the Times Square Visitor Information Center and the official city Visitor Information Center on Seventh Avenue between 52nd and 53rd Streets *(see page 98)*. For information about subways and buses, tel: (718) 330 1234.

Getting from Times Square to TriBeCa

Taxis

These normally have to be hailed, although there are taxi ranks at Grand Central Terminal as well as elsewhere. Only private car services can be ordered by phone.

All licensed (i.e. yellow) taxis have electronic meters that print out receipts if required. A nightly surcharge of 50 cents is in effect from 8pm–6am, and a tip of 10–15 percent is expected.

For lost property in taxis, tel: (212) 302 8294.

Motorists

Driving to New York isn't recommended, mainly because parking is expensive (in garages or lots) and either risky or unavailable (on the streets).

Roads outside New York are in good condition. The road system in the US consists of Interstate Freeways (eg I-84), United States Highways (eg US95), State Highways or Routes (country roads) and Secondary State or County Roads (side roads).

The maximum speed limit outside urban areas is generally 55mph (88kmph), 65mph (105kmph) in some places and 25–30mph (40–48kmph) in built-up areas unless otherwise indicated. School buses that are stationary with their lights flashing may *not* be overtaken.

Car rental

To rent a car you must be over 21 years of age and have a national or, better, international driving license. Some car rental firms add a surcharge for drivers aged under 25.

If you are considering renting a car, check out the conditions. It's good to use larger firms in case the vehicle has to be exchanged at any point. **Credit cards** are necessary for all car rentals in the US.

Toll-free (1)-800 numbers for central reservations can be found in the *Yellow Pages* under **Car** or **Automobile Rentals** (Avis, Budget, Hertz, etc).

Sightseeing tours (a selection)
Bus
- Gray Line New York Tours, 900 Eighth Avenue at 42nd Street, tel: (212) 397 2620. Well-known company with a wide range of hop-on, hop-off double-decker bus and other itineraries. Tours last between two and eight hours.
- New York Apple Tours, 777 Eighth Avenue, tel: (212) 944 2400. More double-decker hop-on, hop-off bus tours.

Boat
- Circle Line Sightseeing, Pier 83 at the western end of 42nd Street, tel: (212) 563 3200. From 30-minute speed-boat rides to a three-hour trip around the entire island, showing all aspects of Manhattan from the water.
- Circle Line Seaport, Pier 16, South Street Seaport, tel: (212) 630 8888. One-hour cruises of New York Harbor, plus special music cruises and more speedboat rides.
- NY Waterway, Pier 78, West 38th Street and Twelfth Avenue, tel: (800) 533 3779. Converted ferryboats; rides up the Hudson River and around Manhattan.

Helicopter
- Liberty Helicopter Tours, heliport at West 30th Street and Twelfth Avenue, tel: (212) 967 6464. Manhattan from the sky – not exactly cheap, but exhilarating.

On Foot
- Adventure on a Shoestring, 300 West 53rd Street, tel: (212) 265 2663. Tours through particular neighborhoods and also special themes, eg sites with literary associations.
- Municipal Art Society, 457 Madison Avenue, tel: (212) 935 3960. Tours focussing on history and architecture.

Guided tours with special themes
- Backstage on Broadway, 228 West 47th Street, tel: (212) 575 8065. Behind the scenes at Broadway's top theaters.
- Bite of the Apple Central Park Bicycle Tours, 2 Columbus Circle, tel: (212) 541 8759. Tours across Central Park.
- Harlem Spirituals/New York Visions, 690 Eighth Avenue, tel: (212) 391 0900. Harlem jazz and gospel tours, plus sightseeing in Brooklyn and the Bronx.
- Harlem Your Way, 128 West 130th Street, tel: (212) 690 1687. Walking tours of Harlem, including gospel churches and jazz clubs.
- Heritage Trails New York, 61 Broadway, tel: (212) 269 1500 or (888) 4 TRAILS. Historical points of interest in the Financial District.
- Urban Park Rangers, 1234 Fifth Avenue, tel: (212) 360 2774. Tours with nature themes in various parks throughout the city. For Central Park tours, call the Ranger Station at (212) 628 2345.

Facts for the Visitor

Travel Documents

International travelers should bring a valid **passport**. No visa is required if your length of stay does not exceed 90 days and you can furnish a valid return ticket. If you want to stay longer, apply for a visa at the US Consulate.

Length of stay is determined by the immigration officer you meet on arrival, so have ready such things as credit cards, traveler's checks or hotel reservation forms.

Customs

Items for personal use can be brought into the USA duty-free. Duty-free allowances include 200 cigarettes or 50 cigars or 2kg of tobacco; 11 alcoholic drinks and presents to a value of $100. Flowers, meat, vegetables or fruit may not be brought into the country.

Tourist information

Useful maps and brochures are available from **NYC & Company – the Convention & Visitors Bureau**, 810 Seventh Avenue/53rd Street, NY 10019, tel: (212) 397 8222, 1-800 NYC VISIT. To speak with a counselor, call (212) 484 1222. Their Visitor Information Center is at the same address; it's open Monday to Friday 8.30am–6pm, Saturday and Sunday 9am–5pm. Alternatively, you can visit their website at: http://www.nycvisit.com

Brochures, maps and information kiosks are also available at the **Times Square Visitors Center** at 1560 Broadway, between 46th and 47th Street, from 8am–8pm. In London, NYC & Company has an office at 33–34 Carnaby Street, London W1V 1PA, tel: 0207 437 8300 (open Monday to Friday 10am–4pm).

Foreign affairs

Currency & exchange

The unit of currency in the US is the dollar ($) = 100 cents (¢). The following coins are in circulation at present: cent (1¢); nickel (5¢); dime (10¢); quarter (25¢); half-dollar (50¢); and $1. Banknotes come in the following denominations: $1, $2, $5, $10, $20, $50, $100 and up. Note that there are two types of $50 and $100 bills.

There is no limit to the amount of foreign or domestic currency that can be taken in or out of the country; travelers checks or cash worth more than $100,000 must be declared, however.

It's best to bring a credit card (e.g. Visa, MasterCard), US dollar travelers checks for small sums ($20, $50), and also a small amount of cash in low-denomination notes. Most hotels, restaurants and shops accept US dollar travelers checks and most banks will convert them into cash. Visitors can use their bankcards in ATMs.

Opening times

Store owners in New York decide when they want to close – there's no mandatory closing time. Large department stores in midtown close on Sunday, and the Jewish-run shops on Orchard Street close on Saturday.

Banks: Usually Monday to Friday 9am–3pm, and on one day in the week (usually Thursday) until 6pm; a few are also open on Saturday mornings.

Post Offices: Monday to Friday 9am–6pm, Saturday 9am–noon. The General Post Office at 33rd Street and Eighth Avenue stays open 24 hours, with counter service until 8pm.

Public holidays

New Year's Day (January 1); Martin Luther King Day (3rd Monday in January); Washington's Birthday (3rd Monday in February); Memorial Day (last Monday in May); Independence Day (July 4); Labor Day (1st Monday in September); Columbus Day (2nd Monday in October); Veterans' Day (November 11); Thanksgiving Day (4th Thursday in November); Christmas Day (December 25).

There are local public holidays too. If a holiday falls on a Sunday, the Monday after is also a holiday and post offices, government offices, etc are closed.

Tax

Value added tax is never included in the prices displayed at tills in New York, therefore, you pay the basic price plus 8.25 percent sales tax. There is also a 13¼ percent tax on all hotel rooms. This so-called room tax is supplemented still further by a transient occupancy tax of $2 per room per night.

Telephone

Local calls (25¢) can easily be made from phone booths (just follow the printed instructions). If you don't know the area code and number **long-distance calls** have to be made via the operator (dial 0), otherwise you can dial directly. **Overseas calls** can also be made directly, but if you're calling from a pay phone your pockets will have to be stuffed full of quarters. If in doubt ring the overseas operator (dial 0). The code for the UK is 0 11 44 followed by the area code minus the first zero, and then the actual number. **Telegrams** can be placed with Western Union or via hotel reception.

At the moment New York City has four area codes: 212 and the new 646 for Manhattan, and 718 and the new 347 for Brooklyn, Queens, Staten Island and the Bronx.

Important telephone numbers:
Emergency (fire, police, ambulance): tel: 911
Doctors on Call: tel: (718) 238 2100.

Phone home from here

Temperature

Temperature reports are in Fahrenheit. To convert to Centigrade: subtract 32, then divide by 9 and multiply by 5. (0°C = 32°F, 10°C = 50°F, 20°C = 68°F, 30°C = 86°F, etc.)

Voltage

110v AC. Adaptors can be bought at most airports as well as local hardware stores.

Time

New York is on Eastern Standard Time (5 hours behind London). Daylight saving time is from the beginning of April until October.

Tipping

Waiters in restaurants expect at least 15 percent of the bill to be placed on the table after a meal. In hotels, bellmen should be given around $1 a bag, and a bit extra if they have to go a long way; doormen expect $1 for merely opening car doors or calling cabs; chambermaids get $1 a night for routine cleaning; taxi drivers get 10–15 percent of the fare; shoe-cleaners and cloakroom attendants get $1 each; and at the bar, it's $1 per drink.

Medical assistance

Medical help has to be paid for instantly, either in cash or by credit card. Europeans and other non-US citizens are strongly advised to take out medical insurance.

24-hour Pharmacy: Genovese Drug Store, Second Avenue/68th Street, tel: (212) 772 0104.

The NYPD

Security Precautions

New York is certainly not the safest of cities, but it's a lot safer than is often suggested. If you follow a few basic rules you won't encounter many problems.

- Avoid wearing expensive jewelry or expensive-looking jackets.
- Don't accept offers from strangers to carry your luggage.
- Use the hotel safe wherever possible.
- In hotel rooms, use the peephole in the door to check out callers before opening.
- Never carry large amounts of cash. Almost all establishments accept credit cards and travelers checks.
- If the character of a street starts to change, turn back immediately.
- If you get mugged, offer no resistance.

Alcohol

The minimum age for consumption of alcoholic beverages is 21.

Where to Stay

One of the city's grand hotels

New York may have some of the finest hotels in the world, but they're also some of the most expensive. Although dormitory-style hostels and budget hotels offer rates as low as $25–$90 a night, the average room costs between $200 and $250 with no upper limits for luxury hotels.

However, even the priciest establishments often have special weekend rates, which are worth inquiring about. In addition, several US reservation services offer discounts of 50 percent or more on upscale rooms, including Quikbook, tel: (800) 789 9887, fax: (212) 779 6120, e-mail them at: info@quikbook.com – or try the online service at: www.hoteldiscount.com

Remember that telephone calls from rooms can be astronomically expensive, so check with the front desk before dialing (in recent years, however, several hotels have begun offering free local calls).

Also remember that state and city levies are high, with a 13¼ percent room tax added to hotel bills, plus an additional 'transient occupancy tax' of $2 per room, per night. It all adds up.

The following is brief selection of recommended hotels, ranging from discreet luxury, to affordable chic, to some of the city's best bargains.

$$$$ (Double rooms from $300 and up)

The Plaza

The Carlyle, 35 E. 76th St, NY 10021, tel: (212) 744 1600, fax: (212) 717 4682; **The Lowell**, 28 E. 63rd St, NY 10021, tel: (212) 838 1400, fax: (212) 319 4230; **The Mark**, 25 East 77th St, NY 10021, tel: (212) 744 4300, fax: (212) 744 2749; **The Pierre**, Fifth Ave/61st St, NY 10021, tel: (212) 838 8000, fax: (212) 758 1615; **Plaza Athenee**, 37 E. 64th St, NY 10021, tel: (212) 734 9100, fax: (212) 772 0958. **The Regency**, 540 Park Ave, NY 10021, tel: (212) 759 4100, fax: (212) 826 5674.

$$$ (Double rooms from $225 and up)

The Algonquin, 59 W. 44th St, NY 10036, tel: (212) 840 6800, fax: (212) 944 1419; **The Plaza**, 768 Fifth Ave, NY 10022, tel: (212) 759 3000, fax: (212) 759 3167; **Millenium Hilton**, 55 Church St, NY 10007, tel: (212) 693 2001, fax: (212) 571 2316; **Morgans**, 237 Madison Ave, NY 10016, tel: (212) 686 0300, fax: (212) 779 8352; **SoHo Grand Hotel**, 310 W. Broadway, NY 10013, tel: (212) 965 3000, fax: (212) 965 3244; **Roger Smith**, 501 Lexington Ave/47th St, NY 10017, tel: (212) 755 1400, fax: (212) 758 4061; **Roger Williams**, 131 Madison Ave, NY 10016, tel: (212) 448 7000, fax: (212) 448 7007; **Waldorf=Astoria**, 301 Park Ave, NY 10022, tel: (212) 355 3000, fax: (212) 872 7272.

The Algonquin

$$ (Double rooms from $150-$225)

The Bentley, 500 E. 62nd St, NY 10014, tel: (212) 644 6000, fax: (212) 207 4800; **Empire Hotel**, Broadway/ 63rd St, NY 10023, tel: (212) 265 7400, fax: (212) 245 3382; **Franklin**, 164 E. 87th St, NY 10128, tel: (212) 369 1000, fax: (212) 369 8000; **Gramercy Park Hotel**, 2 Lexington Ave, NY 10010, tel: (212) 475 4320, fax: (212) 505 0535; **Holiday Inn Wall Street**, 15 Gold St, NY 10038, tel: (212) 232 7700, fax: (212) 425 0330; **Paramount**, 235 W. 46th St, NY 10036, tel: (212) 764 5500, fax: (212) 575 4892; **Hotel Wales**, 1295 Madison Ave, NY 10128, tel: (212) 876 6000, fax: (212) 860 7000.

$ (Double rooms $150 or less)

Best Western Manhattan, 17 W. 32nd St, NY 10001, tel: (212) 736 1600, fax: (212) 790 2760; **Habitat Hotel**, 130 E. 57th St, NY 10022, tel: (212) 753 8841, fax: (212) 829 9605; **Pickwick Arms Hotel**, 230 E. 51st St, NY 10022, tel: (212) 355 0300, fax: (212) 755 5729; **Quality Hotel East Side**, 161 Lexington Ave, NY 10016, tel: (212) 545 1800, fax: (212) 790 2760; **Washington Square Hotel**, 103 Waverly Place, NY 10011, tel: (212) 777 9515, fax: (212) 979 8373; **Wyndham**, 42 W. 58th St, NY 10019, tel: (212) 753 3500, fax: (2120 754 5638.

Washington Square Hotel

Suite Hotels

For $200–$300 a night (and higher) it's possible to rent a one-bedroom suite that sleeps up to four persons – ideal for families. These suites are like mini-apartments, with a kitchen niche equipped for self-catering – a useful way of saving money.

Beekman Tower, 3 Mitchell Place, First Avenue/49th St, NY 10017, tel: (212) 355 7300, fax: (212) 753 9366; **Benjamin**, 125 E. 50th St, NY 10022, tel: (212) 715 2500, fax: (212) 715 2525; **Dumont Plaza**, 150 East 34th St, NY 10016, tel: (212) 481 7600, fax: (212) 889 8856; **Eastgate**

Tower, 222 East 39th St, NY 10016, tel: (212) 687 8000, fax: (212) 490 2634; **Lyden Gardens**, 215 East 64th St, NY 10021, tel: (212) 355 1230, fax: (212) 758 7858; **Lyden House**, 320 E. 53rd St, NY 10022, tel: (212) 888 6070, fax: (212) 935 7690; **Plaza Fifty**, 155 East 50th St, NY 10022, tel: (212) 751 5710, fax: (212) 753 1468; **Shelburne,** 303 Lexington Avenue/37th St, NY 10016, tel: (212) 689 5200, fax: (212) 779 7068; **Southgate Tower**, 371 Seventh Avenue/31st St, NY 10001, tel: (212) 563 1800, fax: (212) 643 8028; **Surrey**, 20 East 76th St, NY 10021, tel: (212) 288 3700, fax: (212) 628 1549.

Suites at all these hotels can be reserved through the central reservation number for **Manhattan East Suite Hotels**: tel: (212) 465 3600, toll-free: (800) 637 8483, or online at: www.mesuite.com

Tips gratefully received

YMCA
(Double rooms from $86)
Accommodation at the **Young Men's Christian Association** is available to both men and women. Reservations should be made well in advance.

YMCA-West Side, 5 West 63rd Street, NY 10023, tel: (212) 787 4100; **Vanderbilt YMCA**, 224 East 47th Street, NY 10017, tel: (212) 756 9600.

Youth Hostels
(Around $25)
Stays at the city's main youth hostel are limited to seven days. Reservations should be made well in advance. There's no age restriction. Discounts are available for members of youth hostel associations (with international identity cards). Dormitories sleep 4–12 people.

New York International Youth Hostel, 891 Amsterdam Avenue/103rd Street, NY 10025, tel: (212) 932 2300, fax: (212) 932 2574, or reserve through their website at: www.hostelling.com

Bed and Breakfast
B&B accommodation is a relatively recent phenomenon in the city and can be a very good way of getting to know the locals. Whole apartments can be rented, or rooms in private homes. It often involves sharing the bathroom with the landlord, but that's only a small sacrifice in return for the personal contact and wealth of information available.

B&B accommodation is often cheaper than medium-priced hotel accommodation, especially since the taxes and surcharges don't apply.

For more information, try calling the **B&B Network of New York**, tel: (212) 645 8134 or **City Lights Bed & Breakfast Ltd.**, tel: (212) 737 7049.

Index